For Claire

Firefighting with God

Peter Hamblin

On your own journey
Truly meant to be.

With Love.

Peter Hamblin

Firefighting with God

by

Peter Hamblin

Copyright 2018 Peter Hamblin

ISBN: 978-1-9164145-0-1

Copy edited by Ian Large

Cover design by Jag Lall

This book is produced by Peter Hamblin in conjunction with **WRITERSWORLD**, and is produced entirely in the UK. It is available to order from most bookshops in the United Kingdom, and is also globally available via UK based Internet book retailers.

WRITERSWORLD
2 Bear Close Flats, Bear Close, Woodstock
Oxfordshire, OX20 1JX, England
☎ 01993 812500
☎ +44 1993 812500

www.writersworld.co.uk

The text pages of this book are produced via an independent certification process that ensures the trees from which the paper is produced come from well managed sources that exclude the risk of using illegally logged timber while leaving options to use post-consumer recycled paper as well.

Contents

Prologue

The Quick Journey through My Life

Life for me meant waking each day and getting on with it. There was no real plan; it was about living with how my life had evolved when I was far from it. Most of the days were what I considered to be normal, either going to work or planning for days off, what someone summed up as to 'keep on keeping on'. It's different when you are a shift worker and your body clock is all over the place. Not sleeping when your body is expecting to makes it a fight to keep going, and just as it begins to readjust from your 'rest days', off you go again on the same cycle. While I was working nights as a shift worker many of my neighbours thought I was unemployed, completely unaware that when I was starting my fifteen-hour night shift they were having their evening meal at what I call tea time and others dinner, before sleeping in their own beds at home. I would arrive back, if I was lucky, just as their new day was starting with breakfast.

Not that I am complaining; when I first started shift work in 1975 I would love being out in fire engines – what we called fire appliances – in the small hours of the morning; there were very few people about then, just foxes and milkmen starting their rounds. Now life has become busy twenty-four hours a day with people and traffic everywhere, encouraging the foxes to do the same and work in the daylight hours because they might as well keep on keeping on.

My family life was completely different to what it had been before marriage and not just because of the shift work. I would work as a carpenter on many of my days off, unless I had no choice but to sleep, and life was far from normal because of the irregular hours.

If I had thought about my plan it would have been about doing the best I could by doing what my dad had done, feed and provide for the family by working hard and playing hard. I believe I succeeded in that, but I was not my dad in so many other ways, one of which was in not keeping my family together, which shocked him. His expectations of me were that I was the stable one of his three sons and as such he bequeathed me his father's charming chiming wall clock with its swinging pendulum. That clock has since become symbolic of my life, having been repaired many times, but despite being in and out of storage boxes it still keeps ticking away the seconds and chiming reminders at thirty-minute intervals that life moves on. I love being the guardian of our family clock, despite it needing to be continually wound up and losing time from the simplest of nudges, unlike myself who always keeps good time. Dad never asked for it back despite me having had eighteen different homes with it, and now he can't.

My life could not continue as it was, and having long since become my own version of being a man I eventually left my wife for a life that was in many ways worse, with Dad's words of advice, 'You've made your bed, now lie in it', ringing around my ears as a constant reminder. I eventually gave in to that struggle too, and after ten years of trying to be happy and failing with the other woman, I left and eventually asked for help.

I didn't ask anyone in particular although I did mention God, if He or She existed. I was drunk at the time and drowning in tears that had been locked away for most of my fifty years and although I didn't understand that at the time either, I have learnt that not only is it good to shed tears, especially for a man, but for me it was essential in beginning to discover the real me and make life as I would have liked it to be rather than how it had become.

These were not crocodile tears, they were floods, released from an overflowing dam of emotions that had been locked away inside from a lifetime of being a 'big boy that shouldn't cry' – and didn't. The tears that night washed away my frustrations and ensured a good night's sleep so that by the morning I had forgotten about asking for help. Not that forgetting was important because my life began to change anyway, although it would be years later before I linked the differences to my cry for help as I got on with life. Getting on with life was achieved by agreeing to go out socially again and it just happened to be at Christmas as I ended almost a year of a self-imposed social solitude that followed the shock ending of a rekindled relationship. It wasn't so much the ending that had caused me to be shocked because I was used to them, it was that for the first time in my life I had not been the one to do the ending. I had been dumped as it is so quaintly put! Looking back, that was the best Christmas present I could have ever wished for.

I am not sure why I had imposed a ban on my social life, although it wasn't really imposed at all, it had just sort of evolved. Maybe I hoped I would gain some sort of insight and answers by avoiding a social life that always seemed to invite chaos, but all I seemed to gain was a healthier bank balance and a happier dog. I knew my career as a firefighter and the regular encounters with death were not the problem, although I had always been puzzled by my lack of emotions when encountering it. No, it was me and relationships and blaming everyone and everything but myself for my perceived inadequacies and failures.

That painful year of looking within, what I would come to call introspection, *'the observation or examination of one's mental and emotional state and the act of looking within'* – did actually turn out to be one of great significance, because it was the first time – ably assisted by John Denver and his wonderful lyrics – that I had taken the time to question who I was. Searching for answers to the chaos I always seemed to cause and my devastation at being dumped was a lonely affair that didn't yield the answers, but at least I had set the ball rolling.

Nothing I ever did in relationships was ever done with the intent to hurt or fail, but being on the receiving end made me feel how others must have felt and forced me to at least try to understand why I had. Later, I realised there had always been a battle within me and would remain so until I began to see my actions were as inevitable as my 'honest ignorance', but I was too busy in the moment to stop feeling sorry for myself and being the victim, which was a battle that I had experienced many times before in my search for happiness. According to this Native American Indian fable there is a battle that goes on inside us all:

One evening an old Cherokee told his grandson about a battle that goes on inside people.

He said, "My son, the battle is between two wolves inside us all. One is evil; it is anger, jealousy, sorrow, regret, greed, arrogance, self-pity, guilt, resentment, inferiority, lies, false pride, superiority and ego. The other is good; it is joy, peace, love, hope, serenity, humility, kindness, benevolence, empathy, generosity, truth, compassion and faith."

The grandson thought about this for a minute and then asked the grandfather, "Which wolf wins?"

The old Cherokee simply said, "The one that you feed."

That I had become depressed is now obvious but it wasn't then; I called it being 'down', which was easier to admit than feeling like a failure and unable to cope. After all, there was, and still is, a huge amount of misinformation, misunderstanding and stigma associated with 'being depressed'.

My depression had sneaked up on me and I guess that's what it always does. If it was a case of arriving overnight it could presumably be removed overnight, but that's not the reality of something that steadily consumes and becomes who we are. Whether it was the depression that had built the wall of self-protection around me because of the shock and the feeling of worthlessness, or the culmination of years of fighting against myself I do not know, but either way it achieved what I needed, eventually.

Anyway, I was probably depressed long before being dumped because I knew once again that the relationship was in some way wrong for me and had only been rekindled by my jealousy in the first place. I was fed up with not understanding and fed up with running. I wanted to stop and be settled, to be calm and at peace, but my unhappiness and need to be loved kept driving me on to add to my lifetime of disappointments; being dumped was just the straw that broke the camel's back by highlighting and reinforcing my inadequacies.

There was so much about my life that was positive; my two beautiful children, my career which fulfilled me more than my wildest dreams could ever have imagined, and my beautiful home shared with my faithful companion, Spot the dog. But the one thing that eluded me, true love, seemed further away than ever as I spent solitary night after night battling with myself to find the truth of who I was.

Depression is said to be the way the subconscious mind saves us from ourselves by shutting down 'normal life' to avoid further problems; a bit like dieting by not shopping. I hadn't sought medical help or counselling because it hadn't occurred to me that I needed it, and in any case I was averse to taking medication to solve my problems. I wanted to be real, not subdued, although I didn't know what being real was then either; who does unless we challenge who we are?

As it turned out, shutting myself away for a year was the very thing that inadvertently saved me by bringing everything to a head. I had known even before I had children that I needed to breathe new life into my old ways, and during those earliest of personal battles – that seemed like a lifetime before – I would often say that it felt like I was on a downward spiral that I couldn't get off.

Although I couldn't see it then my whole life had been dominated in one way or another by my relentless search to find true love and I had been continually encouraged by having an ample supply of opportunities. I was heartened each time I thought I had found it and equally disheartened each time it crumbled. My life had been full of false alarms, one way or another, and it would stay that way for many years to come, spiralling ever deeper out of control and being 'well driven' by my honest ignorance, despite my positive intentions to steer a different course.

Over the years that followed my year of isolation, and having returned to the social scene, I learnt that I had been labelled as a womaniser, although no one said that to my face; it was said in that happy jokey matter of fact way that delivers a message that can be taken any way when delivered with a smile, something I was also good at. Whether my resilience to find love as an antidote for my relationship 'issues' could ever be called womanising is up to the individuals who labelled me and why. What I knew and they didn't was that I had made a promise to myself somewhere in those intervening years between the breakup of my marriage and asking for help that I would never again stay in a relationship just to make it work. I had to be truly happy. I can see now how that must have looked, and if I'm honest I would have probably come to the same conclusions, but that is something else that I've learnt since seeing my life as a journey; never judge another lest we judge ourselves. The Native American Indians had a saying for that too: Never judge another unless you have walked in their shoes!

Ironically, I was always at my happiest when on my own, it was easier just having to be true to myself, there would be no confusions or heartaches, no empty promises of 'lifetimes together', no falling in and out of love and fleeing the scene leaving behind chaos and disappointments. No more womanising! But being on my own and happy was never going to be enough for me either and I broke those honest intentions time after time as well. I needed to be loved and didn't understand the hopelessness of trying to love another when I didn't love myself! So I continued to 'court' women and although it was less of a pursuit than it had been before, it would still be many years before my change of direction could reap its reward and get me even close to my final destination. It was rather like trying to turn around a fully-laden oceangoing freighter from 'full speed ahead'. A very gradual process!

My year alone with my dog and successful and satisfying work life could have been enough if that was my purpose in life. But it wasn't and that's why I believe I questioned the existence of God. I had never questioned God before; desperation does that by encouraging us to be different, but then I had never really thought about what believing in God was about before either. God was just God in my mind and hadn't, so far as I knew, been involved with my life up to then. I have learnt that doubting God is being 'agnostic'.

My parents were what I would call 'non-practising' Christians who would go to church for weddings, funerals and christenings, although Mum would occasionally attend at other times and if I knew she was going I would always beg to go with her. I guess that was a chance to have her to myself and seek the love and attention I didn't consciously know I was lacking, rather than any deep conviction for a faith, which I was too young to understand or have. Anyway it didn't work! All I probably succeeded in doing was to spoil Mum's chance of some quiet time away from her family and the responsibility of being a wife and mother in hard times. Although I would like to think she took me because she loved me, it was probably just the Christian thing to do and how could she deny her son without challenging her own faith?

Like all the young children at church I would be deposited in a supervised outer room to draw and listen to stories. I often wonder what God makes of isolating children like that? We didn't have a Bible to hand at home, which I am sure God would not have a problem with, and my two brothers and I weren't preached at or threatened with God's retribution, so far as I can remember. In fact my parents rarely threatened me with anything; maybe if they had I would have felt loved, although I doubt that too. I didn't seem to have faith in anything, so I guess I must have been a pessimist as well.

Belief in God is a wonderful thing until we have reason to question it and even now, when I wrestle with understanding, the thought of it makes me feel disloyal and uncomfortable.

So does God exist? Was it God that answered my prayer? Well someone or something did because from then on everything in my life began to change. It wasn't the instant answer I had expected or hoped for, in fact it would take fifteen years to turn my ship around from my 'normal way' and achieve my desire to be happy and fulfilled. If it had been God or some other object of worship – both of which according to dictionary definition qualify as something we can pray to – that had helped me then I didn't see it. I put the changes down to coincidence; lots of them, but whatever they were and wherever they came from they made me take notice. Then I discovered what would become my favourite quote from Einstein: *'Coincidence is God's way of remaining anonymous'*, and suddenly everything seemed to make so much sense and it felt like I had found the missing link to God.

For many the belief in things celestial is proof enough of a God or other life force and whilst I really do get that, I also get why many don't. I have a friend who believes that there is nothing more to life than our physical presence. According to him we are born and eventually we die, there is no before and no after. That of course is as difficult to disprove as it is to prove, but whilst being driven by him one day we passed a single magpie on the side of the road to which he saluted and said, *"Good morning Mr Magpie. How is your lady wife today?"* That was new to me and I was amused, so I asked him why he saluted and talked to the magpie? *"Because it's bad luck not too,"* he said, but there was no explanation for why it was unlucky other than he had always done and believed in it... oh, and his parents had always done the same! So I asked him who or what, when he didn't believe in God or any other life force, he expected to prevent the bad luck? The silence filled the car as he became lost in thought and I honoured his thinking and we said no more, although I smiled as I recalled my own superstitions, either inherited from my parents or learnt from childhood play, when on seeing magpies I would recite: *'One for sorrow, two for joy; three for a girl and four for a boy.'* I wasn't smart enough to remember the rest and it would take me many years to learn that it went further with *'five for silver, six for gold; seven for a secret never told'*.

Superstitions of course have been passed down through generations of families and they are willingly adopted without question as we learn from our childhood. Because they are harmless they will probably stay that way, and yet there are other family behaviours that we learn in good faith that can be harmful, which we would do well to challenge, but don't; and why would we unless, like me, we are trying to make sense of our lives?

Stepping on cracked pavements was also said to be unlucky and was another incomplete superstition that I tried for a while – the complete version is *'(to) step on a crack (will) break your mother's back'*, but either way it was impossible to avoid them while walking the two miles to senior school because I had mistakenly assumed it meant the pavement slab edges as well. In fact there were very few cracked pavement slabs that bordered the roads on our new council estate because those who could afford cars were few and far between.

It took becoming a fireman, as we were known then, to stop me from avoiding walking under the myriad of ladders the Fire Brigade has as the tools of its trade, because I had also believed in bad luck. It was the strangest of feelings during my practical training when confronted with the choice on an hourly basis, and even now, out of uniform and retired, it lingers somewhere deep within me.

Although I see superstitions as nonsense, I realise their origins do hint at something else that is bigger in life that is not, but it would take me many years to develop from the child within before I could ditch superstition in favour of personal responsibility.

I have gradually come to believe that life is not about good or bad luck and that life is in fact trying to help us at all times to overcome the consequences of our choices!

Although I didn't see the events that were to follow my prayer as being help there is no doubt in my mind now that they were. I still enjoyed the bottles of red with John Denver while writing poetry that had become my substitute for going out, but after a while I didn't need them so much as enjoyed them. The events that piqued my interest were really quite simple in the end; they were reading books that had been 'put' in front of me that I wouldn't normally have chosen to read. Two of them were books of fiction, because it was fiction that I preferred to read, so I guess it was no real surprise that my cry for help, my prayer, was answered through storytelling, but storytelling that also subtlety hinted at something bigger in life. The third book was said to be about getting answers from God, which I couldn't put down.

Because I wasn't consciously looking for books to help me I would have been unlikely to find any of them without help and there is no doubt in my mind that they had been intentionally 'manoeuvred' in front of me to give me the beginnings of an answer to my prayer. It didn't matter that I had gradually returned to my old ways, what mattered was that the so-called self-help books – found under thinking books now – had piqued my interest and had arrived one after the other through a series of coincidences until the third one delivered what was going to be as close as I was going to get to having pressed a 'magic button' to ensure I was engaged. To say that I enjoyed them hardly seems to do justice to the crucial role that they played in leading me towards the love and happiness I was so desperate for.

I now see life as a journey, a journey that is not easy to identify as such unless we are looking at it as a whole rather than snapshots of events in time. Seeing life as a journey gives us continuation by fitting our lives together one piece at a time to show us the bigger picture and that it is inevitable, if we are looking.

I began to make informed and better decisions as my 'honest ignorance' became opportunities to learn from and missed or taken as meant to be.

I have since taken that further by seeing coincidence, be they meaningful or not, as something called synchronicity, which is *'situations that look like accidents but are not, they are system'* or *'the occurrence of two related things simultaneously without planning'*, both of which are not a million miles away from coincidence: *'a striking occurrence of two or more events at one time apparently by mere chance.'* So if Einstein is right, and I think he is, then coincidence is a great way for any God to draw our attention to the bigger picture of synchronicity and on identifying it as such, offering us the help we so often need in life whilst remaining largely anonymous. As with most people my story is not a simple one, it offers up equal measures of pride and shame. It would have been easy for me to give up many times and hide, but instead I have used my shame to motivate myself to do better and never knowingly accept second best; to have done so would have been to devalue and waste the experiences on my unique road to success.

The Dalai Lama summed up how I began to see life as a journey so well when he said: *'People take different roads seeking happiness and fulfilment. Just because they're not on your road does not mean they are lost.'* That, above all else, was what gave me hope.

PART ONE

THE MAKING OF ME

1

Circumstances and Life Scripts

My parents would have been considered old in having children in their late thirties; my birth, just after Christmas 1949, meant I was the second son of three – the middle child. These are the circumstances that I have come to believe were chosen by me, and the story of how I would have to wait fifty-five years to learn that my lack of self-worth was created by the lack of praise, encouragement and loving attention from my mother, that meant I would never feel good enough unless I changed it.

We lived in a new council house – now called social housing – on a sprawling estate in south-west England, and by today's standards we would be considered financially poor. The poured concrete construction of the house was a cheap way to build that meant the house was cold and damp in the winter. Neither of our two fires were lit frequently or for any length of time; one was a coke-burning enamel stove with a drop-down front that revealed the red hot glowing coke in the corner of the scullery (kitchen) and the other was an open coal fire in the 'front room' (lounge), which was in fact at the back of the house overlooking the large rear garden that sloped gently up to the public woodlands of the Kings Weston Estate behind. A portable paraffin stove was used to boost the heating, especially in the dining room, but it wasn't until many years later that it was understood to be the main contributor of the considerable damp problem that Dad was constantly trying to cure. Similar to life in general really, trying to cure the symptoms rather than the root cause, albeit done with an honest ignorance.

After the Second World War, Dad found work in the stores of a large industrial site where he would work loyally for most of his working life with one promotion to foreman.

Mum had to supplement her meagre housekeeping money by cleaning other people's houses three or four days a week, but despite that we never went hungry and with her 'silver service' cooking skills, learnt before marriage, she produced the most amazing variety of tasty meals for us every day from the cheapest and largely unwanted cuts of meat, including boiled pigs' trotters. Tripe and onions were also a treat and with Dad growing our own vegetables and fruits we never lacked nutrition. Whatever else Mum wasn't to me, she was a brilliant cook.

Most of my earliest memories are supplied by family photographs, one of which was from the age of about eight when Dad began hiring a car for two weeks every summer for holidays; it would be the same routine each year, a week of day trips and then a week in a first-floor flat by the sea at either Weymouth or Falmouth. Once, when we were returning from Weymouth, the car caught fire at the aptly named Canards Grave near Shepton Mallet and we waited in the public house for the Fire Brigade to arrive. Whether that subconsciously influenced my decision to join the Fire Brigade when I was twenty five I do not know, but my older brother likes to tell anyone willing to listen that it was because I caught the long grass on fire in the field behind our house while playing with matches and which our local brigade had to extinguish!

I was not one of those children who longed to be a fireman or a train driver; in fact I don't remember ever thinking about my future at all. When I saw the careers officer in my fourth and penultimate year at senior school to discuss my career options I bizarrely said I would like to be a footballer or a long-distance lorry driver. I have no idea why or where those two unlikely choices came from; I have not achieved either but done both – neither very well.

My earliest childhood memory was of lying on my back in a pram (perambulator) screaming and crying, presumably alone in a kitchen with a wooden rack full of drying clothes attached to the ceiling above me. I say 'in a' kitchen now as opposed to our kitchen because it was only recently that my brother told me that we didn't have a clothes rack in our kitchen so I have no idea where I was, why I was crying or indeed if it ever happened. Two sessions of hypnotherapy have failed to reveal an explanation and it still lives on within me as a puzzle that encourages me to speculate.

I regarded my childhood as an unhappy and difficult one and my face on family photos, as snapshots of time, only served to confirm that, until a particularly important and significant day whilst training to be a personal counsellor. That day would turn out to be another major turning point in my life by helping me to see the reality of my childhood very differently to how I remembered it. The tutor that day had given each of us a large sheet of drawing paper, mine was purple, and a tin of crayons and said we were to draw as many happy memories from our childhoods as we could remember. Straight away I thought, *'Well that's a waste of time for me because I don't have any.'* The tutor went on, *'and all of you who have just said to yourselves "you don't have any", you do, and once you find one you will find others.'*

Everyone except me was busy drawing, my paper remained blank; I was feeling very isolated, awkward and embarrassed, but each time I glanced at the tutor she wasn't looking, although I was sure she was. It wasn't the fact that I'm not artistic that bothered me, but how it highlighted just how different my life must have been to everyone else's. After a very uncomfortable ten minutes I remembered the summer car hire and I began to draw the sweeping front wheel arches and wide running boards that I would step on to climb in; I visualised the polished wood dashboard and the smell of leather from the steering wheel and seats – especially the long front bench seat that are sadly not in use anymore – I smiled at the memory and was lost in a time that I had forgotten as I drew my childlike picture.

Just as the tutor had said, that memory led to another of clinging to my dad's neck and sliding around on the suntan oil applied to his back, just in case the sun shone, while he swam in the wonderfully shallow beginnings of the sea at Weymouth that seemed to go on forever. As I drew I could almost feel the texture of his woollen swimming trunks on my feet and I smiled at the feeling of being happy and safe and a little frightened at the same time. I also remembered the taste and texture of sand that always seemed to be an integral part of our thinly cut cheese and cucumber sandwiches handed out by Mum from her deckchair on the beach and eaten whilst sitting on a small damp towel while shivering underneath the almost inevitable cloudy sky. And then I remembered Auntie Daisy, my favourite person and Mum's sister, who would often come with us on the day trips and sit in the back of the car with us boys and cuddle me, which gave me so much more than she would ever know... or maybe she did! She would cheer us all and lift the gloom on cloudy days by pronouncing there to be *'enough blue in the sky to make a soldier's pair of trousers'* and *'it was sure to be a sunny day'*. I didn't draw that but my clumsy and hastily-drawn memories were making up for lost time with happy memories from Christmas when Dad would light the fire in the 'front room' as a treat, using newspaper to put across the fireplace opening to help to 'draw' the struggling fire into life; the Christmas tree standing invitingly in the corner of the room that we decorated together with wrapped presents placed tantalisingly below and homemade decorations made from paper rings looping across the ceilings with hanging balloons filling in the spaces.

All the memories that came flooding back were not necessarily happy ones but they weren't sad ones either. The point was they were coming back, as if a locked door to my memory had been opened as I drew the extreme cold temperatures with a 'brrrrrr' to represent my shivers when getting into the double bed shared with my younger brother, and kept apart by the long 'sausage' Mum had made from old cloth materials and placed under our soft fluffy winceyette bed sheet, keeping very still as the best way I had learnt to warm up. And on being woken in the freezing cold mornings and told to get up for breakfast when I would get dressed with lightning speed – without washing – to try and be the first down and sit on the only chair we had in the kitchen next to the only source of heat from the coke stove that had been lit by Dad before he went to work. My legs would be bright red from the glowing coke coals until Mum would tell me to move and stop 'hogging the fire'. I didn't move far from the short, stubby-legged chair to stand wedged between the fire and the wall with hands kept for as long as possible on the hot enamel pipe that stretched up from the fire through the ceiling.

The page filled with childish drawings of happy memories and others that were important too, simply because they belonged to my childhood that had for so long affected me. I was excited, a rare occurrence for me even now, and I wished I could have continued drawing all day but in truth I was also frightened that I would run out of happy memories and was relieved when we were told to stop.

It was a very emotional experience which had 'blown a hole' in my belief that my childhood was all unhappy. I hadn't forgotten the days and evenings spent playing in the street outside of our house where all the neighbouring children took part in the fantasy of our own Olympics, football and cricket tournaments, and in the woods behind the house either as a cowboy or an Indian on make-believe horses with plastic guns and real bows and arrows; it's just I didn't have time to draw them. I smiled as I laid down my crayons and sat back feeling a little more normal and wondering why I had buried such happy memories.

Later, on the same course and on what would turn out to be another day of great significance and discovery, I would learn how we all 'write' a 'life script' for ourselves based on the experiences of our early years up to and including the age of seven, and often beyond, and that that life script will influence the rest of our lives as we 'faithfully act it out'; and I began to understand how it had, and in that understanding was the sense that maybe I could do something about my way of life that had always been a puzzle to me. It was not lost on me that my prized childhood picture had begun with a lost memory from the age of eight.

Whatever the truth of my life's earliest years, we were a family and we went through it together, and for me in particular that meant 'hand me down's' extremely well-used from my older brother. Even my mother's excellent needlework skills could not repair them for what she would call *'the umpteenth time'* as they were torn and worn from playing outside, something we were always encouraged to do and which guaranteed my younger brother would have new. Despite that, his enduring and favourite story from childhood is how Mum would scour the second-hand shops for his clothes and how embarrassed he was to have to go to school dressed as a Japanese Emperor!

As well as the clothes being too big for me and often being 'lovingly' described as 'looking like a bag of spuds' by my mother, my biggest issue was the state of my shoes. By the time my brother had grown out of them they already had holes in the soles which would flap up and down, released by tired and rotten stitching, and making rhythmic flapping noises as I walked and often tripped and made far worse in the rain as my too big, heavily darned socks poked out of the front and soaked up the rainwater, making it look like a dog's tongue when panting.

In the wet and colder months I tried to limit the discomfort by cutting out shoe shapes from old newspapers – if we had any to spare as we also used it cut into small squares for toilet paper – or the longer lasting and luxurious but scarce cardboard to use as insoles. It was a blessing to use wellington boots, even in the hot summer months, when they were available, but I couldn't wear them to school. When I was at school, morning assembly would mean having to sit on cold flagstone floors in the high ceilinged entrance foyer of Kings Weston House, an imposing mansion, where I would regularly 'wet' myself and have to wear wet trousers and underpants all day, resulting in sore legs and, I assume, being rather smelly.

I guess it was no surprise that I missed a huge amount of school time unwell and spent lying alone in the double bed at home with Mum often at work. I would spend hours watching the squirrels and birds in the woods behind the house or picking at the lines of lumpy ice along the inside bottom edges of the galvanised windows formed by condensation that had frozen overnight in the winter, trying to prise off bigger and bigger lumps. When I felt well enough I would move downstairs, against my mother's strict instructions and, using the stumpy chair as a step, would climb onto the wooden draining board and sit with my feet in the Belfast sink waiting for her to appear weary from the walk up the steep hill of the adjoining road opposite. I do not remember a warm greeting.

I was ill so often, especially with tonsillitis, that when I was nine the doctor insisted I went to the local chemist once a week to have my weight recorded on a card. My brothers had both had their tonsils removed, but I wasn't deemed fit enough to survive the operation, which has left me vulnerable to throat infections ever since.

Mum would feed me bread – no crusts – and sugar in warmed milk as it was the only thing I could swallow; I only discovered recently that I am intolerant to cow's milk and I suppose I may have been even then, so if I was, the very thing that was supposed to be making me better was probably having the opposite effect.

When I was well I would love to eat sugar sandwiches made by putting spread on the bread and dipping it in the sugar bowl, shaking off the excess back into the bowl. I would also sneak spoonfuls of sugar as if I craved for it, and bizarrely coal dust from the floor of the coal store by wetting my finger and licking it clean like sherbet dip from a liquorice stick. I loved it.

In those days our milk was delivered to the doorstep and I can remember the birds would use the period from between milk delivery and the milk being taken in, to peck holes in the silver-coloured foil bottle tops and drink the milk; there were also gold-coloured bottle tops for the creamier milk, what we would call full fat now, but we never had them and not because they were deemed unhealthy as some would believe today. In the freezing winters the birds would have to be quick or go without because as the milk froze on the doorstep it would expand out from within the bottle, pushing upward in a frozen solid mass with the silver foil cover still on top. That used to fascinate me until at some stage we had the latest clay bottle covers for the milkman to put the bottles under, which must have dismayed the birds.

My parents weren't openly affectionate; I cannot remember being hugged, praised or encouraged, all of which would explain why I was always hanging around my mother, looking for attention.

When I was about eleven we were given an old upright piano and I used to enjoy trying to play *Three Blind Mice* or *Frère Jacques* with one finger. I have no idea who showed me that or who gave us the piano, but it must have cheered Mum and Dad that I actually 'showed an interest in something' because I was asked if I would like piano lessons – I know for sure it wasn't because I showed any signs of being a child prodigy. The arrangements were made and on the afternoon of the first lesson – which involved a bus trip of about 10 minutes – I prompted my mum to get ready as we were going to be late. I remember the fright of Mum saying I would have to go on my own as it washed across my body and my legs became wobbly, but despite my tears and fears she wouldn't relent and handed me the bus fare. I was a timid little boy who had never been on a bus on my own before and had no idea where the venue for the lesson was. I sat on the kitchen chair next to the cold and unwelcoming coke stove and sulked, but it didn't work, sulking never did when I was young, although I made it work as an adult when I became polished and almost professional at it. Mum said not to be silly as I was just having a dose of the collywobbles, but I didn't go and she reclaimed the fare.

Of course I didn't know then that I was sulking to gain attention as well as to get my own way; that was something else I learnt about whilst training to be a personal counsellor when they identified it as seeking recognition – positive recognition preferably but negative would do. Even when I thought I had stopped sulking, it soon became apparent that I hadn't, and like many other things in my life it had merely disguised itself and become much more subtle and 'appropriate' for an adult!

The first time I can remember receiving affection and attention – positive recognition – in my life was from Auntie Daisy who was married to Uncle Harold – they didn't have children. As well as joining us occasionally for holiday time day trips, she would take two buses every other Tuesday from her home on the outskirts of Bristol to visit us. Sometimes she would arrive before I got home from school at lunchtime and on other occasions I would have to wait for her to appear walking wearily at the top of the steep road opposite, just as I had done while waiting for Mum. I would like to say I was waiting for the cuddle I always got when sitting on her lap, but in truth it was more likely to be for the first choice of the cakes she would bring for each of us. What I am sure about is the value of the attention she gave me through the only hugs and cuddles I ever got. That's if my memory serves me correctly!

Since I have already proved that childhood memories can be a misinterpretation of the reality and neither of my brothers felt they were lacking in love, I also questioned the validity of my own feelings that I received little or no affection from Mum and that she was harsh with me right through my childhood to being married and leaving home. Whilst we all agree that we never had a bedtime story or cuddly toys, we do not agree on that and they insist they always felt loved. I would have to wait until I was nearing sixty-five years of age, when Mum and Dad had long since passed, and a chance meeting to get the information that Mum had

·king last as the last one left and no more choices to be made and never on merit.

During the summer months we would spend many hours outside the house using the pavements as an athletics track and mimic real athletes seen on our black and white television. Almost at the end of her working day Mum would sit with her cup of tea and her one cigarette of the day on the top step of the many that approached our back door from the pavement below, and from that elevated position she would love to watch us all playing. Her jobs were not done until the nine o'clock ritual of supper time for Dad, and eventually us boys as we qualified by age to enjoy the cheese and biscuits, cheese on toast or fried sprats and many other delights. It would be many years hence until I managed to break that routine as too late to eat.

Dad's shed was a mishmash of wood, old bicycle parts and prams left over from our childhoods, and a variety of rusty nuts and bolts, screws and nails, all of which we used to make four-wheeled carts whilst avoiding Dad's gardening tools stacked neatly in one corner. Our four-wheeled carts could seat up to five of us at a time and be steered down the pavement of the steep road opposite at great speed. It became a race when we had more than one cart. The drivers had little fear, steering with their feet or by pulling the cords on the front axle of wood that could be pivoted on the single bolt that attached it to the main body of the cart to make a cross member. I would never be at the front and steering! There were enough near misses as it was. The same hill was our track to hurtle down while sitting on a Christmas hardback *Beano* or *Dandy* annual balanced on a single roller skate. It was an art to keep balanced while leaning back with straight legs out in front and the body leaning slightly left or right to steer and I often fell off, scraping my fingers.

There were few events at junior school that I remember clearly; I would spend most of my day gazing out of the window, which for some reason the teacher had placed her desk in front of. On more than one occasion the police would use the area surrounding the school for dog training and I would sit mesmerised while watching police dog handlers train them to flush out and haul down the would-be escaping criminals; I didn't think to draw that as a happy memory!

A not so happy memory from the same classroom was one that would shape my life considerably from there on in when, for the first time ever, thinking I knew the answer to a teacher's question I put my hand up. The teacher must have been surprised and I guess, trying to encourage my new-found bravery, selected me to answer. I got it completely wrong. I felt so embarrassed and uncomfortable and experienced feelings not unlike those when Mum refused to accompany me on the bus to piano lessons. I have found it almost impossible to volunteer in any similar situation ever since. Our life scripts and learnt behaviours are so well embedded into our lives!

One time I fell from the top of a tall tree in the small wooded area next to a beautiful cedar tree and hit what seemed like every one of the many branches on the way to the floor; I picked myself up, sore and dazed and reported to the school office, feeling the worse for wear, where I was told to sit on the chair outside for 'observation'. I can remember it quite clearly now, but didn't draw that either; having gone back to look at the tree I am rather proud and astounded that I was even brave enough to climb that high or that I did not do serious damage to myself. Maybe it was to do with the woods and nature again but whatever it was, climbing that tree doesn't feel like me as I remembered me.

I could even feel alone when I was surrounded by other children playing on the huge sports field at the front of the school, which is where I was hit on the bridge of my nose by a 'flying' cricket bat thrown from somewhere by someone unknown. Despite being knocked over by the force and shocked, I didn't cry and wasn't helped. By the time I got home I had two black eyes, a swollen face and was interrogated by an angry mum. Who she was angry with, me or my assailant, I will never know.

I was not a child at twenty when my Mum's anger towards me surfaced again after my younger brother had been badly beaten up and she puzzlingly marched me into his bedroom and blamed me for not looking after him, despite not being with him.

I do not know when my childhood ended and adolescence began but many believe it ends at twelve, perhaps that's what my Mum believed when she insisted I travelled alone to the piano lesson that wasn't. I could argue that I stayed a child well beyond that and until the time when I began to feel I was in some sort of control of my life, but it's ridiculous to still consider yourself to be a child at twenty five when I joined the brigade.

It seems an obvious truth that I can only talk of the events that I can remember as I remember them. Whether I have blocked out others is probably lost forever now my parents are dead and my brothers' versions are different, but somewhere within that age period up to and after the important age of seven, were the events that shaped my life to become who I was and who I would become.

I was taught as a carpenter and joiner that if you don't start a job properly it won't finish properly, something I have personally experienced as being right. It would be a great analogy for human life from birth if it were not for the fact that I believe, with the right understanding and will, it can be put right to finish right and I am the living proof. But it would still be a long road ahead before I reached the point of understanding as my adolescence continued to be dictated by my life script.

2

Adolescence

My first day at senior school was celebrated by being in my new school uniform with new shoes and a leather satchel; to this day the smell and stiffness of leather still reminds me of that first day as I walked the two miles to school with it empty. My achievements at infant and junior school had been predictably poor, which meant I was allocated a place in the bottom stream of classes and wouldn't advance a great deal in the five years before I left. I was also no less timid, had no ambitions or expectations and my life drifted along, hardly creating a ripple.

I did not seek or make friends; they were my quarter ounce bags of sweets weighed from the tall glass jars with the screw top lids or an occasional penny bag of broken biscuits from the bottom of the biscuit barrel bought each day from the rank of shops outside the school on my way back from a lunchtime at home. I never felt alone and never shared my comforting friends as they were consumed one after the other during afternoon lessons by surreptitiously sliding my hand into the convenient patch pockets of my blazer and manoeuvring them into my mouth as if stifling a yawn or wiping my face. That I was never challenged puzzles me now so I assume being in the bottom class, inconspicuous and turning up was enough to satisfy the teachers to leave me alone with my quiet, undisruptive behaviour.

We were never given pocket money; we were expected to earn it. I achieved that by becoming a 'paper boy', delivering the local evening newspaper six days a week and with no thoughts of entrepreneurship; a Sunday morning paper round soon followed. The Sunday morning bag was bulky and heavy from the tabloids and larger broadsheet papers and with the strap digging into my shoulder it became easier to divide them into two bags for balance as more and more customers chose a lie in with doorstep delivery. Whether that was my initiative I do not know, but it was more likely to be the kind Mr Baldock who didn't want me to give it up, having done the round himself for a while.

Early one Sunday morning I was hit off my bike and left sprawling on the usually very busy main road, only briefly seeing the car as it sped away as I slowly untangled and lifted myself free from the bike and bags. It was at a junction where I would turn right into the road where I lived and my round started, so maybe I didn't look properly. I groggily pushed the bike for a while as I began posting the papers before putting the chain back on its cog ready for when I felt better and our road's steep beginning decreased enough to make it manageable. It was then that I felt a wetness in my left shoe and saw my sock was soaked with blood. Being close to home I called in and showed my mum who was the only one up and dressed besides me. She gave me a hot cup of tea with sugar for the shock and told me to rest on our stubby chair next to the unlit fire until I felt like continuing. What I felt like was a hug and a cuddle and to be told it would be alright; what I got was a bandage made from a discarded bed sheet ripped into strips to contain the bleed. The two deep gouges from the cogs of the chain ring are still visible today as shiny scars on the front of my left ankle, adding to my bent finger and nose as proof that I was alive and at least taking part in life.

My reward for being a reliable and punctual paperboy was being asked to swap my emptied bag of delivered papers on return to the shop every Friday for the well-worn leather money satchel and receipt book and head out again to customers' houses to collect the money due. Tearing the perforations of the small blue rectangular ticket and receiving payment in return made me feel important; some weeks it would be more than one as the customer cleared their arrears and that probably helped my maths. I am proud of those values that were learnt from my parents and that I was trusted; they have served me well most of my life as a positive part of a life script that often wasn't. How and why that script was responsible for me becoming sexually aroused for the first time in my life, whenever I arrived at one particular house in anticipation of the door being opened by a middle-aged woman, which it always was, I have no idea. Although I am sure a psychotherapist would say it was something to do with my relationship with my mother and I would have to agree rather than be labelled a potential sex pest, which I wasn't.

The first girlfriend I ever had was just that, a friend who was a girl from school. I would have been fourteen or fifteen at the time and unless you count kissing it was not a sexual relationship, probably because I didn't have a clue what a sexual relationship involved and that was probably just as well; we would hold hands while walking and look out for each other in the playground and in corridors. She was lovely, as I guess all first girlfriends are, but my lack of maturity was obvious when I asked one of her friends to tell her that I didn't want to be her boyfriend anymore, which was embarrassing and more playground than adolescent awareness. Having several boys approach me menacingly in the playground because I never had the courage to tell her myself was the only confrontation I can remember having at school; they were right of course, I learnt and would never do that again, I didn't like being frightened. It was the beginning of knowing girls and relationships and understanding what doing the right thing was; although that wouldn't make much difference later in life when married!

Like most firsts in our lives I have never forgotten it and if I had been asked to draw memories of embarrassing and awkward moments from my childhood that I regretted, that would be the first thing on the paper; I am constantly reminded of that time whenever I hear one of my favourite songs by Marvin Gaye: *I Heard it Through the Grapevine*, which was released years later in August 1968.

My health steadily improved, but I still shared a double bed with my younger brother, which was the cause of many squabbles until – at what age I do not know – Mum's solution was to make an even larger 'sausage' to place under our bottom sheet to keep us apart.

My older brother eventually left home to live with his girlfriend and that meant that at the age of fifteen I had my own bedroom and bed for the first time in my life, although why I moved into his small room and out of the double which overlooked the woods and not my younger brother I do not know. Did I choose or was I pushed? Maybe I was bored with the view after all those times home alone ill and in bed and I wanted a new view with people and cars.

    The only events that I remember taking place in that bedroom was managing to break a Christmas watch from my Christmas stocking before I wore it – it was never repaired; hiding myself away for hours in fear after being summoned to the front door by my angry mother to be confronted by the uncle of a girl from school who I had knowingly sold a defective car to; and one morning when she burst into my room, obviously planned, full of anger again and spitting with rage, to confront me masturbating and screaming that I was a *"a dirty little boy for making a mess on the bedding and I* (she would) *will have to clean it up*!" It seems quite innocent as I write, but it was frightening as well as embarrassing and damaging. I hesitate to call it a sex education, although I learnt – I never had any sex education from my parents.

My dad was what many would call 'a man's man', 'working hard and playing hard', which he did by enjoying drinking with his mates in the local working men's clubs and pubs, as well as ensuring he took Mum out on Thursday and Saturday evenings as 'her time'. On many Saturday evenings when we were too young to be left on our own we would be taken to the houses of his friends and kept out of the way while they drank, smoked and partied long into the night; when it was the turn of our house I would go into the still smoky front room early the next morning, before anyone else was up and, carefully picking my way around all the empty bottles and glasses that were strewn all over the room, would retrieve the longest fag ends from ashtrays that were sitting on floors and resting on the arms of chairs and settees. Then, with matches stolen from the box in the kitchen – not too many to be noticed – which I would strike on the wall in the outside toilet, I would relight them and choke in my many attempts to 'take back' (inhale) the smoke as I had watched them all do so many times. I never succeeded and I eventually tired of trying, a failure for which I will be eternally thankful for.

Dad's heavy smoking made him cough until he was red in the face every morning in the upstairs bathroom and that also helped to ensure that none of us ever smoked; he finally gave up when warned by his doctor that if he didn't he would be dead within five years. He did, having smoked just one more 'Woodbine' on getting home and in front of me he bravely, and not a little reluctantly, threw the rest of the packet in the kitchen waste bin and lived at least thirty more years.

Friday for Dad was pay day and the end of his working week when he would go drinking with his mates straight from work. Whenever he went to Shirehampton he would take the difficult short cut route home through the woods of our childhood playground and, the worse for wear, we would often hear him careering down the steep hill out of control and using the tightly packed trees to arrest his speedy descent, before arriving at the top of our garden with a smiley red face looking dishevelled and covered in mud, but happy; from there he would climb unsteadily over the wire fence and step down on the large section of a fallen tree trunk that he had placed as his seat for taking a rest from gardening, before walking the length of our generous garden packed with vegetables either side of him. His seat was our step to gain access to the field and woodland behind.

It would be a real treat for me to be taken by Dad to watch his team, Bristol City, play football at Ashton Gate. He would meet up with his fellow 'mad hatters' in the same corner of the lower terracing, where I have vague memories of being passed from shoulder to shoulder and sat on the wall at the edge of the pitch with my legs dangling over the advertising hoardings and passed back again at the end of the game.

Dad was a good, hard-working, charismatic man and a solid, if not hands on, father; most of the parenting was done by Mum. I can't recall seeing any closeness between them even when I was old enough to understand these things, but that doesn't mean there wasn't even if it was in their own way, because I can't remember them ever arguing either. He seemed to be loved and known by everyone and his were easy footsteps to follow in.

My own drinking started innocently enough when Dad's skittle team were looking for a replacement 'sticker up' (of the skittles) every Thursday evening at the local pub. As I lacked the confidence to do it on my own I asked one of the four local lads I had become friendly with to help me. My income gradually increased when other nights and Sunday lunchtimes were added and I was able to resign the paper rounds.

We soon became regulars at the pub and to start with we were bought lemonade and crisps to keep us happy; as we got older, small amounts of beer were added to the lemonade to make shandies, which gradually became stronger with more beer than lemonade. Our income increased even more as we were allowed to enter the Sunday lunchtime skittle competition as well as stick up and with our fair share of wins, along with often being given a small share of the winnings of other beer happy winners, Sundays became very profitable. I would often walk home with Dad when Mum would be impatiently waiting for him to carve the Sunday joint. When it was lamb I always felt I was being punished on being 'asked' to pick and chop the mint with sugar before adding the vinegar to make the mint sauce. Maybe it was because we were more often than not late for lunch, but with my dad a past master in planning and appeasement I witnessed on more than one occasion his ability to soothe my irate mother when we were extremely late by presenting her with a box of chocolates bought from the shop on the way home, that he said had been 'won' in the raffle, which he had been waiting for. He didn't say anything to me, we weren't close. No matter how late we were we always ate together as a family.

The act of learning at a secondary modern school – even in the lowest 'streams' – was a bigger struggle than the infants school had been. I was reasonable at mathematics but nothing else. In 1965, my final year, I was in the first group of students to sit the new CSE (Certificate of Secondary Education) exam which couldn't be failed. It was introduced specifically for pupils like me, who were not good academically, to be able to leave school with a certificate of achievement. Mine showed I had passed all of the seven exams I took with grades from three to five (grades were one to five) with the exception of maths, in which I achieved a Grade One pass, which was regarded as the equivalent pass of the higher General Certificate of Education (GCE). That prompted the Head of Maths to speak to me for the first time in my five years when he asked me if I intended staying on at school. He expressed his disappointment as a '*shame*' because I '*had done exceedingly well*'.

The shame was to be my own personal one, because the Grade One was also a surprise to me. I hadn't meant to cheat, but having finished all that I could on the exam paper, which meant most of it except for the algebra questions which I was useless at, I decided to use my protractor to measure the missing angle on the first algebra question, to my surprise and delight it was drawn to scale and with no requirement to show any working out I simply measured all the missing angles and recorded all the missing answers. It never occurred to me to question why an exam question would be that easy and I must have forgotten that protractors shouldn't be used, let alone be in the large gymnasium exam room. The fact I was so confident in measuring them probably helped me in not being caught, but the whole episode was yet another example of the fogginess that seemed to surround me in life. The paper qualification was and would never be of any use to me, although in some odd way I am proud of it.

3

First Day of Work

My dad, who I can barely remember talking to me about anything, asked me what I was going to do on leaving school. As I still had no idea he asked me if I wanted him to try and get me a job as an apprentice where he worked – something he had already succeeded in doing for my older brother who worked in the offices; I remember shrugging my shoulders less than enthusiastically and saying ok.

It was arranged for me to attend an aptitude test with eight other lads of the same age; there were nine apprenticeships available!

I have a vague memory that most of the tests were of a practical nature but the only part of the test I can really remember in any detail was being shown drawings of a set of interconnecting cogs and being asked if the first cog was turned in an anti-clockwise direction which way the end cog in the series would turn. In those days many companies gave preference to employing people whose close family were already employed so I was almost guaranteed a job offer subject to not doing badly; it was 'who you knew not what you knew'. Later that same day I was told that I finished ninth and was offered an apprenticeship as a carpenter and joiner. The other eight jobs demanded a higher level of technical ability for safety reasons as chemical plant technicians, electricians and plumbers.

To begin with I would travel to work and home with Dad which ensured I never 'clocked in' late or 'out' early. I looked forward to Fridays as the first time in my life that I would collect a wage packet, which was in a brown envelope, cleverly designed to show small portions of all the bank notes and strong enough for the loose coins rattling around within. Mostly I would have to make my own way home on Fridays and it wasn't long before I would ride my bike to and from work.

Although I really enjoyed being an apprentice I still found the practical and theoretical work a challenge because I was not a natural. Working was the beginning of growing up and I managed to pass all the City and Guilds exams necessary to qualify at the end of the five-year apprenticeship and even went further by passing exams at night school to begin qualifying as a building surveyor, which I did not have time, or the need, to finish.

Many of my work colleagues and my dad believed they had jobs for life if they wanted it, but I was keen not to get into the cosiness or familiarity of a working life that held them or indeed what would now be called the 'pension trap' – how things have changed. They would talk about their regrets of not moving on sooner and feeling trapped in some way and it was not a difficult decision for me to take the voluntary redundancy that we were all offered when I was twenty one.

I soon found another job as a carpenter and left the joinery side of the job and working in a factory workshop behind for good. Working on building sites was tough in comparison and it took me at least a year to adapt my skills and become reasonably comfortable and, what I would call, being good at my job. Once again, most of my learning was done the hard way, but I began to find work as a self-employed sub-contractor, which was seen as the way to go; it was more 'dog eat dog' than the cosy world of an apprenticeship, but the rewards were better. Good health and safety did not exist then and personal welfare was considered to be having a concrete building block to sit on in the freezing cold winters while eating my packed lunch and drinking warm coffee from a flask; anything else was considered an unnecessary expense which made the harsh winters with no shelter or hygiene facilities almost unbearable. I was earning £10 a day then which was considered good, and by employing an accountant and paying little or no tax it was even better.

By that time I had established a routine of drinking and dancing at clubs and pubs in town on weekends and more local in the week. Alcohol had already begun to take its grip on me with adverse effects and I would regularly make dates, when drunk, to meet up with girls the following week and, like many others, would arrange to meet them either Monday or Tuesday evenings at 'the map' in the city centre. The trouble was that there were always many girls to choose from as I struggled to identify my own date and I would have to rely on them recognising and approaching me as I frantically searched my memory while looking for signs. The relief on being approached was soon replaced by the awkwardness of not remembering their names, although I did develop quite a skill at negotiating the whole evening without it. There were also many times when I was stood up, either that or they had the same recognition problems, although it never, to my knowledge, got so bad that I spent the evening with the wrong girl.

All these new responsibilities and experiences were gradually inviting me to 'grow up' and it was against this background that I met my future wife when I was nineteen and we were married when I was twenty two. The first time we met was on the last bus home from town where I had been out with friends. When she got off the bus at the same stop as me I asked her out and was surprised that she lived just five minutes' walk away from me.

We got on well right from the start and our relationship blossomed quickly from evening dates to weekend trips to local beaches in my car when she would bring the most wonderful salmon sandwiches wrapped in tin foil. We did all the normal things that girlfriends and boyfriends did, like going for drinks and the cinema, and I quickly stopped going out with my mates. The night I asked her to marry me and she said yes made me feel amazing and I almost floated back home singing and whistling in a state of euphoria as I passed the scene of the bike accident years earlier without a thought. It was the happiest I have ever felt.

We began saving and set a date. As the wedding day approached we began to make the final arrangements and that's when my first doubts about what I was doing began. It was such a simple thing, we were discussing how to best utilise the wedding cars and it was proving difficult. My fiancée suggested that my parents didn't have to come in the wedding cars and could get to the church under their own steam. I was shocked, and I was shocked that I was shocked; I never got shocked about anything because usually I was so easy-going – although now I could probably substitute 'easy-going' for a lack of awareness. I retaliated by suggesting her mum and dad could get there under their own steam and mine would use the wedding cars. Eventually we sorted it out so everyone could use the wedding cars, but for some reason it had left a seed of doubt within me that I couldn't get out of my head and I seriously considered finishing the relationship and calling off the wedding.

But I didn't... and I made all sorts of irrational excuses in my head to convince myself why I shouldn't. Letting everyone down was one and convincing myself it would be alright was another, after all *'I had experienced the most amazing feeling when my fiancée said yes to my proposal'*... so surely everything would be alright and it was only about wedding cars and parents! Or was it? I didn't understand then how the feeling of being wanted and being good enough was probably at the root of it and I can't remember discussing my fears with anyone. Left with my own timidity we married. I had battled against my gut feelings and won.

4

Change of Career

Denis and I had worked together when I was an apprentice and he was fully qualified. We left at the same time and went our separate ways, but kept in touch through our shared passion for football and by attending night school together to obtain further building surveyor qualifications. Denis was learning to drive so he would drive us the fifteen miles to college and back and his wife would feed us with ham, egg and chips on our return, eaten sitting up to their small Formica topped table which has always remained with me as a cherished memory. We teamed up again a couple of years later to spend three prosperous and fun years converting large Victorian houses into student accommodation, but all good things come to an end and it did when the building trade, as it was prone to do, followed the economy into recession and by early 1975 contracts had all but come to a stop.

After a morning in the lounge of my house scouring the *Yellow Pages* for work we applied in desperation for work making wooden ladders in a factory and we were offered jobs over the phone, subject to interview. Neither of us truly believed this was the right solution, but we had the same work ethic that believed there was always work out there and sometimes 'you have to do what you have to do', no matter what it is, to pay the mortgage and put food on the table. But good work ethic or not, on the way there we laughed at what we were doing and turned around, determined not to panic and keep looking. We found a week's work here and there until Denis met an ex-school friend, who was working in the fast-developing dry lining trade on building sites, who offered him a job, which he had accepted.

I managed to find enough work to survive on my own for three months until I was also given an opportunity for alternative employment.

The first time I played organised senior football was with Denis, but at the age of twenty three, a year after I was married, I would end up playing for a team called Filton Old Boys, which I wasn't, on the other side of town. The team shared facilities with a rugby club who had a clubhouse and a bar and it had become a routine to have a drink after the game and it was there, having stayed much longer than usual, that I ended up talking to another Peter who lived locally. Although I knew of him as playing for the first team, being in the reserves meant we hadn't spoken. Within the hour I had learnt from this very proud and gregarious man that he was *'Peter John Dewey, ex Physical Training Instructor (PTI) Royal Navy who had been to Hong Kong twenty four times'*, who had left the Royal Navy two years previously and joined the Fire Brigade. Despite being a fireman, Peter considered himself as a bit of a carpenter and good with wood, which he worked with on his days off from the Fire Brigade to supplement what he said was poor pay. Because of that his solution for my dilemma was simple; join the Fire Brigade and work as a carpenter between shifts.

At that time I knew nothing about the Fire Brigade, except the obvious.

Avon Fire Brigade (Bristol Fire Brigade became defunct in April 1974, with local government boundary changes) were by chance recruiting as I made my enquiries and, armed with what Peter had already told me, I applied. It was not a sought-after job then and it wasn't just the pay that was poor but the conditions of service as well. However, the qualifications for entry weren't demanding, which suited my non-academic abilities perfectly and I managed to pass the basic English, maths and general knowledge tests and successfully carried a twelve-stone person, in the demonstrated manner of a fireman's lift, for one hundred yards and pass an interview. It was clear that my carpentry trade background was considered as a good transferable skill that could benefit the service and I accepted the job offer and started training in June 1975. How things have changed since then when it felt like I was being dragged in, now it's like winning the lottery just to get a job interview.

I soon began to see why my trade background was valued as we were expected to learn very technical information on a whole range of subjects, including hydraulics and the operation and use of a variety of water pumps, which then had to be applied to complicated practical skills. The Fire Brigade is not, as some people would like to think, all squirting water, cups of tea and playing snooker. Firemen – who became firefighters when the first females were recruited into Avon Brigade many years later – have to become competent and skilled team players with a diverse amount of equipment and procedures and able to 'think on their feet' in order to survive in a very dangerous and demanding job.

Fire Brigade life is very much modelled on the Royal Navy and the training is still one of the toughest challenges I have had to overcome in my life, with discipline and obeying orders unquestionably top of the list; there can be no time or place for arguing or discussions when the lives of firemen and the public are at stake at incidents when attitude and resilience is tested to the limit. I was one of thirty trainees who were constantly shouted at and mentally abused to the point of bullying and there were many times during the three months when I felt like resigning. Everything we did was designed to build and emphasise the importance of the team, and because of that I began to understand more about myself and others. I was growing up and, as importantly, I was developing an awareness of life that I had never had before.

We were split into three squads, each of which would have its own trainer allocated for all the practical training that were called 'drill sessions'. Mine was different to the other three, thank goodness. He had just transferred to Avon from another brigade and was much less about the shouting and more about explaining and encouraging, which suited me down to the ground. It was clear that the other training officers did not agree with his softly-softly approach and whenever he was off duty one in particular made it his own personal mission to what felt like trying to break me by making up for what he saw as the easy time we were having. He would scream in my face and taunt me and on one occasion, whilst using the high pressure hose reels, 'mentioned' that he wouldn't even let me water his garden let alone trust me to fight a fire. He was relentless in his aggressive attitude and had probably assessed me as being weak and someone who would buckle under pressure and although I never did, I can see why he would think so. I thank him now for being one of my biggest teachers in life, but I didn't at the time because it was the first time I had been really tested in life. As it was it stood me in good stead for many more tests to come and I grew up in that three months and learnt what working as a team and looking after each other meant.

The kindest thing I can say about him as a training officer was that he was ideally suited to it. He had given me many of the different skills required for surviving on a fire station and at incidents and he was one of the best operational officers I ever worked with and for. He became a good friend, eventually.

As well as the practical aspect of the training I had to pass a written exam each week based on the technical aspects of what we had been taught; failure was not an option and nor were the final exams which we had to 'pass out' from.

I was disappointed, but not surprised, to be posted to the White Watch (the other two watches were Red and Blue) on my local fire station at Station A3 Avonmouth, which I was informed was a 'very quiet station and one everyone should try to avoid'.

My probationary training and studying would continue for another two years and I craved the opportunity to learn how to be good at my job, but they were few and far between.

Like my first job as a carpenter, meeting the cheeky, confident and always grinning Peter John Dewey and becoming a fireman, when it had never been a dream or intentional, would seem for many years to be too good to be true and lucky. Now I see it wasn't about luck at all but meant to be. Being guided into my second job was perfect for me and perfect for my life ahead.

5

Learning to Cook

One of the skills I had to learn quickly was learning to cook. All fire stations employed cooks then, but only during the day shift when they would cook mid-morning breakfasts after the 90-minute practical training and fitness period. A Fire Brigade cheese on toast had become the breakfast of choice for many of the firemen across the UK and was something to savour with its grated cheese and diced onions mixed together and piled as high as possible on freshly sliced thick white bread and grilled until it bubbled and melted; these were not the thin cheese on toast of suppers at home with Mum and Dad. The cooks were sometimes asked to prepare meals for the oncoming night shift, especially if there was a major training exercise involving the whole watch, but normally watches preferred to cook their own and we would all have to take our turn on night duty. The inexperienced ones like me were not trusted with meals that had to be paid for and we were paired with someone who knew what they were doing with a good roast or spaghetti Bolognese a common choice.

Despite the ever-increasing arguments at home, my wife and I continued to work hard together improving our home. One of the projects was building our own fitted kitchen. This was before the days that you could go into a DIY store and pick up cheap readymade units and we were both proud of the end result. With my new confidence in cooking I decided to surprise her by preparing and cooking our evening meal while she was at work. It wasn't the sort of surprise I had hoped for as I struggled with the instructions from the cookery book and the kitchen was in chaos as she walked in. I tried to explain, but there was no appeasing her horror at the state of 'her' new kitchen, and the battle escalated and, as normal, lasted many days. It was rather ironic that having had so many problems with shoes when I was younger that it was my inability to make choux pastry that was my downfall!

I hated confrontation and would withdraw into my own world of quietness instead of trying to sort it out. Although it made me feel better it had the effect of frustrating my wife even more as she pursued me, trying to resolve her own dissatisfactions. Eventually, after many days, I would snap and lose my temper, but once it did the storm would be quickly over as we both calmed down; unfortunately, my version of calming down was to limit my communication and interaction altogether by going into a stubborn sulk that would last for many more days.

Having vowed that I would never make another meal, I didn't. I was also stubborn in refusing to replace a bedroom door that had been damaged by a shoe that had been thrown at me and missed. That's what it is like to behave like a child in an adult body! It was becoming more and more obvious that we couldn't live in harmony together as our many differences hardly narrowed at all and, from my perspective, I had no idea then what was causing the problems and we battled on with no apparent awareness of how to stop. That is not to say that we didn't have good and happy times together because we did, but as with my childhood days it is so much easier to remember the not so good things.

The birth of our daughter, four years after we were married and a year after I joined the Fire Brigade was, next to the birth of our son three years later, the happiest of times, although I was about to find out that as well as bringing joy, children would bring hard and relentless work. As a mother my wife finished work to look after us all and she did it very well.

Although I didn't drink alcohol regularly, and by that I mean every night, when I did I often made up for it by 'binge drinking'. On the celebration drink with friends to 'wet the baby's head' my wife's dislike of my drinking was to be justified, as to my shame I became so drunk that I ended up with what is called a 'love bite' on my neck. When I woke up the morning after I was horrified by what I had done and, despite my attempts to hide it, my wife saw it straight away when I visited her and my daughter in hospital. There is no excuse. The only thing that makes me feel any better about it was that nothing else happened, it was the briefest of encounters when I stupidly, and drunkenly, kissed a girl on the way home with my friends; I realised straight away when she tried to kiss my neck but obviously I was not quick enough and, despite it being very small, it was too late. I promised it would never happen again, but alcohol had not finished playing a big part in my life.

Avonmouth was, as promised, a very quiet fire station. Partly because most of its ground (the area it covered defined by set out boundaries) was packed with 'high risk' and well-protected industrial sites and partly because it had a smaller than average residential area. Being quiet did have one advantage as I had plenty of time to study for my quarterly probationary exams and I also decided to study for the Fire Service's statutory exams that are used for promotions.

Six months after completing my two-year probation I applied for a transfer to a busier station, as I feared becoming stuck in the same way I had witnessed others to be when I was an apprentice and also many of the firemen at Avonmouth had become. Again I reasoned that if I didn't leave quickly, the chances were I never would.

My transfer was granted in 1978. By then I had passed the first of the three statutory promotion exams required for promotion, which was the leading fireman exam in two parts, one written and the other a practical test where I had to demonstrate my ability to command and control a small practical training incident in charge of a fire appliance and crew of five.

My transfer to the smaller but busier station at Southmead on the Blue Watch enabled me to begin learning the practical aspects of real firefighting. It was by no means an easy ride as I came across another vindictive officer who made my life a misery, but I persevered, even trying to win him over by finishing a wooden table off that he was in the middle of gluing together when they had a shout, which I was not attending having been left behind to cook the meal.

Despite all that, my time at Southmead was rewarding and fun but with a real mixture of personalities on the watch I was to learn many more lessons that year. One of them was in the kitchen where I had once again been left behind to cook the suppers and I inadvertently used the top quality mince of a very vindictive fireman who, as a non mess club member, had brought it in to cook his own meal. Ours was still in the freezer forgotten, and was by far an inferior quality, but the lads, who realised when they returned, kept him busy and out of the way while they defrosted ours for him and started to cook it so he wouldn't know. But he did know, he just couldn't prove it as we brazened it out. Nothing more was said.

Another was over Christmas when what was supposed to be an exercise in fun and team building turned into a nightmare. We were in the lecture room when the watch commander asked each individual to write on the chalk board what they would give each of their colleagues as a present for Christmas and why. What started off as funny and ingenious quickly turned into an opportunity for some to use the gift as a weapon to vent personal frustrations; one said he would buy sandpaper so that a certain individual would feel more comfortable when he sat on the fence; the retaliation was quick and equally as sharp when a bottle of milk to neutralise his acid tongue was offered. Others were less caustic, like cookery books or a book on personal hygiene, alarm clocks, easy to open wallets and a lie detector kit. It was quickly stopped, but not before a lot of damage was done; an object lesson in how not to build morale.

On the plus side I did gradually begin to gain experience as a fireman and, as we were short of qualified HGV (now LGV) drivers, I was trained and became qualified to drive the fire appliance – called pumps by firefighters. I also passed the second of the three promotion exams that year, which qualified me up to and including the next rank of sub-officer; it was much the same format as the first exam but with an expanded and more complicated practical scenario involving two pumps and a total crew of nine.

I was offered my first brigade promotion to Leading Fireman, which I didn't want, a year after transferring to Southmead simply because I was one of the few firefighters who were qualified up to and including the first two ranks. The offer came as a result of the first ever national Fire Brigade strike which, after nine weeks, had resulted in a new pay deal and the creation of a fourth watch, to be called Green Watch. It was needed to accommodate the additional firemen employed to reduce the working hours from 54 per week to 48. When I declined to apply I was put under pressure so I asked for time to consider the offer, which would mean a transfer back to Avonmouth. I eventually accepted with the proviso that I would be allocated the next available place on the Junior Officers' course at the Fire Service National College at Moreton-in-Marsh, Gloucestershire.

The college, located on an unused RAF station from the war, had been developed into an international teaching facility and was used by fire officers from across the UK and abroad. It has an extensive range of purpose-built concrete fire resistant training buildings used for both practical firefighting, and command and control training. It includes high-rise buildings with lifts, a concrete ship surrounded by a moat, mock industrial units with basements, sewer complexes and a breathing apparatus training building that can produce extreme temperatures and smoke conditions from real fires burning in fire cribs full with wood and straw. There are also full-scale stretches of motorways for RTC (road traffic collisions) training involving buses and cars, and chemical incidents including sections of railway lines and carriages. It was a place to experience real incidents under controlled conditions and was the perfect place for me to catch up.

I was allocated a place on the six-week course within six months of being promoted and it was everything I had hoped for as academic, practical and tailored for officers like me on their first tier of promotion. I returned full of confidence and a friendship with Iain from the Durham County Fire Brigade.

It would be the first course of many that would eventually accumulate to spending one whole year there out of my 30-year service. The longest course was thirteen weeks and would be the catalyst for my next major life change.

6

An Introduction to Death

I guess it was not surprising that many of the arguments with my wife centred on my drinking alcohol. Any justification I may have had, had disappeared with my own stupidity and lack of control. I would mostly drink at weekends when we were out together, but I did occasionally enjoy going to the pub with my dad, and sometimes my brothers, on a Sunday lunchtime when I was not at work or busy at home.

I still hadn't worked out the connection that I was mimicking my father's behaviour, by accepting it as what I considered to be 'normal life' and my wife was doing the same from a family where the complete opposite was the norm and drank alcohol very sparingly.

That difference meant that Sundays in particular became a battle between our learnt behaviours and, although I didn't understand that concept then, I did agree, as a compromise, that when I did go for a lunchtime drink I would be home for 1.30pm when the Sunday lunch would be *'on the table with or without me'*, and it always was, whether I was five or twenty minutes late; ironically lunch was rarely on the table at the agreed time if I stayed home to work.

It was no surprise then that our battle extended to include Sunday afternoon family walks, something else I had never experienced as a learnt behaviour with my family on any day... unlike my wife. All I wanted to do was to fall asleep on the settee after my Sunday lunchtime drink and a lovely Sunday roast, just like my dad used too. I was fine on non-drinking weekends and the children loved them, and so did I as I relented after a few weeks of stubbornness. Being stubborn, sulking and playing games was another battle going on within me, which would take many more years to overcome. Eventually, Sunday afternoon walks with my new family and often shared with my wife's became my pleasure, with or without alcohol, as I shared my childhood playground of Kingsweston Woods.

I didn't know at the time just how important nature was to me; nor did I see our lives as a battle between what we had both been shaped to be by the learnt behaviours of our respective families.

Compromise is a great and necessary thing, but understanding why it is needed in the first place is greater and essential if two young people from different backgrounds are to grow into their real selves together and not consider the other a threat to who they are; if only we were all born with wisdom and understanding.

My learning within the Fire Brigade was an altogether quicker affair, including how to be a competent young officer at Avonmouth Fire Station and I soon yearned for a busier station to extend my learning. That was soon satisfied when my transfer request to the Green Watch at the brigade's busiest and most diverse station at Temple Back in central Bristol was granted much earlier than I could have hoped for or expected. I soon began to panic at the reality of being a leader of very experienced firemen. I had been married for eleven years, was thirty-four years of age and my daughter and son were seven and four respectively.

Firemen at busy stations were considered, mainly by themselves, to be the best because of the confidence they gained from being busy and the status that goes with it, but we would all do well to remember that thinking we are the best at anything transcends that fine line between confidence and arrogance; confidence is empowering, arrogance is dangerous! Yes most of them were good, experienced firemen, but not all, and it was a far less an intimidating place than I expected. All those who held themselves back for the fear of being inadequate were wrong and I have learnt there is nothing to fear about change other than the fear itself. I was not confident, but I harnessed and overcame my fears by being determined to become the best I could be – without realising it, I am a typical Capricorn who are said to be steadily ambitious.

Staying in comfort zones for the fear of change can be so limiting and difficult to overcome, whether it is in the workplace or in your personal life. My early work years as an apprentice carpenter and a probationary fireman were comfortable experiences because no one expected me to know everything. Those who were willing to teach me mostly took pride in watching me grow, but I have also encountered some who jealously guard their knowledge lest, God forbid, others become more competent than them; a trait that is born from a lack of confidence and self-belief created by a lack of support and encouragement in our earliest years. They mask their lack of self-worth by seeing others as a threat to their own status and use phrases like *'I had to learn the hard way so why shouldn't you'*.

I had already experienced the difficult times transiting from the comfort zone of the carpenter's workshop to the tough environment of building sites and survived; it was unbelievably hard at times and I made many mistakes, some of which cost me my wages to put right, but it had shown me that it could be done and my fears overcome.

Low or limited self-confidence is born from a lack or limited self-worth. Self-worth, or the lack of it, lives within our subconscious mind as our life script that was formulated by the circumstances of our early years. I had to wait for fifty years of chaos and mainly disappointing life before I asked for help and questioned who I was. There are many people who will not or will have no need because they have adapted or accepted their lack of confidence as normal behaviour and in doing so have reinforced it through an 'honest ignorance' to accept who they have become, and that is ok if that is how it is supposed to be. Knowing if it is meant to be is the tricky part of our journeys and that is why many of our actions should not be considered right or wrong within the context of how we live our lives; that is personal choice, but a choice driven by our circumstance that we can change if we choose to and know how. At thirty-four years of age I was still sixteen years away from the beginning of that particular journey.

At Temple Back Fire Station I would be one of a team of six officers who managed the watch of eighteen, mostly experienced firemen. Of this twenty four there would always be a minimum of seventeen on duty at any one time to crew the three frontline fire appliances, a specialist rescue appliance, and a turntable ladder for working at heights. We also had a command and control vehicle for use at larger or unusual incidents and a specialist rope rescue team for cliff faces or any other high or awkward places, both of which were 'alternatively crewed' when needed.

In my early years we talked of 'manning' the fire appliances, but with equality and fairness issues encouraging political correctness we soon began to use the term 'crewing' instead. One of the more crazy decisions we had to abide by was to drop the term '**man**hole covers' for 'metal or drain covers' but that, like many other crazy decisions at the time that did nothing for equality or fairness, has been sensibly reversed over time.

To survive I had to grow up fast and the best way I considered to do that was to stay in the background while I observed, listened and learnt from everyone and everything. What others on the watch considered to be banter and having 'the craic' around the mess room table, as they discussed everything happy, funny, sad and unusual that they had experienced, I looked upon as a rich source of knowledge, whether it was about incidents attended on 'shouts' – Fire Brigade slang for incidents – or the sometimes unusual and even bizarre situations that always seemed to occur around firemen on fire stations.

I enlisted the help of senior firemen as well as my fellow officers and was honest with them about my lack of experience and desire to learn. This was no time to bluff my way through and it worked, as bit by bit I learnt the job of being a good fireman and a junior officer at the same time; in at the deep end but the best place to learn.

Nine years after joining the brigade, and for the first time, I would be introduced to what would become a regular meeting with death and serious injury and I still didn't know how I would react. It was well-known that some operational personnel could not deal with them at all and would manoeuvre their career choices to avoid it as much as they could.

My first fatality occurred around 0200hrs one morning when we were 'turned out' to a 'persons reported' fire – which means somebody was believed to be within a building that was on fire; possibly trapped, but not always. The time taken for crews to turn out from a station from first receiving a call is incredibly quick but when the words 'persons reported' are shouted it gets even quicker. As was the way then, we were alerted to the 'shout' by way of ringing bells (bells have since been sensibly removed as being a hazard to health), activated by the central control room staff, who had taken the 999 call. Their job is to professionally extract the correct location from the caller, to dispatch the correct 'predetermined attendance' for that area and type of incident and anything else that could possibly help the crews, all of which is not an easy task with 999 callers who are often distressed, not thinking straight and desperate to get off the phone to help.

We made our individual ways to the nearest of the many dispatch boards that were strategically placed around the large station and always next to the firemen's poles. The boards were divided into sections, each of which represented a different appliance call sign that could be illuminated by the control room staff to give instant visual information as to which appliances were needed. On our way to the appliance the OIC (Officer-in-Charge) would go to a teleprinter where all the relevant details of the incident were printed out on what is called a 'tip sheet'. That whole system has since been replaced by a softer alerter tone that emits a series of high-pitched notes through a loudspeaker system that the control room staff would also use to announce which appliances were required, incident location and type of call; always backed up by a 'tip sheet' (hard copy) to eliminate mistakes.

On arrival at the lower ground-floor flat we were met by a police officer who confirmed the fire and that somebody was still believed to be inside. As the crews prepared to enter with their breathing apparatus I went around the back of the building to assess the situation more fully; this is standard practice on any incident, with the OIC staying in control at the front. I was met by another police officer who was looking through a partially open ground-floor window. He told me there was too much smoke to get inside and left to return to the front. I also looked through the gap and saw that the light smoke-logging (used by firefighters in a similar way to water logging) was much clearer at floor level and looked to be what we would call 'clean smoke' – meaning not acrid – so I took a deep breath and climbed in.

I found the girl of about twenty in a room at the front of the flat lying on a bed with just a mattress that was smouldering slightly and producing the smoke. I picked her up and was surprised at how light she was; it was like picking up a young child. My colleague, Brian, who had already forced open the front door to allow entry of the breathing apparatus team had come in to help me in response to my fire ground radio communication informing the team what I was doing. After a very quick briefing to the breathing apparatus team as we passed, Brian and I assessed the young girl to be not breathing, no heartbeat and no visible injuries.

We worked together, as we had been trained to do, with me administering mouth-to-mouth resuscitation and Brian the heart massage. It sounds so simple writing that, but the truth was it was far from that, with the reality that we were fighting for someone's life. No matter how well-trained at resuscitation, doing it for real is completely different to practising on a manikin. It was to be the first and last time in my career that I carried out mouth-to-mouth resuscitation. We continued for what seemed a lifetime, but in reality was less than ten minutes until the ambulance crew arrived – this was before the days of paramedics – who took one look at her eyes as they assessed her and told us we were wasting our time.

On our return to the station I asked my boss – he was the same training officer who had said that I was so useless he wouldn't let me water his garden – if I could attend the autopsy; he agreed and made the arrangements for Brian and I to attend at 0930 that morning.

It was the saddest, most thought-provoking experience of my life, and definitely the worst. The doctor performing the autopsy asked if either of us smoked, which neither of us did. *"Shame,"* he said with a rue smile pointing to the heavily nicotine-stained fingers, *"because if you did you wouldn't after seeing this."* He prepared the body and removed the lungs and then cut them in half; we looked on, awestruck and in amazement, as he began to fill a glass with black tar poured from each lung and then showed us how it had clogged up the delicate alveoli within it. We both began to feel queasy.

I had nearly fainted with the shock of seeing the body being opened for the removal of all the major organs for inspection. It made me question whether I had performed the mouth-to-mouth resuscitation correctly and it put a completely different perspective on the value of a human life. From that day on, training professionally and regularly with a heavy accent on practical skills, not only for myself but for those who I had the responsibility to train, took on a whole new meaning and purpose. I learnt so much from the whole experience from beginning to end that it reinforced my determination to be as good a fireman and fire officer as was possible. As a start I requested permission to attend the inquest at the coroner's court.

Although the smoke from the fire was not what we would have called acrid, and even though I referred to it as clean, it was not; all smoke is full of the 'silent killer' carbon monoxide and the inhalation of carbon monoxide had caused the blood vessels within the windpipe to change from the normal blood red to a much deeper shade of red. The distinct change in colour was easily visible at the autopsy, and with the absence of any further evidence from the very thorough autopsy, the doctor attributed it as the cause of the young lady's death.

The coroner's verdict was that the young lady died from the effect of smoke inhalation caused by the slowly smouldering fire in the horsehair filling of the mattress ignited by her cigarette after she had fallen asleep whilst smoking in bed. One of the most poignant facts from the autopsy was that there was nothing except a small amount of cider in her system, which meant she hadn't eaten for some while and that made me feel emotional as I tried to work out what sort of life she was living.

At that time, the 'careless disposal' of smoking materials was one of the two most common causes of fire, and sometimes death in the home, the other being unattended chip pans, both of which have substantially increased risk factors when alcohol is involved.

7

Peter John Dewey

A year after the death of the young woman, my stay at Temple Back Fire Station came to an end when I was offered a temporary promotion to sub-officer and a return to Southmead to cover long-term sickness. Temple Back had been everything I wished for with an increase in confidence and knowledge, which was one of the reasons I asked for time to consider the move. The other was because I would be in charge of the Red Watch, and Peter John Dewey, my friend and mentor who was 'ex PTI Royal Navy, been to Hong Kong twenty four times' would be my second-in-command. I talked it over with him and, with the understanding I could be returned voluntarily or due to a change in circumstance to Temple Back at any time, I accepted.

During that second spell at Southmead I was approached to become the manager of the brigade football team; word had got around that I was a manager at Filton Old Boys. Again I had my doubts, mainly because I would be losing my last connection to a social life and friendships outside of the Fire Brigade, which had become so all encompassing. In the end, flattery from the football club chairman, who was also the 'I wouldn't let you water my garden' officer, helped to persuade me.

Life at Southmead with Peter and Red Watch was fun. We attended a variety of incidents when my learning continued as I tactfully learnt to ignore Peter's gentle promptings and subtle suggestions, always delivered with his testing smile as confirmation I was getting it right. It was the beginning of being able to put into practice my intentions for regular and professional training sessions as I developed my own methods to gradually silence the whingeing complacencies of the so-called 'older hands' who thought they had nothing to learn.

The Fire Service is the one service that the public and

businesses can turn to to provide professional, trained personnel and a diverse range of mobile, fixed and portable equipment to deal with and co-ordinate major and unusual incidents beyond any other, and my mission was to keep it that way on my watch.

Firemen are just a small but important part of the team, from control room staff to civilian support, that delivers a service to the public who are their paymasters. Gone are the days when insurance companies were the paymasters through premiums and fire brigades were just for the financially rich. Personally, I believe insurance companies should make contributions to a service that continually saves them money, but that's another story.

Calls attended by the brigade that are classified as fires or humanitarian are free at the point of use; however, so-called non-humanitarian calls can be charged for unless they are turned into humanitarian or training exercises by the resourcefulness of the crews. Emptying or filling private swimming pools is a good example of a non-humanitarian call that can be used as a training exercise and calls to gain entry to locked properties by occupiers are reclassified by suggesting to occupiers that they have *'surely left a pan cooking on a stove'*, which is a potential fire risk.

Unfortunately, the public could often be even more resourceful than we were at being one step ahead and, on one such occasion when we used our ladders to gain access into a second-floor apartment through an open window, the grateful client removed items that he was not legally entitled to. Despite carrying out our normal checks to confirm genuine occupancy, which he had done by describing the location and description of certain items within, what we didn't know was that he had been locked out by the authority of a court order in an ongoing domestic dispute. No wonder he was more than normally grateful and a happy man for the free service we had supplied as he enthusiastically waved us goodbye on entering the apartment. His estranged wife called the police on discovering the burglary on her return. Our systems were updated following that so that the police are asked to do the verifying before we gain entry.

Another unusual incident involved a fire that caused extensive damage to the roof of a bungalow when my fire investigation and the evidence showed that the fire had started in timbers surrounding and close to a boiler flue and then spread to the roof. According to the occupier she had last lit the boiler three days earlier, which was queried by the insurance loss adjustor; we agreed it as the most likely cause but he was insistent the fire would have taken hold before the three days. When I returned, at his request, he took me to one side and said if the occupier continued to insist that the boiler hadn't been lit for three days the claim would be denied because he could see no other cause. Away from the assessor, who knew exactly what I would do because he had hinted at it, I explained to the claimant that if she wanted the insurance to pay she would have to tell a 'white lie'. She was a very honest lady and found it all very difficult, but she did what she had to do and was paid out; I just wish there were more people around like that assessor who was human enough to do the 'right thing'. Not all incidents are true to the text books and neither is life either.

Another incident involving money was when we were called to a pub where the landlord had put a large amount of rolled-up bank notes from the Sunday lunchtime takings in an oven as a temporary hiding place while he cleaned up. It's not rocket science is it?; he knew, but someone else didn't and turned the oven on to heat themselves a snack. The bank notes were well done and badly burnt around the edges and we were all politely amused.

Not all incidents were about people and money, although when animals were involved humans always had some sort of a role to play. We received a call to a bird of prey caught in overhead telephone wires in the middle of a large grassed area that formed part of an overspill car park at the Bristol County Ground where Gloucestershire County Cricket Club play. The bird was alive but hanging upside down and frantically trying to free itself from what turned out to be kite wires that were wrapped around the telephone wires. The only way we could reach it quickly was to 'pitch' our thirteen-and-a-half metre ladder, the longest and heaviest ladder we carried, which was capable of being manhandled with its long poles, or props as we called them. As it was in the open we had nowhere to rest the ladder against, which was always the preferred option, so we pitched the ladder beneath the bird and stabilised it by holding its two props while Peter who had 'volunteered' – in truth no one else would have been have been allowed to – climbed the ladder and untangled the bird. He was protected by safety glasses and gloves and a total trust in his colleagues to keep the ladder upright. As there were some doubts as to whether the bird was injured and could fly, it was decided to place it in a cardboard box and take it to a vet who gave it a clean bill of health. We returned to the fire station with the bird in the box and, because it was near to the evening shift change-over time, Peter 'volunteered' to take care of the bird, which meant taking it home and training it.

The incident caused a lot of local media interest and became a front page story with the *Bristol Evening Post*, who published the story with a large picture of Peter proudly holding the bird. Five days later I was invited to his garden to see the progress the bird was making flying – tethered – from his perch to Peter's arm; he was so proud of his quick achievements as the bird swooped many times to take its reward. Unfortunately, or fortunately if you were the bird, Peter was never the most patient of people and while I was there he decided to try the bird off the tether and, much to his disappointment and surprise – but not mine – the bird flew happily away; we laughed.

After a happy year of subtle mentoring by Peter and with the long-term absence through sickness continuing into the foreseeable future, I was substantially promoted in post without assessment, a rare occurrence that I was thankful for because it suited me to be judged on what I was best at rather than an interview which I wasn't. Peter and I would spend a total of two-and-a-half very happy years together managing Red Watch and having fun at work.

8

Marriage Guidance

The Fire Brigade had become my school of excellence for maturity and awareness and it felt like I was catching up quickly from a very slow start. My parents' gift of a good work ethic would stay with me for life as a complementary learnt behaviour; in a perfect world I would have chosen for it to be like that for emotional issues, but I had no awareness of such things then. My dad's attitude of 'work hard, play hard' meant I always had money in my pocket to spend, but my wife had learnt from her parents to be more cautious with money than I had.

The renovation and modernisation of our home was almost complete and, having spent years doing it for others, I was developing a taste for doing it for myself and my family, so when a dilapidated three-storey Victorian terraced house in our area came up for sale by auction I became excited and interested. My wife was not. Although it was probably the right decision not to live under a badly leaking roof and a house that would have to dry out, I saw it as symptomatic of our battle that was by then a normal part of our lives. I know I was wrong, but that didn't stop me from using it as a weapon in our other battles.

Many years later after Mum had died, Dad, trying to ease his financial commitments and do his three boys a favour at the same time, offered us the opportunity to buy his council bungalow for him at a ridiculously low price under the right to buy scheme. Although it would have meant another financial commitment it would have been a sound investment for our futures. Once again I was disappointed to get an absolute no. Many people have said to me why didn't I do it anyway and fund it from my growing carpentry side line, but I couldn't no matter the battle, that would have been disrespectful, although I did think about it. No matter what my wife was, she always well-intentioned and, although I didn't use it as a weapon per se, it was just one more incident that reflected our differences as it quietly put another 'nail in the coffin' that was our marriage.

We had tried to sort our marriage out over many years but we both acknowledged, with a widening gap becoming a chasm, that we needed help and we agreed to go to couples counselling with what was then called 'The Marriage Guidance Council' and later became 'Relate'. In total we would attend three separate sessions of six weekly meetings over many years with little sustained improvement, which was hardly surprising when I was not honest on any of the three opening sessions when we were asked individually to answer honestly whether we wanted the marriage to work and be together? We would both answer yes, but with mine the voice in my head was saying NO.

What is it they say about speaking your truth; why couldn't I? Because if I had maybe it would have been different, maybe they would have suggested individual counselling, which in hindsight was the very thing I actually needed, or maybe they would have said we will help you to separate amicably? Although I think that was the very thing I was afraid of, and anyway none of it was my fault, it was my wife that would have to change, not me because I was ok! Wasn't I?

Not speaking your truth will always make things more difficult and it did as the hole I was digging for myself became deeper and deeper. I feel we did both try to change in our own ways, but it didn't make living together any easier. I read somewhere that when in a relationship and we start to look at other women or men as potential partners it's usually a sign that the relationship is over, which is exactly what I had started to do.

We continued doing all the things that families do together; in fact we did a lot more than my family ever did. We had good family camping holidays and continued decorating and improving the house; I demolished the old garage and built a new one attached to the house and we had UPCV double-glazed windows installed to replace the original galvanised ones. To all our friends and family it looked like we were the perfect family and when we finally split up it was a shock to them, but behind closed doors nothing we did to improve the house seemed to improve our life together. I know I loved my children because I felt it and they made me feel alive, but my wife was different, not bad, not wrong; just different to me. In my heart I really did want everything to be ok and to be the happy family people saw, but I didn't know how to and my feelings were both confusing and relentless. At its worse it was like trying to hold back a high spring tide of doubts and unhappiness; at its best we had built a lovely family home with a lovely family and a growing financial security. I looked at all that I had and what we had achieved and easily pushed my doubts to one side, hoping, I guess, for a miracle because I felt we were never going to sort it out and I couldn't face the alternative.

I really wanted to love my wife and rekindle the ecstatic feelings of joy I had experienced at the time of my proposal and I would keep on saying to her after every row that somehow I needed to stop and get off the spiral of escalating arguments. I needed to wipe the slate clean of the hurt used as ammunition and start again.

The problem of course was that I didn't love myself and until I did I would never be able to love another properly, or let them love me as an equal. My life as a child seemed ok to me then, but how would I have known if it was or wasn't. You live the life you're in and accept it as normal and you take that forward with you until something happens to challenge that idea; and that wasn't very far away.

9

Promotion

There is a lot of rhetoric in our society about the importance of having a good education, which I would only partly agree with. My education was good; it was me who couldn't respond. Some people, like me, for whatever reason are late developers or are just more practically inclined than academic. There are many more ways to display intelligence than just passing exams; intuition, wisdom and life skills all count and yet, because it is difficult to measure, it is often ignored, although many employers are now beginning to recognise the value of life skills and offer apprenticeships or internships straight from school based on potential. There is a stigma attached to our education that you can only achieve by passing exams and attending university, which seems to have become a must-do whether the subject taken is suitable for an onward career or not. Whilst I welcome with open arms the opportunity for all, university, for many, has become a 'club' to attend for the experience rather than as a necessity for a specific career. Of course, everyone should be encouraged to strive to fulfil their own potential for excellence, but passing exams does not guarantee an ability to do any job or live life in a fulfilling way. What it does is to indicate an ability to learn at a certain level, which can determine the possibilities of suitable chosen life paths, whilst not necessarily supporting instincts or personal ambitions.

Parents of a child who is desperate to be a firefighter or a train driver could quash that ambition 'because he or she is too bright'! Who would ever know, if not encouraged and allowed to follow the 'dream', whether that child could 'rise amongst the ranks' and one day become a chief fire officer and pour water over the parents' ideas, or a chief executive of the railways and deliver a first class service?

There are so many children and adolescents who have been pushed into areas of education to suit a profession that their parents would like them to follow for no better reason than to follow in their own footsteps or to relive their own disappointments or missed opportunities; while others, somehow, even manage to judge themselves as successful or not, by the success, or not, of their children. Whatever success is!

Good intentioned parents really do believe that they have their children's best interests at heart, but often simply follow what was done or not done for them as children. There should be a balanced and sympathetic approach to suit each individual child, without undue pressure or force. Let them find their own way!

Many employers now look for a good basic education and prefer to nurture the potential of future employees themselves by taking them on straight from school and shaping and tailoring their on-going education to suit their business. I applaud that.

Had I been good enough I would loved to have gone to university, but I wasn't and I did what my life had qualified me for with a little help from a father who offered me the opportunity of a job. I want to say thank God I trusted him; and I do. Both of them for different reasons; one because I chose him as my father on Earth and the other because I believe He is the father of us all. The truth of my life as I now see it is that it was more or less a fait accompli and meant to be before I was born.

Later in my life I was denied the opportunity to continue my training as a personal counsellor when the University of Bristol changed the qualification criteria half way through my four-year training course. They insisted it was due to new guidelines issued by the British Association for Counselling & Psychotherapy (BACP) that all future students could only sit for the diploma part of the course if they already had an existing university degree, in any subject! Would that have made me a better counsellor? Absolutely not! Would I have been a good counsellor? Absolutely yes. And there are many reasons why, but top of the list would not be because of the standard of education I achieved, but because of my life experience and the wisdom I had gained.

So what is success in life? How can it ever be judged or measured by anyone else other than by the individual? For me it has been about passing the only test in life that really matters; understanding what life is all about and becoming real enough to fulfil a purpose which is so often shrouded by misinformation and a way of life that does not exactly encourage free thinking.

Success and purpose go hand in hand with living; to live life to the full we have to understand we have choices and that it's ok to be unique and challenge ourselves when we feel unfulfilled or lost in life. Break free from the mould of learnt behaviour cast innocently by your parents to create your life script that may or may not be always appropriate for you as an individual, and walk a road unmarked by the footsteps of others by being a pioneer of invention through freedom, and turn hope into the reality of what you believe. You cannot make a mistake per se, because all roads will lead to your successful conclusion of life as a human simply because if you were meant to be on a different road you would be!

That doesn't mean you can't change the road.

I finally passed the one remaining Fire Brigade exam, the 'station officers', at the third attempt but I needed a helping hand to do it. Fifteen minutes before the exam was due to start I was talking with a colleague from Southmead Station when he said he had studied the previous ten years of exam papers and was sure a certain question would come up. I hadn't looked at it so I looked it up in the appropriate fire service manual and memorised the only list I could find as they were always popular questions. It was the first question on the exam paper and worth ten marks; a month later I received notification of a pass! Was that lucky, was it a coincidence, was it neither and just pure chance or was it meant to be? Whatever it was, my success ultimately led me to attending the longest course available at the Fire Service College, where I made one of the craziest decisions I was ever likely to make in life.

There was to be an expansion and upgrading of the traditional roles within Avon Fire Brigade with the creation of a number of additional departments for both uniformed and civilian staff. As a result of that, twelve station officer vacancies were created for a variety of established and new roles and I was by then qualified to apply. Once again I was hesitant, but I applied along with 34 others, which meant for the first time in my career I would have real competition and be officially interviewed and assessed over a whole day.

The day was hard, with a succession of interviews interspersed between dealing with the sort of problems we could expect on a day to day basis if promoted; in effect we were sat at a work desk with a full in-tray and expected to prioritise and deal with them. Our fates were announced at the end of that day when we were called in one by one. I had finished thirteenth and just missed out; the consolation was that I would be top of the list and next in line for any future promotions within the next year. I was naturally disappointed but felt reasonably pleased to have finished above halfway at my first attempt at an assessment.

Before I had time to leave for home I was called back in and was for the second time in my career offered a temporary promotion into the Fire Safety Office. It would mean coming off shift work and operational duties on fire stations and working normal office hours on what was called a nine-day fortnight, Monday to Friday one week and four days the next. This was much better for family life, but it was also well-known that many relationships struggled with the change from shift work to days, not just with a potential loss in income from part-time working that was barely covered by the increase in pay that came with promotion, but being home every night and weekend together with what some wives and partners considered a loss of personal space.

I accepted the offer and the 'white shirt' that came with it. The white shirt was significant in the Fire Brigade at that time because up until the rank of Station Officer all firemen and junior officers wore blue shirts; for many, the old-school firemen especially, it signified the dividing line between 'us and them'.

So I joined 'them' on a temporary basis by the 'skin of my teeth' in October 1986 at a time when there would never be a better chance. Once again I seemed to be in the right place at the right time; whether I could turn it into a substantive promotion or not, it would be good experience.

Even when I look back at my original posting to the quiet station of Avonmouth, a posting that new recruits dreaded, it had worked perfectly for me, with plenty of free time to study and make a start on passing the promotion exams. Had I been posted to a busier station I do not know if I would have had the time or been bothered, but I wasn't and I did and I became a station officer, albeit temporary, within eleven years, when I had never had any real intentions of trying to be anything other than a good fireman. Whatever happens in life, I have learnt from times like that to trust it as what is meant to be will be and as being in the right place at the right time and to follow the journey I am being invited to take by going with the flow. I have learnt to know when to stop fighting for something that is a lost cause and trust the reasons why. That can be timing, circumstance or a myriad of other reasons, but I have always found when looking back that there was something 'better' and meant to be on the horizon. I am not one to give up a fight easily, but it has often been for the wrong reasons of previous disappointments spawned through apparent injustices. It is very easy to become a victim, a status that has controlled much of my life.

Fire safety as a career path, like being posted to Avonmouth as a recruit, was to be avoided at all costs by many officers who wished to do nothing but firefighting at what they saw as 'the sharp end', but I embraced the change and the opportunity to learn about keeping the public safe and, in particular, 'the means of escape from fire in public and private buildings'. What the job lacked in excitement was more than made up for in the opportunities to have the craic. One such occasion occurred when a member of the public had brought some out of date fireworks into the office for our safe disposal, something which we didn't actually do, but one of the most infamous jokers in the brigade had also recently been posted into fire safety and, unbeknown to anyone else, had gratefully received them. It started on a lunch break when we were all sat quietly reading or chatting at our desks and there was a curious whistling noise followed by a loud explosion that made us all duck. A 'whistling banger' had been taped to a homemade paper aeroplane, the blue touch paper lit and thrown into the air. The consequences could have been awful, but that didn't stop others from breaking in to the source for their own supply as the office became a less than relaxing and safe place to be, albeit filled with laughter for many days; you would think firemen would know better but you can't take the boy out of the man.

On a less dangerous note, one of the jobs in the office was 'duty Busby' for the day when one of us would have to stay in and answer all the many incoming telephone calls. It soon came around to my turn, something that I was not looking forward to as many of the queries were quite technical and difficult to answer. One was from a gentleman who said he represented an organisation called 'ASH' (I looked it up after and found they did exist and it stood for 'Action on Smoking and Health'). It was a very difficult and uncomfortable call when I seemed unable to pacify the caller who was asking for confirmation of the existence of a self-extinguishing cigarette that would go out if the smoker didn't 'puff' on it for a specific time and what the Fire Brigade's stance was on it. Despite the obvious benefits in reducing the risk of death or injury I had no idea whether such a thing existed. My suspicion of a prank call from one of my colleagues, who if it was, was not in the room because I had checked during the call, was raised when I offered to call back with an answer and the line went dead. Such a cigarette does exist, but has never become law in the UK whilst it is encompassed within a European directive, so maybe it was a genuine call. As always in the Fire Brigade you have to learn quickly.

Away from the fun times there was also important work going on as fire safety officers designed, implemented and ensured compliance and maintenance of fire prevention and the means of escape from fire. One of the most prestigious projects in the office at the time was working with designers and architects to provide a safe shopping experience on the proposed new shopping centre, 'the Mall' at Cribbs Causeway just off of the M5 motorway in Bristol. The solutions were both complex and brilliant and if you know what to look for you can see some of the more obvious ones with large areas of special glass fixed above head height in the pedestrian galleries. They are designed to confine and stop the spread of hot fire gasses and smoke from individual shops or restaurants on fire to within the controlled area, from where it can be safely ventilated outside by huge specialist exhaust fans at the top of the atrium. They are actuated automatically by the fire detection and/or alarm systems, all of which allows the time needed for the public to be safely evacuated.

That's why ignoring fire alarms can never be sensible. Whether they are actuated by automatic fire detection systems or by manual call points they should be observed, because to do otherwise could one day turn out to be fatal. I saw once that some wag had penned graffiti under an official fire door sign that stated 'This door is alarmed' by adding, 'Oh dear, tell it not to worry'! That was funny but it also demonstrates how lightly we take fire safety measures in public buildings. We have all become very complacent about alarms ringing simply because there are so many of them around and the vast majority turn out to be false alarms, but one day the 'crying wolf' situation may not be.

The Woolworths department store fire in Manchester in 1979 is a prime example of that when many of the occupants became trapped by a fire that was developing in the second-floor furniture department because they ignored the fire alarm. There were distressing images of people trapped behind metal security bars fitted to windows with firemen using cutting equipment to remove them and perform rescues. Firemen will tell you something has gone badly wrong with fire protection systems and the means of escape measures when people have no choice but to escape through a window in any property. Ten people died that day and many more were injured, some seriously. The fire was thought to have been started by a faulty electrical cable close to soft furnishing displays where the highly flammable and toxic polyurethane foam used to make the furniture was a significant factor in the rapid fire spread. As a result of that fire, and many other deaths in people's houses where polyurethane foam furniture was in use, the legislation was eventually changed in 1988 in favour of the safer materials now used in furniture.

Investigations into the behaviour of people in the store that day showed that a large number of them (predominantly in the public second-floor restaurant area) chose not to leave the building despite the sounding of the fire alarms and repeated requests to do so by the staff. According to the report, even with the smell and visibility of smoke in the area, some people actually continued to queue at an abandoned check-out whilst others insisted on finishing their meals.

A year later, my temporary promotion was again made substantive and one year on from that, at thirty-eight years of age, I made a positive decision to stop spending so much of my time thinking about how unhappy I was. If I was still unhappy when the children finished full-time education, I would leave then; they were twelve and nine. The decision felt good and it was like having a weight lifted from my shoulders, but it didn't last long and not for the obvious reason as it was about to be put back on with interest as my life as I knew it was about to come tumbling down.

10

Alcohol and Crazy Days

Within weeks of making that decision I was informed that I was to be sent on the thirteen-week 'Specialist Fire Protection Course' at the Fire Service College. It would be the fourth course I had been on, the first one of more than six weeks and the first time that a senior officer called me in for a pre-course interview. Amongst other things he asked if all was well at home *'because the length of the course was known to have caused trouble with relationships before'*. Maybe I should have taken it as an omen and an opportunity to open up, but he was my boss not a counsellor, so I said everything was fine; whether that was lying or trying to be positive depends on why he asked; was he just being a good boss or a good boss with perception? I don't know, but whatever it was it made me think.

On each course I had attended before I had always been in the group who would go off camp to socialise for an evening. This one was no different other than the fact we would spend day after day in the classroom with no practical firefighting to wear me out physically and it seemed like an even better idea to break the monotony. I didn't need much persuading.

Three weeks into the course I was approached by a woman in a club who just stood in front of me and smiled. I returned the smile and she started to talk to me. I told her I was happily married with two children and just out for a night with the boys and turned away. She returned twice more and each time I politely asked her to leave me alone and she did, until late into the evening when, besotted with beer, she reappeared to say she only wanted to talk. So we did, then we danced, I went home with her, three weeks later, having become besotted with her, I left my wife.

This is the one thing that if I could change in my life, I would. I should have been brave enough to leave with no other female involved, but I wasn't and I have paid for that in regret and shame. It was a decision fuelled by a drunken mind that removed inhibitions and common decency and which had plunged me into a false world of fantasy when flattery becomes the love of being wanted; it filled one void within me and created another just as big.

Since that time, and more recently especially, I have argued with myself long and hard over the rights and wrongs of my actions and find it hard to imagine it could ever be right, but what I do know is that what I succumbed to that night and the weeks that followed created the biggest storm I had yet to encounter in my life. And yet, had I been asked to return to my marriage, which I wasn't, I wouldn't have.

I have no idea what it is like to be in a real tornado that does so much damage and causes death and destruction, but it felt like I was in my very own as my life spun out of control and ripped my family apart in the process. I had caused even more emotional damage to two innocent children in their formative years, especially up to and around the age of seven, that had already witnessed parents that continually argued. That 'damage', which cannot easily be repaired, would remain with them, manifesting itself through their own particular way in their life ahead with every step of their onward journey guided by the consequences of my decision. It would be fair to say that whatever the force was that was propelling me forward on my journey allowed for hardly any thought for anybody but myself, with little or no perception except the wonderful feeling of being wanted. Many people believe that emotional turmoil experienced as a child cannot ever be fully repaired and, whilst I accept it can be difficult, as I have discovered in trying to repair the cracks of my own childhood, I believe it can with the right positive intentions and if you want to. I have also come to understand how the most idyllic of childhoods can cause adult relationships to be difficult simply because it could be difficult to replicate in the reality of your own life.

All I could do was to survive and do the best I could in the reality of the circumstances I had created as I became a Saturday parent with little, if any, influence on the development of my children.

My mum and dad had moved from my childhood home into a bungalow and it was there that I went to ask if I could stay for a while. Dad took me out for a beer almost as soon as I arrived and for the first and only time in my life that I can remember he tried to talk to me about life, but despite saying all the right things it was too late. He said he and Mum had not always been happy and that you had to work at it; that by marrying, *'you make your bed and lie in it'*. But it wasn't just my stubbornness that wouldn't let me change my mind, it was the predominant feeling of unhappiness experienced over our seventeen years of marriage and, despite the awful mess I had created, there was also a relief that I was at last free to pursue a love that was true, not just one that had to be worked at.

I saw my children only on the legally agreed access day of Saturdays between 10.30am and 5.30pm, no earlier, no later. I didn't agree it, I had no choice; I understood that. My punishment may have been legal, but the retribution was debatable whilst also being understandable. My wife was the judge of my crazy decision and it would be her alone that would determine the length of my sentence; my guilt was overwhelming, but it helped with my acceptance as a new battle raged within me, as I became lost in new experiences that I had no understanding of as a child in an adult body. I needed to grow up and from the darkness of my despair a glimmer of doing so had begun to grow; had I known that then it would have given me hope, but I didn't and I slid deeper into a way of life that I had no idea how to cope with as an adult with little grown-up awareness.

I went back to the marital home on just three more occasions; once to tell my wife and children of my decision, once to collect my personal things and once, eighteen months later, to apologise properly.

The mess I had created was easier to bear at first because I could 'hide' at the college for the remaining eight weeks of the course, but once it had passed I was exposed and shocked that the people who I thought were my friends would literally cross the street rather than be put in the awkward position of ignoring me from close quarters. I am not sure what I had expected, but I soon realised that another reality of my decisions, and there were many still to come, was that all but a very small proportion of our/my so-called 'friends' were taking sides and I was also being judged by them as jurors who had made their own majority decision. Of course they were not friends at all; real friends are not that hollow and do not abandon you by taking sides, but they did so I returned to hiding, driven out of town by my guilt and my unwillingness to face confrontation.

I see it all so differently now, I realise that most of us judge others all the time in one way or another because we must compare to make ourselves feel better. I naively thought that they were all happy in their own relationships, until I realised that actually, many of them weren't and were trying to stay their own course by having to work at it or not. Many of them remain unhappy to this day and are far from being together with their partners and no longer share beds to lie in, let alone make them.

Those long-forgotten friends have reappeared in my life as my teachers, helping me to understand a life that cannot be judged by anyone other than the self. I didn't like me then either, but I have learnt to and now I am happy I hope they are as well. They are still my friends wherever they are and if I ever see them again I will not cross the road unless that is where they are walking.

My office job meant I could leave work on Friday one week and Thursday the next at 1700hrs and return to the Midlands where I was living at weekends. I would then return to spend Saturday with my children and then back to the Midlands on Saturday night.

My colleagues at work were all aware of my circumstances and made no judgement on my bowed head supported by my hands as I stared at my work unable to concentrate; they were as brilliant as you would expect caring people to be. I was an emotional wreck and my depression deepened; on more than one occasion the thought would enter my head about ending it all, but it was never a serious possibility, simply because my desire to live outweighed the finality of death and the thoughts were only fleeting and part of so many others in my head at that time as I tried to make sense of how I felt. Beneath all the chaos I suppose I hoped one day that I would find the missing happiness in my life as a way of making my life and my decisions worthwhile, but my thinking was not that clear cut.

I can see now how death can be an option for so many when the circumstances of our lives combine and align in such a way that offers no hope that we can see for a future. My hope was lost in the grief of loss, and the guilt and blame attached to it, despite it being self-inflicted; but who can see that from within the storms and tribulations that blinds us to everything reasonable? We all need hope and we all need help at some time in our lives too; my help was needed for emotional issues and in particular the lack of love I felt for myself that sabotaged my marriage, but there are a myriad of manifestations from our life circumstances that are endured by so many with no reasonable understanding of why or the possibility of help and understanding. That's what can make life seem hopeless, and without hope I can see how we can give up and how it can seem easier to be dead. But to die through our own choices when the balance of our minds are in trauma by somehow judging ourselves as inadequate and failing is a tragedy in itself. None of us are ever inadequate!

Living back at home with Mum and Dad for the first time in seventeen years, little had changed except the location was comforting in an odd way but awkward in so many others. I would return home from work each evening to find my cooked tea on the table and the food still tasted wonderful; my laundry would reappear – repaired where necessary – ready to wear and I would be gently questioned as to where I was going, what time I would be home and if I would like supper. One of her sons had come home and Mum slipped straight back into being a mother. I may be wrong in considering she may have been trying to make up for something, but it certainly felt different and not because we were all older.

Alone with my mum when Dad was out I tried so hard to talk with her, especially about her past, which I knew very little about. It was as if there was a secret never to be told as she mentally refused to go any further than what I already knew and in the end I gave up out of respect to whatever it was. It could have been the war or other traumas but whatever it was, if I was right, it died with her. After Mum's death I tried doing exactly the same with Dad, aware that his death would be the end of knowing anything that could help me in my search for myself and some sort of belonging, although I was still not consciously aware of searching then either. I was not alone in my desire to know more and account for what seemed like missing years in both their lives, I was just more curious than my brothers because I had to be to find clues to the real me, but like Mum, Dad did not respond as he continually and skilfully steered the conversations in another direction.

Six months after meeting my new partner, as she had become, she sold her house and moved to Bristol. On the plus side I was tired with all the travelling, which had at least been made easier by selling the motorbike I had when we met and buying a £50 Astra van. That van, bought from Ken the garage owner next to Avonmouth Fire Station for what he paid for it, would become the most reliable, enjoyable and cheapest vehicle I had ever owned.

When my partner asked me if I was sure about her, the NO in my head automatically became a YES with a total disregard of the consequences once again. And therein lies one of the legacies of having a lack of self-worth that I didn't even know I had that was still creating an imbalance in my life through the fear of not being good enough and needing to hang on to something that was anything but love, but made me feel worthy.

My children had unsurprisingly found the situation they innocently found themselves in difficult. We had spent months of access days visiting museums, swimming pools and places of interest while eating at McDonald's or Burger King, something I would never have normally supported, but did in an attempt to make life better, which it never would. After a while my new unsatisfactory routine and life with the children became the norm and one which we would share with all the other dads and their children who were as easily recognisable whilst trying to find things to do on 'access' Saturday. The availability of my new home, where I lived with what had become my extended family, gave me hope that we could all integrate together, but all it seemed to achieve was removing the need to wander and occupy my allocated time. I tried everything I was advised to by those who understood these things – in this case the new family arbitration service that was being trialled locally – and which had been reinforced by all the books and leaflets on the matter.

It included what my children could consider their own corner of the lounge – as there were no spare bedrooms, even if they wanted to stay, which they didn't – where they could keep their own possessions and make it feel more like home. Some chance! They looked at me like I was from another planet and couldn't wait to leave on every occasion I tried to play happy families, which neither was nor ever would be.

I watched them struggle through my choices every Saturday as we sat together in one room, split and distant from my partner and her children in another. And I began to realise my unhappiness had been passed onto them as they battled to come to terms with something they had not asked for or wanted and with it my own ever-increasing realisation that it would never work easily, even if I had forced or cajoled them; I saw the deep unhappiness in all the children's faces week after week and eventually found the backbone and common sense to make a positive decision to change it and in doing so challenged the ultimatum of the strictly enforced access hours by giving my children their freedom and a choice to spend Saturdays either seeing me or at home and with their friends.

I never consulted my wife, I just discussed it with the children and we agreed that the routine Saturday access would stop unless they chose to see me. Instead, I would always be available to see them at any time that suited them, either together or individually and that turned out to be a great decision which made a positive difference to all of our lives as the tide began to turn and life became easier. I had found my voice as the guilt began to ebb away.

Eventually I left; I suppose it was inevitable. It must be a true and honest love for all those who have overcome all the obstacles and made it work. I had battled with myself and my feelings for over a year and I could no longer live with my guilt and, more importantly, I realised that, as lovely as she was, and having been all I had ever dreamt of in a partner, I didn't love her. I was in love with the idea of being in love.

The small consolation I have brought with me from that chapter of my life has ensured that I would never do such a thing again and I haven't. If I am unhappy in a relationship, I leave, but even then there are plenty of people who will say I have not given it a fair chance or a decent amount of time; everyone seems to have an opinion about relationships, but few have the answers other than those that are informed by their own and willing to voice it. Twenty-five years on I see life very differently and have built upon the experiences as opportunities to learn, but it hasn't all been plain sailing, far from it, because life cannot be like that if you're truly honest with yourself in trying to become real.

We all travel the road we have chosen. That is not a statement borne from seeing our lives from a soul's perspective but from being human and gaining an understanding through taking part in life and learning to get by. What that soul perspective does for me is to give me some respite from that awful feeling of somehow making a mistake by acting against society's rules. I no longer look for excuses because I have for a long time now stopped blaming others and eventually myself, although it would be true to say that after the initial impact of my actions I found comfort in being a victim and blamed everyone but me; now I am merely trying to understand. To believe my actions were not a mistake full stop, is of course not the whole picture because I do not want to trivialise the hurt I subjected my wife to, but if I am correct then she must also be walking her chosen road with golden opportunities and to not believe in that is to place all faith in life on chance and luck as a never-ending fairy tale or horror movie.

Whilst I will always regret the way I allowed it to happen and see my fears to leave the marriage and my children as being weak, it was at least to be the catalyst for a major change in my life which would eventually bring me to complete happiness. I could discuss forever whether, if I had found the courage to do what my instincts were telling me, the outcome would have been the same, but of course I will never know. Had I not got married in the first place when something was telling me not too, I would never have my children and I can't imagine a life without them because they were in part instrumental in showing me what love was, although my 'foolish' behaviour tested that in all ways. If I had married someone else then I presume I could have had different children but they would still have been my children. I could go on and on but 'ifs and buts' will never change the facts or outcomes of what we actually do in life. Can what we do be seen as being on the wrong road of a lifetime's journey and who can possibly judge?

Are there many roads that lead to the same destination which changes dependent on our chosen route or just one road as chosen? And how will we know unless we try? Surely the road we are on must be the right one just because we are on it and to believe anything else is to say our whole life has been a mistake.

11

Forty and Single Again

Returning to live with my parents for a third time was never going to be an option because that wouldn't have been fair on them or best for me. Because I had time to plan moving out I eventually made arrangements to share the house of Terry, a fireman from Southmead Station who lived on his own. The new arrangements with my children were working well and I was spending much more time with them without duress. They would often come back with me after school and be disappointed if Terry wasn't there; he was amazing with them and his delight in them being there was obvious, that he was better qualified to help them with their homework was a bonus. Terry was a confirmed bachelor who is now happily married with a family of his own and I like to think we played a small part in that.

Despite the good arrangement with Terry, after about a year I was offered the opportunity to move into the empty house of my sister-in-law's parents, which was within walking distance of the centre of town where I worked. I loved the house, its location in a vibrant area and being on my own. I began saving hard with the intention of buying my own house nearer to my children as the next step in reclaiming as much of my old life as I could.

Mum died unexpectedly while she was in hospital waiting for a routine operation for gall stones, but had a heart attack while out of bed at 2am; the staff believed she was going to the toilets. Dad rang me and my brothers and we agreed to meet at the hospital as quickly as we could get there. I arrived first because I lived easily the closest and the nurses asked me if I would like to see her. She looked peaceful in her bed and I sat with her for a few minutes and talked to her. I cannot remember what I said but I do remember returning to the waiting area where Dad and my two brothers were sat waiting for me; no one had told them I was already there. Dad was angry with me and asked why I hadn't waited for them. Anger was becoming a recurring family theme for me, except this time it was not Mum, she was at last at peace.

My dad and brothers were really upset and emotional at Mum's death but it had little effect on me and I began to wonder why. I wrongly assumed it was the Fire Brigade for conditioning me to death.

Within a year of living on my own, with my children able to visit and stay whenever they wanted, it all changed. I was approached by a work colleague who asked if I would be willing to share my home with a fireman who was having relationship problems at home and needed to move out. I wanted to be selfish and say no, but having been rejected by two work colleagues who lived on their own before Terry finally agreed to help me out, I reluctantly agreed.

Once we got used to 'living' with each other, John and I had a lot of fun together at home on our days off and out socialising in town, which was in easy walking distance. John was an incessant joker, especially around the house, he even managed to make light of my polite request to be more considerate of me and tidy up now and again; he listened carefully and agreed. When I arrived home the next day he was lying face down on the floor whilst trying to balance some waste packaging on top of the already full to overflowing kitchen bin. He thought it was hilarious as he achieved it and proudly announced that it wasn't yet full and as such it didn't need emptying, something I had mentioned as an example.

Another day was to highlight the difficulties we all face living apart from our families and the tensions it will inevitably cause, when I came home from a day spent working on the building sites to find John knelt in front of the front door as if in prayer, but he wasn't, although he might have been wise to as he was finishing off puttying in the replacement glass of the door that had been smashed by his angry wife on leaving earlier. She also left her presence in the lounge after breaking most of his extensive collection of music CDs and shredding all his shirts. They are now happily reunited, but not before he had moved out because I had saved enough to buy a small house back in the area my children still lived with their mother.

After four years in fire safety I successfully applied for a transfer back to operational duties and was disappointed, although not surprised due to living in the same area, to be transferred back to Avonmouth for the third time in my career, where I would have more responsibility in charge of the White Watch. I went with an open mind and an awareness of the difficulties associated with managing a watch of seventeen personnel on a quiet station as opposed to a busy watch of eight at Southmead. But nothing could have prepared me for my first personnel issue on my first day on duty five minutes before my official start time of 0800 hrs.

I was in my office preparing for the day and about to get ready for the on-duty parade when I heard raised voices. I didn't think too much about it until one of the watch officers came into my office and said that there had been a disagreement between two members of the watch and one had punched the other. My first thought was that it was a windup, but as I smiled the young officer assured me it was not. Having been party to many windups myself I was still pretty confident that's what it was until a fireman – who I knew from brigade football – walked into the office with blood over his hand from his bleeding knuckles. He was visibly shaken and said sorry that he had punched the other fireman who, according to him, had been winding him up. I cancelled parade and went to find the victim.

Those were the days when some of us, rightly or wrongly, were still prepared to at least try to keep incidents in-house and unofficial. I knew I was walking on thin ice because this should have been an immediate disciplinary case of gross misconduct which, if proved, would probably have meant instant dismissal. I found the 'wounded' fireman tending his bleeding nose in the toilet; I knew him as well and we sat down in my office with both of us temporarily 'off the run' with a concocted excuse and a cup of tea as I listened to his side of the story before discussing the options. My preferred option was a handshake and a sincere apology from the aggressor to the victim and when he agreed I asked him to be as sure as he could be because of the possible repercussions on me if he changed his mind. I made it clear to the aggressor that there would be no more chances, but he made life easier for us all by achieving a quick transfer to another station within weeks.

I gained a lot of respect for the victim that day because I believe by putting his own feelings aside he probably saved the other person's job, whatever the right and wrongs of the attack. Unfortunately, there were many officers then who would not have given either of them that choice and by the end of my career the many had become the majority as managers increasingly followed the rules for fear of not being promoted. Somehow, time had changed the balance from using a common sense approach, gained from real work life experiences, to become less important than the discipline regulations and personal ambition.

On a lighter note, one of the funniest experiences that I experienced in the brigade happened during that spell at Avonmouth as a station officer. We had started our night shift and, as usual, after doing all our safety checks, the watch sat down together for a cup of tea before training and other routines. After a while I was becoming aware of a different feeling in the mess room which I couldn't quite put my finger on. It wasn't until five hours later that I did. With our routines and evening meal finished I was wandering back through the station from the mess room to my office when I noticed a light on and noises coming from our small workshop/store room. To say I was surprised to find a fully-grown sheep stood on the worktop looking at me would be an understatement.

Graham, an experienced fireman and a generally nice guy, apologised profusely whilst pointing out a now very obvious wound on the sheep's neck that his dogs had attacked that afternoon. As it had been the second time it had happened he felt unable to report it to the farmer again because he had been warned not to walk his dogs off lead on his land. Graham, who was in the process of packing the wound with sugar – something he had been advised to do – was stitching up the wound with the intention of returning the sheep to its field the next day.

All the earlier references to what's for supper tonight, is it lamb? Have we any mint sauce? Feeling a bit sheepish and flocking together for training, accompanied by giggling and whispering that I was not party to, suddenly became clear.

Although I would have done anything to support Graham and the sheep, and was unaware of any rules forbidding what I was witnessing, I left them to it, advising him to keep the sheep under control and not to let him graze on the small patch of grass, on or off lead, at the front of the station. I heard no more that night and as normal went to the mess room very early next morning to make myself a cup of tea. I popped my head in the workshop and thankfully the sheep was gone; where I had no idea. As I walked back to my office I had to laugh at one of the most bizarre and surreal sights that I had ever seen when I was confronted with the sheep stood proudly on the back seat of Graham's car, looking expectantly straight at me, presumably waiting for his lift home.

After that unusual start the rest of my posting to Avonmouth passed without serious incident. Most of my time was spent raising morale through inventive training sessions on and off the very quiet station. One area that did cause me concern was not unique to Avonmouth but to all of Avon's fire stations. At that time we still had bars on stations that could serve alcohol during what is called stand down times – the time after all our training, safety checks and routines were complete – that was 2100hrs through to 0700. This policy had never been changed or apparently questioned since the war days when firemen would spend days and sometimes weeks at a time on duty at fire stations and were allowed a drink as a dispensation.

Being in charge I would always try to be what I thought was sensible and limit myself to a maximum of two drinks over two hours whilst the sensible majority wouldn't drink at all. My first real experience of the problems associated with alcohol on stations had occurred years earlier during my second spell at Avonmouth as a junior officer when we were invited to Avonmouth Docks for a familiarisation visit on board a Royal Navy ship that was moored up on an official visit. I had no idea how strong Royal Navy beer was until I walked out into the fresh air, having had two pints of the specially brewed beer in the petty officers' mess. My first inkling came when our station officer for the night, who I had rarely if ever seen drinking, whilst walking with me towards our parked fire appliance on the quayside, walked unsteadily past it and asked me where we had left it? He sensibly took the rest of the night off and a taxi home while myself and a few others sat sobering up and prayed we would not get a 'working job' until the effects wore off. We didn't.

That should have been a 'warning shot across my boughs', but even that was not enough to prevent my embarrassment when on my return as the station officer I was in charge of a road traffic collision (RTC) with someone trapped in a car. As I was talking to the trapped person through the open car window, with a paramedic and a police officer close enough to hear, I became acutely aware that I had had a pint of beer and spent the entire incident embarrassingly trying not to breathe over the casualty or the other emergency services. I never ever drank alcohol on duty again.

The only rule our brigade had for alcohol at that time was that we should never become unfit for duty because of it; the only trouble with that was identifying what was unfit. We had one individual in particular who would drink steadily from when the bar opened and would consume what for me would be considered an excessive amount. I also suspected he drank before coming on duty and I asked him privately to limit his drinking, but it didn't make any difference as he continued. In the end the problem began to solve itself when, over a six-month period, he started to miss shouts in the small hours of the morning (I later learnt that this had happened continually before I was transferred onto the watch but nothing had ever been done about it). This only happened when his best friend was not on duty to 'look after' him and nudge him awake. I gave him two chances, both times appealing to him to be sensible and consider the consequences and, to be sure of my ground, asked for guidance from my bosses at HQ, but they would only confirm that the person had to be fit to work and that was down to my judgement.

He had always refused offers to become a 'blue light driver', although he could be called upon to drive the station van at any time, but other than calling the police we had no means of breathalysing individuals. As I had no idea how I could prove that he was unfit for work one way or another I started staying up late with him and playing chess, but I soon abandoned that because, despite considering myself reasonable, he always beat me and in some ways it seemed that I was condoning his drinking.

When he missed his third shout with me on duty I made it official and informed my boss. Against my wishes he was given one more chance. My only consolation was that at my insistence the boss attended the station in his full 'undress' uniform, which was normally reserved for important occasions and which at least demonstrated to the watch that I was trying to do something about a situation that they were nearly all unhappy about.

He soon missed another shout and I again made him subject of a report and a disciplinary charge followed; not for being unfit through alcohol, but for missing the shout. He was found guilty and transferred to non-operational duties at HQ and given counselling under the watchful eye of the brigade welfare system. He never returned to operational duties and two years later was medically discharged from the brigade with a pro-rata pension only to die two years later with cirrhosis of the liver. He was a lovely intelligent man who would do anything for anyone and was an excellent fireman unless asleep. It was another sobering reminder to me on the dangers of alcohol.

Soon after it was made an offence to drink alcohol on duty or report for duty unfit for work through alcohol and/or drugs and the only bars on fire stations that remained open were on stations that had regular social functions for off-duty personnel; the majority were closed down by the member themselves.

My children, who had both been given keys to my new local home, would come and go as they pleased and I loved coming home to find their unwashed coffee mugs, it made me feel part of their lives again.

During this time my son, who by then was fourteen, had come to live with me for a short period and I loved having him there. One night while he was asleep in bed and I was in the front room something very strange happened. My small terraced house had no front garden and a small rear yard that backed onto a cemetery. He had been asleep in bed for over an hour when I heard footsteps walking around upstairs. I went to see if my son was ok and as I entered the hallway I could smell cigarette smoke; thinking my son must be upstairs walking around and smoking I went up. He was fast asleep; I had a quick look around before returning downstairs and, despite it seeming unlikely, I opened the front door to see if anyone was still visible up and down its 400 metre length that could have blown smoke through the letter box. Puzzled, I went back into the lounge and could still smell the smoke as I passed through the hallway. As I sat back down I felt a chill go right through my body more than once and my hairs stood up on the back of my neck. The next day I asked my next door neighbour if anything strange had ever happened in the house and he told me the story of a tragic event in the house when the then owner's fourteen-year-old son, Stephen, had committed suicide by hanging himself from the first-floor landing; another chill ran through my body.

A friend at work suggested it could be the young man who had killed himself returning and I should see a clairvoyant who could be of some assistance. Clairvoyance was something I knew nothing about, but he did and as I was curious he gave me the contact details of a clairvoyant friend and I made an appointment to see her. During the appointment at his house she 'picked up' on the death of the young man and confirmed it was the presence of my son in the house that had drawn him back. My colleague assured me he had not said anything to her, but whatever, I was happy to leave it at that and with an open mind I was satisfied with the explanation that more or less fitted my neighbour's story. However, the clairvoyant wasn't satisfied and was quite insistent in her offer to come to the house to explore more. When she did she gave me more details of the suicide including his name, Stephen, and explained that the chills I was still experiencing were known as 'truth chills'! Being curious I did an Internet search on what I had been told and much to my surprise found the incident in the archives of the local paper from that time.

I told my son what I had been told and the build up to the story and I was shocked and disappointed when he told me he was in fact a smoker. Although he did assure me that he had never smoked in the house it was something else to feel guilty about that had reinforced my lack of involvement in his life from the age of nine. He promised me he would stop and he returned to his mother's about a month later.

12

A Lucky Escape

After spending two more years at Avonmouth and feeling comfortable that my apprenticeship in charge of a large watch on a quiet station was complete, I applied for a transfer back to Temple Back, which was granted within three months; I would be in charge of the Red Watch.

It was during this period at Temple Back that the brigade accepted their first female 'fireman' who had applied to transfer from London Fire and Rescue Service. She would be posted to my watch and that only concerned me because we did not have any written or verbal policies regarding female firefighters. At that time many of the firemen saw it as a controversial decision with concerns over strength, fitness and the ability to work at the 'sharp end'; they were wrong.

Everything in my life was excellent. I loved my house with the new bathroom I was so proud of and I was seeing much more of my children. My return to a busy fire station was fulfilling all my expectations and I became confident in my work, which was providing a rich variety of incidents, especially RTAs, for which I had enhanced my own ability to manage with the most up-to-date techniques learnt from attending a Road Traffic Accident Instructors' Course at the Fire Service College. My attitude about off-site socialising also changed and I didn't.

All RTAs are difficult but some are more so than others with challenging circumstances, and this one was firmly in that category. It was about midday on an approach road to the M5 motorway, near Junction 19 at Easton in Gordano, when we turned out to an incident that would prove the value of the rapid increase in vehicle safety at that time. Two cars, which were being driven between two large and fully-laden aggregate lorries, were crushed and sandwiched by the second lorry that had failed to stop in time when the front lorry had stopped abruptly. The second car had ended up balanced neatly on top of the other; significantly the bottom car was a brand new Ford Escort estate.

When we arrived, both lorry drivers had already removed themselves from their lorries and I was able to talk with both the car drivers who were still in their vehicles. The driver and sole occupant of the top car was not trapped other than being unable to open the doors and the sole occupant of the bottom car said he couldn't feel or moves his legs, but was not in any pain and felt quite comfortable, albeit a little concerned; I was able to open his driver's door to check what I could see and feel of his legs, but was unable to get my hands past his knee area to help determine if his legs had been impinged below.

The rear seats of his estate car had been folded flat to carry his builders tools and the floor panel had buckled up tight to the back of the two rear seats, preventing the front seats from being slid backwards. That meant our only option to free his legs, which was in fact nearly always our preferred option, was what we called a 'dashboard roll'.

Before we could start work to remove either driver we would have to stabilize both cars, in situ, and once that was achieved we were able to open the door of the top car and the driver used our ladder to climb down. We then lifted away and removed the top car from the bottom one with our HI-AB rescue crane.

During the twenty minutes that took I had noticed a small medical team wearing hospital uniforms laying out a large collection of surgical tools on the side of the road. On asking I was informed that they had arrived from the Frenchay Hospital, about ten miles away, and consisted of a doctor/surgeon and back-up staff that had, unbeknown to me, been requested by the paramedic. This was very unusual and the only time I would encounter it in my career.

As the doctor made himself known to me he asked how long I thought it would be before the remaining casualty would be released. Medics are very aware of the crucial 'golden hour' at incidents, which starts from the time of the accident to the casualty's arrival at hospital, although with modern techniques and the ability to assess and stabilise the casualty in situ that is not always as crucial as it was, and accordingly my estimation of at least another thirty minutes served to reinforce his intentions – arrived at following consultation with the paramedics – to amputate both the driver's legs, in situ, to hasten his removal from the car. I was horrified!

The reasoning was based on the casualty being unable to feel or move anything of his legs, feet or toes below what was visible and the probability that they had not had any blood flow to them for what by then was probably an hour; he argued that if he was correct, then amputation would be required anyway and to do it at the scene would save 'valuable' time. I was fortunate – and the driver even more so – to have had that recent training which crucially included information about the latest safety technology built into cars.

I explained to the doctor that this new car would have 'crumple zones', which were designed to do just that; crumple and absorb much of the effects of 'end on' crashes and protect the legs and feet in a cocoon formed from the mangled metalwork, and as such there was a very good chance that, despite not having any feelings in his legs, they may not have lost circulation. Despite that he was still less than impressed with what I said and I had the feeling that he just wanted to perform the 'in car' amputation because he could and it would be great for his 'CV'. I was very persistent because I had a strong feeling that the driver was not badly injured or had any or little impingement on his legs. Only very reluctantly did the doctor surgeon agree not to proceed.

During this time of discussion the crews carried on working to create room for the dashboard roll by pulling the damaged lorries away from either end of the car. To achieve the dashboard roll we have to almost cut the car in half by cutting through and across the top of the front windscreen and the top of the two front door pillars – called 'A' posts – at either end. That would have the effect of the car being cut in half from the top of the windscreen down to the floor panel which would be left intact to act as the fulcrum or hinge point. To make pushing the front of the car away from the rear easier we had also cut the sills under the front doors either side of the floor panel. One end of a hydraulic ram was then strategically placed at the bottom of the passenger side 'B' post – between the front and rear doors – and the ram itself held diagonally up towards the bottom of the windscreen level on the 'A' post. It was then held in place while the ram was extended, which had the effect of pushing the front of the car up and away from the driver as the floor panel also buckled upwards in an inverted 'V' shape to gradually expose the casualty's legs. In effect, the dashboard and steering wheel was moved up and away from the casualty in the front seat, which is why it is called a dashboard roll.

We were able to see all the way through this operation that the casualty's legs were not impinged or trapped by any car parts and the driver was able to walk away once he had been assessed by the doctor; a lucky escape in more ways than one and a victory for modern car safety technology, experience and common sense.

13

Dawn Brings a New Era

My ability and confidence at work was growing, whereas my private life and relationships in particular remained chaotic, with many girlfriends coming and going over the four-year period since I left my wife. The decisions to finish these relationships were always mine, although I would nearly always agonise over my feelings and the ending could take weeks. When it came, the self-recrimination and analysis of what went wrong was reinforced by the confusion and sadness of the exes who I had often promised *'love for ever'* and *'of never feeling so sure about anything in my life'*! Almost without fail I would 'beat myself up' and question my actions as I asked of myself, *'what is wrong with me'*? Of course I know now you can only be as genuine as your state of being will allow at any particular time and I desperately wanted to love and be loved. It was some time before I realised the length of my relationships was more or less dependent on how they treated me. The chase for me was a measure of my lack of worth; the more I had to chase the feeling of being loved, the longer the relationship lasted. When I secured it, if only in my own mind, I would leave and search elsewhere. When you don't feel lovable, you can't feel loved.

Although I didn't understand then that I was searching, that's in effect what I was doing. My inadequacies, if that's what they were, could have encouraged me to stop inviting partners into my life, but they didn't as I continued to fuel my hunger for love with false hopes. My last search had lasted well over a year, which was a testament to her beauty inside and out, but it wasn't enough, it never seemed to be enough; the only consolation was that I hadn't promised her the world. I walked away with another difficult ending, exacting a promise to her and myself that I would stay on my own until I sorted myself out. And for a short while I achieved both, until embarking on a very different relationship journey that would last for six years of highs and lows in a determined attempt at being normal. Rather appropriately her name was Dawn.

The first time I saw Dawn I was out for the night with friends and she instantly stood out from the two other ladies she was with as they walked into the bar. I watched her with surreptitious glances until they moved next to us and her glamorous friend started to talk to me while Dawn stood quietly in the background. It never occurred to me that her friend may have mistaken my continuing glances as intended for her. Later they appeared in the same club which pleased me.

Very few women have ever had any real instant impact on me but there was something about Dawn that was very different. I asked her to dance and she declined on the basis that she thought that I already had a girlfriend. It buoyed me to think she knew something about me despite being rejected. I tried unsuccessfully on numerous occasions that night to talk and dance with her but it wasn't until the very end of the evening that she agreed and almost reluctantly took my telephone number that I was trying to force on her. It was to be two weeks before she contacted me.

We agreed to meet for a drink and followed that with another date a week later when we would go to the pictures to see Whitney Houston in *The Bodyguard*. The euphoric and exciting feeling of new love was as it always is in the early days of romance, until we went for a drink after the film and a man she knew, and who kept looking at me with looks that could kill, came over and started talking to her. I was not introduced. He left and Dawn said nothing, carrying on as if nothing had happened, so I asked who he was and why she had not introduced us. Her explanation was that he was a mutual friend of hers and her husband and because they had only very recently separated, he was one of the many friends who didn't know. Although that made sense, for some reason it also made me feel very uncomfortable and I thought about it when I got home. It was the same feeling of doubt and uncertainty that I had been left with when my wife and I were organising the wedding cars and she suggested my parents could make their own way to and from the church.

We did see each other again but somehow it didn't feel quite the same and I could feel myself backing off. Whether it was a problem with confrontation that I knew I had I do not know, maybe somehow it was a feeling of rejection, of not feeling good enough. I was conflicted by being really attracted to her, and it was more than just her looks, whilst also having doubts. I did see her again, and again, until two months had passed and I finished our relationship, only to go running back, three times in total over as many weeks, once at my instigation when I panicked at what I had done and twice when she chased me. Each time I did the finishing; I was obviously very confused by my feelings. In the end my mind was made up for me when she arrived to tell me she was pregnant. I wasn't particularly shocked as I rarely used condoms, especially when I was drunk, so I accepted that I had a responsibility and, telling her that 'I loved her', we agreed to make a go of it.

Dawn sold her desirable house in a desirable location as soon as it went on the market and we had begun to make plans for her to move in with her two young children when she informed me she had had a miscarriage. I did consider finishing the relationship but, driven by the embarrassment I would feel if I did, I convinced myself, once again, I could make it work.

My house also sold quickly and I transferred the increased mortgage to a larger Victorian property in need of modernisation that we had chosen together that was even closer to my children. Once again I didn't find it easy being the man around the house for someone else's children while missing my own, but as they would spend every Wednesday evening and alternate weekends with their father it wasn't too bad. They were in fact two delightful children who were well behaved and likeable.

We stayed together and added a puppy to the family when we bought Spot the dog and began to forge a close relationship between my older brother and his wife as everyone fell in love with Dawn. The task of modernising the house turned into a renovation as everything we touched disintegrated. Peeling wallpaper pulled the plaster off the walls to reveal the damp and rotting wood everywhere; my dream to renovate my own house, which had been scuppered by my wife, had become a reality I should never have wished for, but it kept me busy and distracted from a relationship I also wished I hadn't got into.

Unlike with my wife, when we argued over our differences, with Dawn we hardly ever argued and my battle was with myself; one part of me was struggling to play what I considered to be happy families, which seemed as if it was almost impossible without having my own children to look after and guide, despite them being much older teenagers, and the other part that desperately wanted to be settled, knowing that I was being given every opportunity with a happy-go-lucky attractive woman who looked after me like a king and took everything in her stride.

I had no idea how to control my feelings; how could I claim to be such a loving man around children when I so often wasn't? As with my marriage I tried to ignore the feelings of wanting to leave and be on my own, but they would not go away and I became more and more difficult to live with. I would like to say I returned to being a child as I sulked and made life really difficult but the truth was I had never really stopped being a child. Despite that and very much like my marriage, we did have many good times together, especially walking the dog in the woods I spent so much time in as a child. Our successes were largely due to Dawn loving me and my children unconditionally and treating them as she did her own; to my shame I could not claim the same with her innocent children. It is hard to truly understand the strange dynamics of what happens in those situations but if you have or are experiencing it you will know what I mean. What I do know is that it wasn't the children's fault, it never is!

14

How Can This Be 'Joy Riding?'

Deaths at fires, suicides and accidents had become a regular part of my life but one in particular affected me like no other had or would again. We were 'turned out' at about 0100 hrs to a person's trapped Road Traffic Accident in an isolated country lane about ten miles from our fire station. Although this was not our 'station ground' it was in the county of Avon, the whole of which was our 'turnout area'. We were the first to arrive at the scene with a fire appliance and rescue tender, with crews of four and two respectively; there were no street lights and it was a desolate and eerie scene in the gale whipped up by heavy rain and winds. Two cars had come to rest, facing and opposite each other on the wide grass verges that bordered the road. One was badly damaged, the other not so much, both were still on their wheels. Someone was shouting loudly for help from one of the cars, the other was quiet. As the crews began illuminating the dark and gloomy scene my initial assessment concluded that the lone male in one car who was shouting, swearing and gesticulating with his arms, did not appear to have life threatening injuries, nor was he badly trapped. By contrast, the lone female in the other car, although conscious and able to talk, was very badly injured and trapped. As we could only work effectively on one car, because of our limited crew numbers, it was an easy choice to begin extricating the female. Another crew were already on their way and I had requested another as well. It was explained to the male they would arrive soon and, having checked the car was 'safe', one firefighter was left to reassure him as the remainder started work on the difficult and delicate job of cutting the mangled car away to gain access to remove the female; it would not be a quick rescue! Although it was by no means certain, experience had taught me that casualties that were shouting and gesticulating animatedly were not usually as big a worry as the quiet ones. That was subsequently proved to be correct at this incident.

Just after we had started work freeing the female the local retained (part-time and on call from home) fire crew arrived. They were tasked with ensuring the car with the male was stable and to begin freeing him; they achieved that quickly within fifteen minutes and he was taken to hospital by ambulance from where, sometime later, he was reported as being stable without life threatening or life altering injuries, 'just' broken bones to one leg and cuts and bruises.

A paramedic, who had arrived on his motorbike at roughly the same time as the local fire crew, carried out his own assessment of the scene from a medical perspective and had requested an air ambulance for the female casualty as he started to stabilise and monitor her. The additional crew requested had still not arrived so we were still short-handed. That meant I had to free up one of my crew who would normally have taken the casualty liaison role by taking that role myself. In this case it involved holding the lady's hand to reassure, comfort and explain to her what we were doing, and whenever she was about to hear bangs or breaking glass as we cut, spread and removed parts of the car to make room for her extrication. She was able to tell me her name was Margaret.

I kept an eye on how the rescue was proceeding, but with a well-trained crew there was no need to tweak it. We had already been working for twenty-five minutes and were all aware that the air ambulance helicopter had landed in a field close by when I began to notice a change in Margaret; she had become less responsive and, although I was still holding her hand, she was no longer holding mine. The paramedic, who was monitoring both her physical and medical condition, was also aware of her deterioration and he looked at me and whispered to get her out as quickly as we could because she was 'going'. I said we were nowhere near ready and it would cause her a lot of additional damage to pull her free, but he said it would make little difference; she had to be freed quickly by whatever means necessary no matter what.

The terrible sound of forcing her extrication from the car will stay with me forever but we were able to remove her and she was quickly put on the prepared stretcher and taken off to the air ambulance.

I know that she had died holding my hand. I can still feel the tears within me as I write these words now. Margaret was officially pronounced dead by a doctor at the hospital. Her death was the first at work to affect me badly and I have never forgotten it; I can still see the scene in my mind even now.

At incidents with persons reported or trapped we would never be without a paramedic and crew and so they were either alive when we arrived and alive when they left or dead when we arrived. That helps firefighters not to get too emotionally involved. Yes I cared, we all cared, firefighters are sensitive people who learn how to deal with these things and stay professional; if we didn't, we could not have done the job properly, but when you feel someone die holding your hand it is almost impossible not to be more involved emotionally. The only consolation was that it at least proved I could have feelings about death.

The police at the scene said they had received calls prior to the one for the RTA about the 'joy riding' of a car in the area. If ever there was an inappropriate use of the term 'joy riding' that was it!

15

Female Firefighter Dies

Avon Fire Brigade continued to recruit additional female firefighters and one of these was Fleur Lombard, who at that time was one of just 8 out of 700 firefighters employed by Avon Fire Brigade.

Fleur, who had won the coveted 'Silver Axe Award' for the most outstanding recruit at her training school, was posted to Speedwell Fire Station in 1994 and died aged twenty one whilst fighting a serious supermarket fire in Staple Hill, Bristol; she was the first woman firefighter to die in peacetime service in the UK.

Although I didn't know her personally, the death of a colleague whilst on duty shook me and the whole brigade badly. In this particular case there was nothing that anyone could have done differently; it was just one of those events when a series of factors align to produce a risk that can happen at any time and that firefighters face every day. Fleur died doing what she had always wanted to do and loved doing, being a firefighter. She died because she just happened to be searching in dense hot smoke directly underneath a very deep beam at ceiling level that deflected the fire down on top of her when it 'flashed over' across the ceiling, having reached a super-hot temperature.

Fleur was posthumously awarded the Queen's Gallantry Medal.

Death seemed to be becoming my ever constant companion as, about two months later, I was back in the coroner's court. We had attended a serious house fire close to the station at about 0200hrs and we could see the thick acrid smoke of the 'persons reported' fire whilst en-route. On arrival we were met by one of the three occupants who had managed to escape and, despite being frantic and upset, she was able to tell me that her friend was missing and assumed to be still inside – she had last seen him on the first floor from where he had roused her and two others from their sleep. The three had left the house and assumed he had as well but he never appeared.

The house was what we called 'well alight' and the seat of the fire was in the ground-floor lounge and spreading up the staircase to the first floor. Firefighters made their way in to search the house whilst having to fight the fire to make progress at the same time. The first crew, wearing breathing apparatus (BA), made their way up the staircase, which was just inside the front door, but weakened by the extensive fire under it in the lounge; it collapsed under them when they were halfway up. They withdrew temporarily and a metal ladder was quickly put in place and they continued successfully reaching the first floor; at the same time a second crew, also wearing BA, were searching and fighting the fire in the ground-floor lounge which they declared clear of casualties. A third crew also wore BA and were up a ladder opening the first-floor windows from the outside to assist with ventilating the fire, hot gases and smoke from the first floor.

Everything was happening very quickly and the first crew radioed that they had located a casualty at the head of the stairs on the landing, but as there was no doubt that he was life extinct they informed me that they would leave the body where it was found to aid the fire investigation that always followed; this was exactly what they were trained to do. Just after that the woman who met us on arrival became quite hysterical, screaming and manhandling me to do my job and rescue her friend; she could not be placated but I could not tell her what we had found until we had finished searching the remainder of the house. I asked two police officers, who knew we had found a body, to take care of her and she was eventually taken away in an ambulance before I could speak with her.

Our investigations found a melted plastic bucket beside the casualty who was found lying face down on the floor close to the bathroom. We knew from witness statements that the four occupants of the house had returned home after a night out and the deceased man, who was a smoker, had stayed downstairs when the others went to bed. We pieced together all the evidence and the most likely scenario was that the man had stayed downstairs to have a last cigarette and fallen asleep on the settee. He had been woken, either naturally or because of the developing fire, between two and three hours later to find the settee on fire and filled the bucket, which was known to have been in the kitchen, with water to extinguish the fire. We could not guess at how many attempts he made at extinguishing the fire but at some stage he had warned and evacuated his friends who were asleep upstairs. It was a possibility that in not being able to extinguish the fire and being unable to re-enter the kitchen for more water because of the intensifying fire he decided to warn the friends upstairs and get more water from the bathroom on his way out.

I did understand how the lady must have been feeling; he had saved her and her two friends, so having just seen him alive she couldn't understand why he had not been rescued. From my perspective I had more work to do in ensuring the house was clear of further casualties, the fire was under control and my crews were safe.

At the inquest the same girl stared at me the majority of the time and, although I was able to personally explain to the maternal family all the circumstances around their son's death, it was obvious that she still blamed me for his death and, in her opinion, for not doing my job properly. It didn't seem like the right or appropriate place to explain my actions of that night.

The careless disposal of smoking material is a very common cause of fire. A common scenario is for the smoker to fall asleep on a chair or settee with the cigarette in hand, which eventually falls from the hand onto, or as in this case, into the fabric of the furniture. A cigarette is not hot enough in itself to cause a fire on the settee unless its resting place is nestled between adjacent seat cushions, or anywhere where it is thermally insulated and can increase in temperature; as it does, over a period of between two and three hours, it will begin to smoulder before eventually becoming hot enough to ignite the material. That is what we believe happened and the coroner found the fire to have been accidental with a carelessly discarded cigarette as the most likely cause. Once fires get a hold they develop and spread incredibly quickly and the foam filling used in the furniture of that home had been of the old type; had it been the newer type that conformed to the new regulations made following the Manchester Woolworths fire, it would probably not have started in the first place.

In normal circumstances, if any fire can be called normal, firefighters would not be sent deep into buildings like his one that were well alight until the fire was brought under control, but when it is believed someone is inside, a so-called 'persons reported', firefighters will take a 'managed risk'. That is why they are so highly thought of. It is also why firefighters die on duty.

16

Death of a Child

Death continued to surround me and, with the exception of the lady in the car, rarely affected me until my first death of a child.

It was late afternoon when we were turned out to a child trapped under a car. It took five minutes to travel the two miles, battling against the rush-hour traffic full of commuters making their way home in the darkness of an early evening in winter and hindered by the 'clever' few who would always try to outrun us or use our appliances as a slip stream by following closely in our wake, gaining valuable distance over those who were more sensible having pulled over so as not to impede us. The less confident would often panic and, being unsure what to do for the best, would unintentionally block our way. All these things we were used to and quite normal, unlike the tragic scene we arrived at in a poorly lit car park obscured further by the lashing rain drenching the scene as if venting its own fury and trying to wash away the anguish and disbelief of the people stood watching, awaiting our arrival. I had fully expected, or maybe hoped, that the child would no longer be under the car that he had apparently wandered behind as it was reversed out of its parking place, but I knew by the distraught mother having to be held back by the small gathering and a quick briefing from the paramedic confirmed that we had work to do.

There were six of us, eight with the paramedics. Our rescue tender was packed full with various types of lifting jacks, heavy duty air bags and lighting but it was clear to me that there was no further time available and the procedural manual and health and safety rules were abandoned. Six of us surrounded the car wearing heavy duty gloves out of necessity with each one of us aware of our personal responsibility to the young boy and to the paramedic and firefighter who were about to crawl beneath and do whatever was necessary to release and rescue the child. I prayed silently for the child and that we would be successful in our attempt to lift the car up off its two nearside wheels to allow access beneath and to hold it up and for long enough. And we were, seeming to take on superhuman powers to lift and hold it safe and steady as the boy was gently pulled clear, but our elation and relief soon disappeared as we gently lowered the car and read the body language of the paramedics that said all we needed to know. They continued to treat the child as they climbed aboard the ambulance, and I imagine as they made their way on the short journey to the hospital where someone senior would have made the call feared by everyone. No one ever wants to give up.

I can only guess at the range of emotions experienced by those who would feel the loss the deepest. The disbelief and shock at the time of the accident; the anguish and desperation waiting for something to be done; and the frustration of being held back by good-willed onlookers keeping them away from the car for whatever reason whilst doing their best in an unfamiliar situation; the relief as the emergency services arrived one after the other in expectation and hope that everything would be ok and then a slow realisation that the young boy was not moving or crying and hoping for a miracle.

It was not a common occurrence for parents or other family members to be present to witness the distressing scenes like this but the few I were yet to experience were enough to not want more. As a father I could only imagine the terrible feelings and raw emotions that are felt watching and waiting for the rescue of your own child.

On return to the station we were all silent. I felt it best that we were not made available to attend further incidents until we had sufficient time to gather our personal thoughts and, if necessary, talk about how we all felt. Although we had a welfare and counselling system in place to help in these circumstances, all six of us decided to have our individual space and to continue the quick debrief we always had before leaving incidents later. This was a sombre and deeply unsettling time for us all and for me personally would turn out to be one of only three incidents involving the loss of a child's life during my career. Anything that could help was tried. Firefighters with children at home would call home to see if all was ok; gaining comfort from the voices of their loved ones. Many would cry in a quiet place, hoping to wash away the pictures in their minds whilst trying to come to terms with the unfathomable reasons for the loss of a young child. Not once in my career have I been aware of firefighters using 'dark humour' to dehumanise incidents involving children; although I believed in a God then, I questioned it that day. Many years later I was to recall these types of incidents and question my new-found belief that we choose our life circumstances for the experience. The emotions of loss, especially of those of a child, are unbelievably strong. If I could feel them when it was not my own children how must a mother and father, a brother or sister feel? No wonder we question God.

On a personal note I considered the implications of our actions and my decisions going wrong. Health and safety can be the best thing in the world but it can also be the worst. I knew of many officers, mainly young but some older, who would be frightened to do anything other than 'by the book' and become 'risk averse'; some because of the repercussions for career advancement and others who just didn't have the necessary skills or experience to do things differently and would not challenge what they have been trained to do; and who can really blame them?

Sometimes it is necessary to do it by the book, but on this occasion it would have taken at least twenty minutes to 'block and chock' the car as it was raised mechanically, and time was something that, if the young boy was to have any chance, we did not have. On this occasion I would not have done anything different, but being able to back my own judgement was crucial, as was trusting the ability of the crews, which I did 100%. No words can begin to describe how I felt that day and neither can I do anything but imagine the pain and lifetime of grief for a mother and father to experience the loss of their precious child. To call it a tragedy is not enough.

17

The Demise of Common Sense

I questioned the brigade Health and Safety Officer once and asked him what had happened to common sense and he said there is no such thing! Typical of the language used in an attempt to build an empire. Common sense – *a sound practical judgement that is independent of specialised knowledge or training* – is no more than a developed intelligence based on your experience. Risk assessments have developed into a must-follow manual and remove the opportunity to learn, they take no account of experience or natural ability, which has gradually diluted knowledge and wisdom that should have been passed on; and that is why all services that rely on them in isolation are producing officers who either cannot or will not make their own decisions because to do so will end up as a disciplinary offence, no matter what the outcome. That is to the detriment of any service organisation working in unusual and fluid circumstances and stifles free thinkers. If we were to apply it to living our lives as humans we would stagnate and not discover the power and beauty of life and I do actually see that happening now; not everything can or should be controlled in life, there is a balance and that is called a free-willed experience that I believe will ultimately open doors of empowerment through personal challenge and growth.

My common sense and ability to adapt would be questioned many years later by one of two officers from the ambulance service who had arrived at an incident with the obligatory clipboard to assess the performance of the two ambulance paramedics who were assisting us at an incident.

I had been promoted by then and attended incidents in my Fire Brigade car and, while returning from an incident at Temple Meads Railway Station early on a New Year's Eve, I was sent on to a persons trapped in an overturned car. I was literally 400 metres away when I received the call and I was by some way the first emergency personnel to arrive at the incident. Despite hanging upside down, suspended and supported by the seat belt, the sole occupant of the car was talking on her phone to her boyfriend when I approached and, despite my advice, she insisted on ending the call. She explained that no other vehicle had been involved and that her car had overturned after driving across a patch of ice and losing control. Other than a sore shoulder where the seat belt cut across her shoulder she said she was reasonably comfortable.

It would be five minutes before the first two fire crews arrived and they were quickly followed by the ambulance, so I had plenty of time to assess the situation and casualty. The ambulance crew also assessed her and agreed with my plan of action to return the car onto its four wheels in a 'controlled roll over' operation by the use of our rescue ropes – called lines in fire speak – strategically placed and held by firefighters; the danger point of this manoeuvre would be once the weight of the car transferred at its fulcrum point while balancing on the two offside wheels. So at that point, as well as holding the weight with the ropes, we would also use our heavy duty metal short extension ladder wedged into the ground and held in place along the underside of the car by two firefighters to help control the descent until the two nearside wheels were on the ground. I was disappointed that the car was allowed to drop the last two inches faster than I would have hoped for and it bounced very slightly. Other than that it worked perfectly. The alternative would have been to 'block and chock' the car on its roof and try to support the casualty once the seat belt was released, which was impracticable because she would almost certainly fall onto her head and neck.

The assessing ambulance officers who arrived halfway through turning the car left without saying a word.

The female was taken to hospital as a precaution and released an hour later with no injuries.

Nine hours later at 0400 on New Year's Day, the same two officers and clipboard turned up at a persons reported fire, this time to assess the two different ambulance personnel at the incident. The small fire in a refrigerator unit had smoke-logged a ground-floor shop with accommodation above it and the incident was quickly dealt with. As we were all leaving, one of them approached me and, discussing the previous incident, asked me why I had not 'chocked and blocked' the car in situ, which all the text books described as the correct course of action for that scenario. This was not a casual enquiry but a direct challenge to the way I dealt with it. When I asked the officer what the text books said about how to support a near eighteen-stone casualty suspended upside down once the seat belt that was holding her was released, she walked away with no further comment. Not everything in life is text book and those who work that way without adapting to individual circumstance can easily turn a simple job into a difficult one. I have absolutely no doubt that if we had performed it the text book way – and it must have been an ambulance service text book because I had never seen a Fire Brigade one that says that without a qualification to adapt where necessary – the casualty would have never have been able to have been adequately and safely supported.

Life is about the experience gained, and used to inform good judgement.

On another occasion we were called to an RTA on the motorway simply to assist the coroner's office to remove the body of a lorry driver who was sat upright high in his cab above us with his seatbelt holding him; he looked so peaceful, as if he was waiting in a traffic jam. He had died of a heart attack and wasn't trapped in any way, but his weight made the recovery of his body difficult without the manpower and equipment we could provide. As I looked at him I became affected by the sadness of the occasion and my thoughts drifted to his family who would be getting on with their lives and expecting him home and completely unaware of his passing; their lives were about to be changed forever by a police officer arriving to tell them of the tragic news. It was a strange feeling. Death does that, whether you believe it is so final or not.

I had another of my own family deaths to deal with when Dad died unexpectedly at eighty-six in 1997 and, just as when Mum had passed away, his death had little effect on me. While both my brothers displayed the sort of emotions I would have hoped for I was once again left to puzzle why I didn't. For many years I had harboured what seemed like a totally irrational thought that I was adopted – which I definitely wasn't – and his death brought that to the surface once more. Whether that was because I hadn't ever felt close to him or Mum was something I would have to wait to discover.

It was two months after that, on my forty-eighth birthday in 1997, when I was offered a temporary promotion for the third time in my career to Assistant Divisional Officer (ADO) as Station Manager at Temple Back; ironically to cover the same colleague whose long-term absence with sickness I had covered at Southmead Fire Station as a sub-officer in 1984. During the eleven happy years as a station officer I had gained invaluable experience and a confidence in my ability at work, but managing the biggest station in the brigade felt like a daunting task and I was nowhere near as confident in my own self. Despite that, I overcame my hesitancy and reluctance to change knowing I had nothing to lose by giving it a go. Four months later I applied for the substantiated vacancy and it seemed once again that good fortune was involved when I was informed I had been successful at interview and my temporary promotion would be substantiated on April 1st. Three out of my four promotions were on April Fools' Day and I was beginning to see it as my lucky day until years later I realised it was because it was the beginning of a new financial year; so maybe an April fool after all!

My brigade car was replaced by the first new car I had ever owned and it was fitted with a siren, blue lights, a flashing headlight kit and a Fire Brigade radio.

Of the four promotions in my career I was only assessed and interviewed for the last two, which, not being my strong point, I considered at the time to be lucky; many years later when I began to look at (my) life in a different way it was another life event that I saw as having the potential of being meant to be.

My first promotion to leading firefighter became possible only because of my first disappointing posting as a recruit to a very quiet station, but it encouraged study and, having passed the first two promotion exams, I was promoted back there, without interview or assessment, because there were so few candidates qualified for the unusually high number of vacancies.

My second promotion to sub-officer started with it being a temporary promotion at Southmead, which was eventually substantiated 'in post' with no interview or assessment having proved I could do the job.

My third promotion to station officer also came about because of an unusually high number of vacancies for promotion just after passing the qualifying exam, after many failures, courtesy of being innocently gifted the answer to a question minutes before the exam was due to start and by then scraping through the assessment day by finishing thirteenth out of thirty five candidates, when there were only twelve vacancies, which was turned into thirteen by an extra vacancy created by the movement of personnel for the other twelve. I was then substantiated in post a year later without further interview or assessment.

My fourth and final promotion was helped by yet another temporary promotion and a successful interview for the substantial vacancy that followed and aided by a slip of the tongue comment from around the mess room table the day before which alerted me to an area that I wouldn't have otherwise looked at.

Was it all luck? Maybe. Was it all a coincidence? Maybe. Was it synchronicity and meant to be? Maybe, I think yes, but if it was, why?

My brigade life continued to grow and fulfil me every day whilst my personal life was still the very opposite and became ever more restless and unhappy. Not long after my promotion Dawn and I split up for the fourth time, my choice again. We had been together for six years and the house renovation was nearly finished. My two children had both started work and would pop in regularly, but nothing is ever perfect in life and this was certainly no exception; four children thrown together by the choices of their parents and inheriting step-parents was not easy for any of us which my intolerance to Dawn's two boys demonstrated perfectly.

I had planned the move before announcing it and moved back into my sister-in-law's parents' empty house. Apart from having to repair the collapsed and damp kitchen floor, the house remained eerily the same. It was strange, but somehow comforting to be back where my life as a newly single man had begun six years earlier. My stay lasted for just two weeks when Dawn let me know she had moved out and I moved back in. I decided to sell the house after finishing the remaining renovation works, but it didn't sell nearly as quickly as I was expecting.

It was a relief to be on my own again and I quickly picked up my old routines of going out with my mates. I was happy and didn't look back, I loved my new job and life was good. Three months later and halfway through a round of golf with a work colleague he told me he had seen Dawn out with her friends socialising in town and that she *"looked absolutely amazing, was the centre of attention and having lots of fun"*. It was like being hit by a sledgehammer and I was instantly consumed with jealousy as the picture it painted in my mind pressed a panic button; I could think of nothing else as my imagination ran wild. I thrashed around the course as quickly as I could. I had to have her back!

I didn't see it as jealousy then, although I knew what jealousy was; I seemed to be in the grip of something that allowed no recognition of it. That's why I believe it was meant to be experienced exactly as it was; how else could my jealousy have fulfilled its purpose without disguising itself, hidden and lurking somewhere within my fragile self-confidence and a lack of understanding of what a lack of self-worth actually means as it breaks free from somewhere deep within our subconscious mind with feelings of not being good enough? Jealousy is so powerful, it has the ability to control and influence our deepest fears by encouraging us to lie bare-faced, knowing full well what we are doing as we kid ourselves that we are not; although lying was something I didn't need much help with when it came to feelings and emotions.

If I had known about self-worth as the domain of jealousy and how together they live at the centre of our emotional body as a subconscious and delicately balanced force, then maybe I would have been able to stop it. But I couldn't and I rang her!

I pleaded with her to see me again *because I had made a mistake'*. I lied, to her and to myself, and I believed it when I said I couldn't live without her as I unashamedly played on her desire to be happy. She was understandably reluctant to get back together but I was relentless in my pursuit, having lost any ability I had to control my actions, and eventually she agreed to the possibility of meeting up, but not until after she returned from the family holiday abroad with her children and ex-husband.

I was beside myself, it was as if my life had just shut down as I analysed our previous time together over and over again and convinced myself that I could put right my unhappiness as failures that could be worked at. I couldn't concentrate on my work and became completely irrational during the longest two weeks of my life. On her return we arranged to meet up but she sensibly made me wait. A complete role reversal from our beginnings together, me chasing – Dawn unsure.

We gradually rebuilt our relationship whilst living apart and Dawn continued to hold all the 'power'; events were happening very quickly and a month later we agreed to get back together again, with the proviso we should get married and buy a brand new house on the opposite side of town – a fresh start! Our house sold with perfect timing because Dawn had already identified our brand new house. I was excited about owning a new house for the first time but it was soured because my doubts had already returned. It was a repeating pattern of more lies and a lack of honesty but with a slightly different twist which I had not experienced before; I may not have wanted her but I certainly didn't want anyone else to.

Within a month of moving into the house Dawn moved out, saying it didn't feel the same.

Just as I had planned my departure months earlier so had she. Her children were elsewhere and she would be sleeping at a friend's house the night she told me, only returning the next day to get her things. That night was as difficult as it was long; even though I had also been unsure almost as soon as I had 'won' her back, I was devastated. I had been dumped for the first time in my life and it reached parts of me that I didn't know existed; the same place as the jealousy had risen from, but deeper.

The next day I was due to sit the NEBOSH (National Examination Board in Occupational Safety and Health) Diploma exam. It was always going to be a hard exam for me to pass and this didn't help. Our instructors for the ten-week course were also the exam invigilators and before we started they asked if anyone had any circumstances that could be a disadvantage on the day; I am not sure if I understood it in the way it was meant but needing all the help I could, I privately explained my circumstances away from the prying ears of my eleven work colleagues.

It was a course that had provided me with one of the funniest moments I had experienced when, one afternoon during lunchtime, we hatched a plan to have some fun and break the monotony of what was at times a very boring, albeit necessary subject. We would try to work names of as many vegetables into the afternoon session as possible. The easy ones were carrots for incentives, peas for watching our P's & Q's; sprouts, turnips, mustard and runner beans all found their way in as we giggled, with the tutors aware something was going on but not sure what. But the ultimate show stopper at the end of the afternoon was the comment from a colleague who closed the day by saying, *"We would all like to thank you for today which has 'broadly bean' ok."*

I could have done with something to make me laugh on the day of the exam but it got worse. After the exam we all went for a drink and I stayed as long as I could to ensure Dawn would be gone. But she wasn't and I arrived home to apologies and giggles from her and her four friends who were all 'glammed up' for a night out, which really put the 'boot in'. They eventually left and it was to be the beginning of one of the hardest years of my life. Rejection was something I had never experienced before, or so I thought, and I desperately wanted her back. I was living on the wrong side of town and on a material note I had a massive mortgage and steadily rising interest rates, financially life was difficult albeit helped by my recent promotion; on the positive side the guilt this time was not mine and she left new custom-made furniture and made-to-measure curtains which she had paid for.

During the emotional and difficult year that followed I refused all offers to go out socially. Work fulfilled me and kept me busy and it was a Godsend to be on call regularly from home one evening each week and one complete weekend from Friday morning through to Monday teatime each month. When off duty I would enjoy driving to remote beaches to walk my dog, and on evenings would pull

Dawn's wonderful choice of curtains in my lounge and listen to what I call emotional music and my friends would call sad. I drank red wine and joined many wine clubs to enjoy the opening offers of a free case which kept me well in stock as I wrote poetry and letters to Dawn that I never posted. Many years later she surprised me by saying that when she didn't have her boys she would often sit outside the house in the evenings agonising over whether to come in. I am so pleased she didn't although it would have been so welcomed.

For the best part of a year the voluntary isolation designed to keep me out of relationships had worked, but it came at a price when one unremarkable evening a glass of wine became two bottles and I started to cry and it became remarkable! I had already decided to sell the house that by then was in my sole name and to move back nearer to my children and my roots, and maybe that's what caused the floodgates to open and release every tear that I had ever stored. My mother's words that 'big boys don't cry', so long an impenetrable obstacle, was breached by the combined power of sadness and loneliness and the effort and confusion of the relentless soul-searching of the year; a year of trying to be different but instead deciding to 'run back home' to an area of comfort and familiarity in my early years and where my children still lived; I cried like I have never cried before with the powerful message in the words and music of John Denver encouraging me and, remarkably, when I was almost cried out, I looked up to the ceiling and challenged God, if there was one, to help me!

I didn't know it then of course but those tears and asking for help would herald the beginning of the end; ironically the dawning of a new era as I went to bed, slept it off and forgot all about it.

PART TWO

THE UNPICKING OF ME

18

Coincidence and Meant To Be

That I had become depressed during that year of social isolation seems beyond question now, but I didn't feel or recognise it as depression then; depression does that, it creeps upon us unknowingly by integrating into our adapted lives and by reshaping our futures, despite having only the best of intentions to protect us from further harm.

Had I thought about it I would have seen the avoidance and control of that year as achieving nothing but my breaking point, but as it turned out that would be exactly where I needed to be. As it was, on the back of a good night's sleep, I got up, washed away the tears, went to work, returned home to my dog and opened another bottle of wine to continue where I had left off. What I would come to call 'to keep on keeping on'; being resilient.

That my breaking point was my saviour and that everything would be ok would take a while hence to be revealed, but crying certainly hadn't harmed me, despite what my mother had threatened, so that was ok, as was asking for help. In fact, everything was ok because nothing had changed, or so I thought. But it had, which means of course somebody or something must have been listening and was already helping me, I just hadn't noticed. Nor did I make the connection then, or for many years to come, that if I had been helped, then I must have been helped all my life and not just because I had asked. I have learnt since that asking for help opens a door of opportunity to believing through the power of intention, and any increase in our awareness and trust in life must be considered as being empowered by belief.

That time would mark what was to be the beginning of the second part of my life, which would eventually change almost beyond recognition to save me from myself, and all because I had been dumped; who would have thought it? There is a reason for everything in life if we had but the courage and wisdom to live it as it is put before us! Acceptance is another lesson learnt but not always followed.

What happened next was a sequence of events that I will hardly be able to do justice to. I thought the scenario of an attractive single next-door neighbour knocking on my door asking to borrow sugar only happened in sitcoms and films. We had barely nodded to each other up to then and obviously walked our dogs at different times as we had never met face to face. What I knew of her was what I had observed over the previous six months since she had moved in with her daughter. She introduced herself as Jane – 'coincidentally' the same as my ex-wife's – and forgetting about the sugar, having been offered a coffee that turned into a couple of glasses of wine, we agreed to talk more often and not be strangers. We weren't for very long, despite my attempt at caution, and despite agreeing that it was best to leave our relationship to being friends and neighbours, because we gradually slid into a two-month relationship. It wasn't exactly what I was looking for following my year's self-imposed exile, but once again it was exactly what I needed.

It had been two weeks since I had drunkenly asked God for help, but that had been well forgotten by the time I started to become disappointed with myself for doing the 'same old things' and getting involved in a relationship almost for the sake of it; Groundhog Day.

My disappointments at myself were of course the forerunner to pulling away because had it 'been all I ever wanted from a relationship' I would probably have taken more notice of the trip to Cornwall – my favourite place – to meet her Dad, something she had convinced me of by saying she thought it could be good for me. And she was right, eventually, because the visit was undoubtedly the beginning of the answer to my 'cry for help', but I was already planning my withdrawal and was keen not to get involved, despite being intrigued by her father's devotion to an apparently famous healer called Sathya Sai Baba whom he had pictures of everywhere I looked. He explained he was a healer himself, which interested me, and asked if I meditated, which I didn't then, but in my head I was gone and thinking about it later he was probably sounding me out as suitable or not for his daughter who was, like him, interested in things spiritual. But I knew nothing of such things then and anyway I was too engaged in not sending the wrong signals as I tried to keep the relationship low key, although I accept now, because I have learnt, that sleeping with someone is not keeping it low key at all so far as most people are concerned. My only consolation when it finished was that on that occasion I had not made promises of a 'lifetime together' or 'being the right one' and would ensure I would be wary of any future relationship with a neighbour.

Jane's disappointments at the ending led to a comment that I thought odd at the time, but made much more sense later when I too became interested in things spiritual. She said she had been told by a spiritual medium that our relationship would last for two years.

My house eventually sold, thankfully to ease the awkwardness, and the selling agent asked me where I would be moving to. He was a bit puzzled about my plans to move back to the other side of the city because I had previously told him that I had grown to love the area, so when he told me about a new house on the same development which had unexpectedly come back onto the market I was interested. The house was ten minutes' walk away in a cul-de-sac of just five homes that backed onto the playing fields of a junior school; it was smaller and perfect. I loved the house, bought it and settled into a new beginning on my own with new neighbours.

I know that selling agent was just doing his job and earning commission but I can't help thinking it was more than coincidence and business. The fact that it was unexpectedly available at the right time kept me on the side of town that I had come to love and would remove many of the temptations to slip further back into old habits and comfort zones by moving back.

Meeting Jane and her father may have been an opportunity to be different and if it was then it was ignored. On the other hand it may have been just an introductory wake-up call for what was soon to follow; either way it wouldn't be much longer until I found myself in a more obviously spiritual place which I did take notice of, but not before I had returned to my previous way of life by joining my friend Steve at a Boxing Day evening dance for single people. Looking back it became obvious that having asked for help someone or something was trying to wake me up to something different as an answer.

One of the most important things that I have learnt through the experience I was about to step into was that if we ask for help it will be answered, but we also have to realise that the help can come in many ways and does not always present itself in the way that we would probably expect it to.

The sequence of events that I believe were started as the answers to my prayer – for surely that is what looking up to the skies and asking, or maybe challenging God for help is – was absolutely meant to be where one event must follow another to allow for the seamless transition of our lives; surely our lives cannot possibly exist of standalone events that just happen to follow each other, that would be too lucky or unlucky for words.

The magazine that came with my regular Sunday newspaper had been running a regular feature of interviewing famous people and one of the questions asked was what book, if any, they had read which had made a difference to their lives? My interest was piqued only because the same book was nominated two weeks running and I decided to buy it on the strength of that. The book was *The Alchemist* by Paul Coelho, which I found in the 'Mind Body and Spirit' section of the bookshop, a section that I didn't know existed until then. The fictional book is about a boy's search to find the meaning of life and I enjoyed it because it made me think.

Not long after, a book called *The Celestine Prophecy* by John Redfield was also nominated twice, not consecutive weeks, but with a week in-between. Once again it was the double nomination which led me to buy it and I found it in the same section of the book store. It is a story built around there being no such thing as a coincidence, although the irony of that didn't really sink home until the sequence of events happened for a third time when a book called *Conversations with God* by Neale Donald Walsch was also nominated twice in one month. I knew by then exactly where to find it! Whilst the other books were good, this book was incredible, it was as if had been written just for me and I understood what it meant; not as if I had read it before, but something deeper! I couldn't put it down. I would read and reread the same passages over and over again, trying to unravel and fully understand some of the quite controversial messages, which were a revelation to me.

It was year 2000, the new millennium, when I was reading the book. I was fifty with twenty four years' service in the brigade and managing two fire stations. It was my on-duty weekend and I was re-reading *Conversations with God.* Having spent Saturday morning in my office I returned home waiting for the telephone call or pager that would mean work. It was mid-afternoon when my pager activated and I was sent to an incident in Avonmouth, close to where I lived with my children, where grass was on fire and spreading to a pile of old railway sleepers saturated with creosote – normally I would not be sent to this type of fire, but it was adjacent to a high risk, above ground section of a major petroleum pipeline that runs from Fawley in Hampshire to Avonmouth.

As the fire was also close to where I grew up, and where my older brother Robert and his wife June still lived, I decided to pop in on my way home. They 'happened' to have two guests staying with them from Australia, June's sister Christine and her husband John, who, unbeknown to me, had already been there for a week. We had briefly met once many years before, but I knew little about them as they had lived in Australia for over thirty years. John was reading a very large book and I asked him what he was reading. He said it was a book about philosophy, something I knew nothing about so he explained as best he could before asking me what I was reading. *"Conversations with God,"* I said. He had barely stopped looking down at his book since I had been there but he looked up at me with an intensive stare and asked, *"How are you getting on with that?"*

I was only too pleased to share my enthusiasm about the book and I tried to convey how fascinating I was finding it, but it was obvious from his smile that he was aware of it because he asked me if I did anything spiritual? I asked him what he meant by spiritual.

It was as if he had been woken from a deep sleep as his quiet disinterested manor changed and he animatedly tried to explain it. He could see I was puzzled and eventually said, *"Look, I am a spiritual minister in Australia and I am going to a spiritual church tomorrow, I feel you should come.'*

I explained it would be difficult because I was on duty, but he emphasised that he thought it would be really good for me and added the incentive that I would be helping him because he wasn't sure where it was and I could take him.

I looked at my brother, but could tell by the body language and the mumbling as he turned away that they had probably already had a conversation about lifts and he didn't want to know or get involved. I was intrigued enough to think about who I could get to cover my duties for the five hours I would need, not an easy ask when we all valued our off-duty Sundays, but Robby Roberts was like me, he loved the job and would do anyone a favour.

I picked up John at the agreed time and on the way he talked almost nonstop about his work as a minister at his spiritual church on the Australian Gold Coast. Not much of what he said meant anything to me at that point but he tried to explain that 'we are all spirit' and when we die a part of us returns to a place called the spirit world. When we arrived at what we thought was Belmont Road Spiritual Church, his chosen church for the night, we tried to get inside the brightly-lit building, but soon realised we were at the wrong building, which oddly enough turned out to be an ex-Christian church that had been converted into apartments. The spiritual church – which was actually called a spiritual centre on the outside notice board – was across the other side of the road and was within what had looked like a normal Victorian residential house. John strode confidently in with me following and although he had never been there before he approached the people within with a confidence of someone who had.

The meeting room itself was on the ground floor and consisted of two rooms that had been knocked into one. It was big enough to seat about fifty people and had a raised platform (or stage) at one end. We sat together more or less in the middle row of the plastic seating; I was even more intrigued as this was not what I had expected from a church. As I was an avid people watcher it wasn't hard to notice that most people knew each other.

There was still about fifteen minutes before the service started; John had suggested we arrive 'nice and early' which was ok by me because that's the way I am as well. As I sat there I began to have a feeling of what I can only describe as being 'home'. I was feeling very calm, reasonably peaceful and comfortable; there was a nice 'energy' about the place – the word 'home' was, many years later, to mark another big turning point in my life. There were about fifteen others present in the room, the majority of who were female. The service began with two people walking into the room and making their way to the raised platform from where we were all formally welcomed to the 'divine service'. The smartly dressed guest speaker, or demonstrator as they are also known, without 'dog collar' to signify anything religious was introduced by the chairperson and delivered an opening prayer. This was followed by *The Lord's Prayer* and the first of five painful hymns that were mumbled through by us all without music. (Why is it always like that unless it's *Songs of Praise* on the television?) The hymns were interspersed by what was called a 'reading' from a book, not the Bible, although I have heard that infrequently as well, and a philosophical talk, generally called 'the address'. The second half of the near ninety minute service was taken up by what was called 'The speaker giving proof of the continuation of Life' and despite the rather grand title of guest speaker/demonstrator, John informed me they are working spiritual mediums who are either: clairvoyant, clairaudient, clairsentient or clair-cognisant or a combination of them all. The service was closed by a delightfully and thankfully easy to sing hymn with these simple words:

'Lord keep us safe this night; Secure from all my fears; May angels guard us while we sleep; until morning light appears.'

Since that first time I have come to realise that most people go to a 'spiritual church' meeting in the hope of receiving a 'message' of some sort from a loved one who has passed away. I sat quietly intrigued but did not get a message.

At the end of the service John was up and circulating and I just sat quietly until someone asked me if I would like a cup of tea. Quite a few people came up and talked with me, making me feel very welcome while John was mildly, but firmly, rebuked for entering 'the office', which was apparently 'out of bounds as there was healing taking place'. John explained to them that he was a minister in an Australian spiritual church and he was in fact a qualified healer, but it made no difference. He was still firmly, but politely, denied entry.

I took John back to my brother's house and agreed to pick him up again to return to the same church/centre on the following

Wednesday for an 'awareness and development evening'. This had been announced on the Sunday as being open to everyone, experienced or not, to attend for personal development. John explained to me that this was an evening of meditation and a common event for most spiritual churches. I find it hard to believe at fifty years of age I had not heard of meditation, or at least had never thought about what it might consist of, or indeed the term 'spiritual', but once again John did his best to explain both during our short time together.

We returned on the Wednesday and John once again strode confidently into the church. I recognised just a few of the twenty or so mainly female people from the Sunday and that the room was set out differently with the plastic chairs now rearranged in an oval shape, which was all that was possible in the rectangular room, but I smiled that the evening was actually described as a 'meditation circle'. One dictionary definition of meditation describes it as *'to focus one's mind for a period of time, in silence or with the aid of chanting, for religious or spiritual purposes or as a method of relaxation'*.

The leader was a lovely lady called Betty who introduced herself and welcomed us, asking if anyone was there for the first time or had not meditated before. Without putting his hand up John offered that he was new to this church, but as he was an Australian spiritual church minister he was very familiar with this type of event. Out of my comfort zone, the little confidence I did have out of uniform drained slightly and I half-heartedly raised my hand to acknowledge that I qualified on both counts. *'Nothing to worry about, just close your eyes when I say and be quiet,'* she said. So I did. I closed my eyes when she said and apparently we had started.

The room and everyone in it stayed relatively quiet except for a few sniffs and coughs. When Betty next spoke some twenty minutes later she said to *'bring our awareness back into the room, and to open our eyes when ready, but not to rush'*. I did as I was told. So far so good I thought, I felt ok, nice and calm and relaxed actually. Betty asked if we were all ok and then, starting with the person next to her, she asked each of us in turn if we had anything we would like to share with the group. I remember thinking 'Share, share what?'

I must have been sitting about halfway around the group from Betty and as she progressed around the room, everyone had said that they had 'enjoyed it but had nothing to share' until someone's 'feedback' mentioned that he had *'seen a person in an RAF (Royal Air Force) uniform standing in a corner of the room'*. I looked to the corner but saw nothing. Betty discussed this statement but I can't remember what was said. Then another person said they had seen *'a lady in a nurse's uniform'* also standing somewhere in the room. Again this was discussed. My turn came and I said that I had *'felt very calm and relaxed'*. *"Good,"* she said and that was that. I don't remember anything else about that night except that there was no chanting or music. I returned John to my brother's house and we had a discussion on the way about whether I would go again as he and Christine were returning to Australia later that week. Although I said I wasn't sure, there was really no doubt that I would return.

Although at the time I hadn't connected the sequence of events as coincidences, or as the beginning of the answer for the help I asked for, I could feel that something different was going on. To be fair, even for me it wasn't hard to recognise that long sequence of events since asking for help as unusual. Meeting my neighbour and starting a relationship from the need for sugar; being encouraged by her to meet her father because she thought it would be good for me and having my first real introduction to the world of healing and being spiritual; the repetition of books offered as having made a difference to people's lives – life changing; attending a fire incident near to my brothers and popping in to see him, and unbeknown to me his family visitors who were staying with him from Australia and one of whom just happened to be a spiritual minister; being encouraged by him, because of the spiritual book I was reading, into a spiritual church that he thought would be good for me. It's hard to imagine that it was all coincidence. Something was going on.

What was going on would only start to become a little clearer by my continued presence at so-called spiritual events at churches, centres, meditation groups, development workshops, and mind, body and spirit fairs. For some time now I have been able to see that 'life' will, at many times in our lives, create opportunities for us to what I call 'wake up'; whether we take that opportunity is entirely down to us as individuals and how we see life, but there is more to it than that, as I have discovered, and that is dependent on our life purpose. My immediate purpose was to meet a medium called Lisa who worked the very next week as the guest speaker/demonstrator at the spiritual church and who would change my life forever with events that followed, which I had no real explanation for.

19

Lisa and an Important Flight

With John back in Australia I returned to the spiritual church on my own the following week. Out of the uniform I had covered the previous week I wore my smart, but casual, Jaeger suit – no tie – and I was heartened by the warm welcome I received; some even remembered my name. I arrived early, sat in a similar place, and watched the room fill to near capacity, doubled from the week before. I was to learn that attendances at these events fluctuate for no apparent reason and was usually nothing to do with the guest speaker/demonstrator, but that was not the case that night with Lisa, a bubbly and bright lady who I had never met before, who, it was explained to me, was extremely popular 'on the circuit' and a 'brilliant spiritual medium'. The evening progressed much as it had the previous Sunday, but I was taken by the wonderful 'reading' that Lisa used. It was called 'The Cracked Pot' and I still love the deeper meaning it delivers each time I read or hear it.

THE CRACKED POT

A water bearer had two large pots, each hung on each end of a pole which he carried across his neck. One of the pots had a crack in it, and while the other pot was perfect and always delivered a full portion of water at the end of the long walk from the stream to the master's house, the cracked pot arrived only half full.

For a full two years this went on daily, with the bearer only delivering one and a half pots full of water to his master's house. Of course, the perfect pot was proud of its accomplishments, perfect to the end for which it was made. But the poor cracked pot was ashamed of its own imperfection, and miserable that it was able to accomplish only half of what it had been made to do. After two years of what it perceived to be a bitter failure, it spoke to the water bearer one day by the stream.

"I am ashamed of myself and I want to apologise to you."

"Why?" asked the bearer. "What are you ashamed of?"

"I have been able to deliver only half my load because this crack in my side causes water to leak out all the way back to your master's house. Because of my flaws, you have to do all this work, and you don't get full value from your efforts," the pot said.

The water bearer felt sorry for the old cracked pot, and in his compassion he said, "As we return to the master's house, I want you to notice the beautiful flowers along the path."

Indeed, as they went up the hill, the old cracked pot took notice of the sun warming the beautiful wild flowers on the side of the path, and this cheered it some. But at the end of the trail, it still felt bad because it had leaked out half its load, and so again it apologised to the bearer for its failure.

The bearer said to the pot, "Did you notice that there were flowers only on your side of the path, but not on the other pot's side? That's because I have always known about your flaw, and I took advantage of it. I planted flower seeds on your side of the path, and every day while we walk back from the stream, you've watered them. For two years I have been able to pick these beautiful flowers to decorate my master's table. Without you being just the way you are, he would not have this beauty to grace his house."

Author unknown

Each of us has our own unique flaws. We're all cracked pots in one way or another; well I certainly was and still am to a certain extent. That's why I love The Cracked Pot, although I have learnt not to see the cracks as flaws, but instead as our unique and individual characteristics that give us opportunities to discover who we are.

Like the alchemist's journey to find the secret of turning metal into gold, The Cracked Pot is a beautiful analogy for helping to find ourselves on our journey through human life.

Lisa's performance was charismatic and enjoyable to watch that night; it was more than obvious why she was so popular and I relaxed a little when the chairperson began to indicate it was time to finish the service by the rustling of papers. Lisa ignored him and carried on, eventually forcing him to stand abruptly and asking her to finish by beginning to thank her, but she hadn't finished and, unperturbed, she said confidently, *"I have to give one more message and I will make it very quick".* The chairperson was quite insistent; Lisa ignored him and carried on, he sat down. *"I would like to come to the gentleman with the suit on sitting about halfway back."* I looked behind me as she added, *"It's you, the man in the suit looking behind with the white shirt on."*

My heart was beating so strongly it felt like it was about to jump out of my chest and I could feel myself colouring up and feeling very hot. I just sat there staring at her.

Lisa explained that she was drawn to come to me with a message at the very beginning of the evening, but chose not to because she felt *"I would not be receptive to it"* and didn't want to start her messages part of the evening in a negative way, but her guide had insisted that she deliver the message before she finished.

I wondered what a guide was.

"Can I work with you?" I nodded a yes.

"I need to hear your voice so I can make a stronger connection."

I explained that I was a little nervous because this was all new to me. Lisa went on to describe the person that was communicating through her to me, which was without doubt my dad who had passed away three years earlier. The evidence was both credible and meaningful as she detailed his character and work life for about three or four minutes until she sat down and the meeting was brought to a close. I sat quietly thinking about what had just happened when someone asked me if I would like a cup of tea; I walked over to the area where the cups and teapot were and Lisa approached me and started to talk. There was a small amount of small talk and the main thing I remember from the conversation was me saying something to the effect of *'I don't know Lisa, I am fifty years of age and such a simple guy who doesn't want much from life other than to be happy and to love someone, and yet I keep making a mess of everything.'*

Lisa's reply was simple, direct, completely over my head and said something to the effect of *'your heart chakra is blocked and I can help you with that'.* I asked what a heart chakra was and Lisa said it was best described in private and if I would like to go to her house she would give me a private reading and healing. She also asked if I was a firefighter and, as I had never met her before, I was intrigued and I asked her why she thought that. She explained that she often went out with friends and remembered me being pointed out by one of them who knew one of my friends to be a firefighter, and thus assumed I probably was as well; she added that I had seemed quite aloof at the time, standing alone at the end of the bar drinking. I defended myself as not aloof by explaining how my hearing was not good when loud music was being played and had given up trying to listen to conversations and continually having to apologise for being unable to hear.

Many cynical people would enjoy pointing out that Lisa could have known enough about me because she had talked to my friends, but whilst I understand the cynicism the facts are my firefighter colleagues had never met my dad and knew nothing about him. I accepted her business card with the promise I would call her to arrange an appointment if I felt I needed one.

At home later I sat and thought about the evening and my message in particular. Compared to the messages that many of the others over both weeks had received mine was very simple and distinctly different with no more than a description of my dad and his character. The other messages had seemed to be more personal and I remember feeling slightly disappointed. Much later I worked out that just receiving a message, from a father who was dead, was the message, by confirming the principle belief of spiritualism that death is not the end but is in some way continuous.

A week later I called Lisa and arranged what I was told would be an hour's appointment. She started by explaining that the heart chakra was one of seven main energy centres within our human body, each of which had a specific colour attached to it; the heart's was green although some saw it as pink; the others being the crown on the top of our head – purple or sometimes white; the brow or third eye on the forehead – indigo; the throat – blue; and then the heart with the solar plexus below – yellow; the sacral – orange; and finally the base, at the bottom of the spine – red. They follow a line from the crown of the head down the spine and the colours, which will differ depending on who you talk to, are the colours of a rainbow.

The proposed hour with Lisa turned into three and I walked from her house completely amazed by what she had told me. I was given proof in abundance of a life after death by being given details of me and my life that she couldn't possibly have known.

Two things from the three hours stood out above all others; firstly, how Lisa had described exactly the position I had seen my dad in after he had died while living alone in his bungalow; and secondly that the 'spirit world' were celebrating and waving flags because I was now starting to do what I was supposed to be doing and that they were going to ensure I stayed involved because I had been close before and didn't. I had no idea when that might have been although I guess it could have been either the unexplained happenings when my fourteen-year-old son had stayed with me or the more recent events when I met my neighbour's 'healer' father; maybe it was both.

Dad had been discovered by his neighbour, and platonic friend, Rhoda who had gone as usual to his bungalow to share breakfast with him. Unusually there was no reply to her knocking so she let herself in to discover him slumped in the bathroom unresponsive. She called for an ambulance and then called me. I lived close but the paramedics were still there before me and informed me that Dad had passed away from what looked like a heart attack and advised me not to go into the bathroom as it would be better to remember him as he was.

I thanked them and bullishly explained that I was used to seeing dead bodies in my job and went in. I should have listened because it shocked me; he was wearing his pyjama bottoms and sleeveless white vest and was crumpled in the corner of the bathroom between the white hand basin pedestal and the wall, a scene that Lisa had described very accurately.

Before I left, Lisa invited me back to her house for healing to hasten the process of 'opening' my heart chakra. I arrived at the agreed time about two weeks later and, after a brief catch up, I was invited to sit on a dining room chair facing a wall and to close my eyes and relax. I felt Lisa put her hands on my shoulders from behind and from where she quickly removed them. How we got to what happened next I do not know but it was an incredible experience that I will never forget and which I will not be able to give justice to.

Somehow I experienced that I was actually flying through the air, it wasn't like a dream or in my imagination, at least not in the way I had ever experienced before. It was so real as I flew over a succession of fields below, each one full with its own beautiful and vividly coloured long stem flowers that were swaying gently in the breeze. The first field was full of red flowers and there was a lady stood in the middle of it dressed in a long-flowing bright and colourful dress and wearing a wide-brimmed hat with a ribbon around its rim tied in a bow under her chin. She had a shallow scallop-shaped wicker basket with a large handle that looped over her arm and she was picking one red flower at a time and laying them very carefully in the basket; as I flew over her she looked up at me, waved and said, *"Hi Pete, I'm ok it's wonderful here, don't worry about me".*

I recognised her instantly as a lady that had died in a fire I had attended in Bristol, and although for that split second I saw the scene of her death and remembered the location, I had no recollection of her name or any other circumstances. It was not a particularly memorable incident from my point of view, although I understand all deaths, especially the unexpected, are memorable in their own way, especially for family and close friends. So how I was able to identify her and link her to a specific incident, when I had been to hundreds of deaths and never remembered faces, I have no idea. Although I do remember certain memorable incidents and locations better than others this had not been one of those.

I flew on. The next field was full of the same beautiful flowers but they were blue and this time there was a man stood picking the long stem flowers and laying them very deliberately in the basket he was holding. I have no recollection of what he was wearing but once again he looked up at me, waved and said, *"Hi Pete, I'm ok too, don't worry about me, it really is wonderful here".*

As with the woman, I recognised this man as someone who had died following a road traffic accident and once again I was able to visualise the scene and remember the location as one I had attended. This particular death, however, was a memorable one because it had puzzled me at the time. Although the gentleman casualty only appeared to be stuck within his expensive and very secure car, that was proving hard to open by virtue of the central locking having jammed in the locked position, he was able to inform us that he was not trapped or obviously hurt. The paramedic, who examined him before he was taken to hospital, quietly pointed out a small red mark on his chest that he was worried about. It was less than fifteen millimetres in diameter and seemed to me to look harmless enough, but what did I know, I was no expert in medical knowledge. Two months later I was shocked to read in the local paper that he had died from his injuries.

The colours in this whole experience were like I had never seen before or since, they were so bright and vivid that I cannot do justice to them; they were out of this world. There were more fields that stretched away in the distance all with different coloured flowers, but that is where my experience of them ended.

My next recollection was of being a baby lying in a pram in a kitchen, distraught and crying uncontrollably whilst looking up at a wooden drying rack hanging from the ceiling; I had always thought it was in our family home, but when I eventually shared it with my brothers they both assured me we did not have a clothes drying rack on the ceiling so I have no idea where I was or why I had been shown it. The scene was as real to me as the flower scene and it has also always puzzled me. While I can see that the flower scene enabled me to link two humans, who I knew to be dead, to somehow appearing to be alive in a magnificent place other than Earth, I have never been able to understand why the kitchen scene seems important enough for me to be shown it in the same experience.

The healing experience ended there and I became aware that I was back in the chair with Lisa moving to stand in front of me; *"Wow. What happened there?"* she said. I didn't know either and all she could add was that as soon as she put her hands on my shoulders my guides had told her to step back and to leave the rest to them. I explained what I had experienced, but other than seeing parts of my life clairvoyantly she hadn't experienced any of what I had.

Clairvoyance is defined in dictionaries as *'The supposed faculty of perceiving things or events in the future or beyond normal sensory contact'.*

Since then many people have suggested that what I experienced may have been astral planing, which is defined in dictionaries as *'relating to a supposed non-physical realm of existence to which various psychic and paranormal phenomena are ascribed, and in which the physical human body is said to have a counterpart: Spiritual beings from the astral plane'.*

That does seem to fit with my experience and I cannot emphasise enough how real and incredible that flying through the air experience was or how I was able to identify and hear two people who I knew to be dead. It was a mystery and one obviously not of the worlds I was aware of and I can only assume it was a way of ensuring I would not walk away from the spiritual experience I had been introduced to by grabbing my attention; and what better way could there possibly be to grab my attention, as someone who was used to and surrounded by death, than by using two people who I knew to be dead. Lisa's comment from the first appointment that the spirit world was going to 'ensure I stayed involved', seemed to have occurred.

I said goodbye to Lisa who was standing in her doorway and walked down her garden path to my car that was parked outside. Just as I reached the car I heard a voice that clearly said, *"Tell her everything is going to be alright and not to worry".* Words not unlike those spoken by two supposedly dead people earlier. I turned around to see who had spoken, but other than Lisa there was no one in sight. I asked her if she had spoken to me and she said no. I told her what I had heard but she didn't make any comment. I sat in my car and thought about those words and wondered if they were meant for my friend Rita who I was worried about at that time, but when I rang her she said she was fine.

I have never forgotten those words that were clearly spoken by someone or something that was close enough for me to hear. I had not imagined it so the only possible explanation was that they were what I now know to be 'direct voice' from one of our guides, but if it was I have never experienced it since and that has always puzzled me too; if they can do it once why not always and why is this so-called afterlife always such a mystery? It capped off a second wonderful and mysterious afternoon with Lisa.

Four years later in 2004 Lisa died from cancer. Although I was never able to link her death to those words it is entirely possible that Lisa was aware she had health issues at that time and the words were for her. She was a brilliant teacher and a wonderful and inspirational human being who I learnt so much from. She had set me, and so many others, on our spiritual pathways – or journeys as I prefer to call them – and had become my best friend in the process; I still miss her even now. Lisa left behind the most wonderful family, husband John and two children, who welcomed many people into their home each week to meditate and work with Lisa; until her passing I had hardly grieved or felt the loss of anybody in my life.

20

Suicide and Blood

My life was beginning to change quite considerably as my interest and fascination with everything I was discovering about a spiritual side of life held me secure. My career remained consistently good with the additional responsibilities that my new role had supplied, ensuring that I would remain motivated until my retirement five years hence. At work we had a variety of specialist crews spread across the brigade area that had plenty of water and cliff rock faces for leisure activities. One such team was the Vertical Line Rescue Team, sometimes referred to as the Rocks Rescue Team, that were based at my station, Temple Back, and who were trained to perform rescues, recover bodies or any task involving working at heights where our aerial platforms could not get access or reach. They would also attend incidents far away at other brigades, but most of their work was around the well-known beauty spot of the Avon Gorge in Bristol and in particular the Clifton Suspension Bridge that is famous not just because it was designed and built by Isambard Kingdom Brunel, but because it is a well-known suicide spot.

One Sunday morning I was 'turned out' with the team to recover a body from beneath the bridge. When we lifted the body there was an A-Z map book underneath, open at the page of the location of the bridge. The thought of this suicidal person having to search for his choice of location to end his life had a big impact on me and made me feel sad and reflective. Here was a young man, possibly a university student, with all his life before him who, for whatever reason, had had enough. Had he sought help? Did he have a family or friends or anyone else he could have talked to? Had anyone noticed he was unhappy, disturbed or preoccupied by something? Had anyone tried to help him or was everyone too busy minding their own business or just getting on with their own complicated lives? And what of his parents or other significant persons in his life, how would they be feeling when they were informed? Who was he and what drove him to suicide?

Death can bring up all sorts of issues, but unexpected death can seem so unfair with the power to change lives in an instant, as those who remain alive try to understand and cope with the various stages of a grief that is so powerful, and capable of producing emotions and feelings that many did not know they had, and wished they had never discovered.

This young man had made his own choices but clearly we can all make choices which we would later regret when the balance of our mind and thoughts are not working logically and in tune. This death was planned so any small intervention may have helped him to make a different choice or at least to postpone it. Our decision-making processes and their outcomes are 'balanced delicately on a knife edge' at many times in all of our lives and I felt a deep sadness and bubbling anger that this young man's personal circumstances could be so difficult as to make him feel that his life was no longer worth living.

Although I or anyone else can never know how anyone is really feeling, I had momentarily felt like ending my own life during the imbalance created by my decision to leave the marital home and start a new life with a new partner, but although I was depressed, it never developed beyond the thought. I would have liked to have been in a position to help and listen to that young man and anyone else whose lives seem not worth living; instead I could only wonder at the reasons and the despair he must have been experiencing. Not much later I became a volunteer for The Samaritans.

On another occasion early in my career and off duty, my son had managed to get his head stuck in the railings at Bristol Zoo and I was lucky to have Iain, my fire service colleague from Durham Fire and Rescue Service, and his family staying with us. Although this was apparently a common occurrence, I had yet to attend anything like it, but Iain knew exactly what to do when he picked him up and turned him upside down to face out from the enclosure, which meant of course his ears would not obstruct his head from coming out the same way it had gone in. Life is so simple when you know how. Like at a children's nursery where we were asked to assist in the release of a child whose head was firmly wedged into the gap created by two upright and one horizontal handle section of a walking frame on wheels, and was screaming in panic as she was forced to sit there adorned with the walker. We had no need to use our cutting equipment as we easily pulled out one of the two poles from the holes they were pushed into and freed the child. The whole occasion was turned into a fun event with four firefighters in uniform playing briefly with some of the children and the giggling staff!

Sometimes when you are too close to anything in life it is hard to see the obvious solutions, but if we want to we can learn. One such occasion for me was as a young officer in charge of an incident in a field with a chained and padlocked gate and I asked for the bolt croppers to cut the chain to gain access to the field. The experienced firefighter I had asked gave me a knowing look and a wry smile as he walked to the hinged end of the gate and, without saying a word, lifted the gate up and clear of the hinges attached to the metal post and opened it. I learnt; that's experience.

Many of the incidents we attended would involve a lot of blood and not all firefighters and officers were good with that. One attempted suicide that had gone terribly wrong was when a large man in a homeless hostel had jumped from a third-storey window, but had only succeeded in smashing into the reinforced glass of a first-floor pitched roof below, which had left him badly cut and unable to move, sat upright with one leg bent behind him. We eventually removed him from the roof on a stretcher using our specialist aerial platforms, but it had taken a long time for the inexperienced ambulance officer faced with this upsetting and graphically difficult incident to get him ready as she struggled to stem the flow of blood or sedate him. In the end she was rescued herself by a back-up colleague who had been sent to assist because of the time taken and the casualty was finally given a sedative and painkiller before being manoeuvred into a comfortable position and put on the stretcher. No judgement; just an understanding of how hard it can be, physically and emotionally.

On another occasion we had to be helped by a local authority plumber who we had asked for when we arrived to find a partly disabled man who lived on his own lying in half a bath full of warm water heavily stained with blood. He had slipped while getting into the bath and 'speared' his arm with the top of a cross shaped 'tap top' that he was holding onto to take his weight while lowering himself into the water. He was a very brave man sitting up uncomfortably but calmly with blood continuing to ooze from the gaping wound that stretched from his wrist, where the tap top had pierced and entered his arm, to close to his elbow where it had stopped, embedded deep in his arm. He was sedated by paramedics while we waited the short time for the plumber, and when he arrived he was magnificent in skills and attitude as he lay on a groundsheet covering the blood as best we could as he worked with no concern for his own well-being to disconnect the tap from the bath. The man was taken to hospital with the tap fitting still embedded to be removed under surgical procedure.

I wrote a letter of thanks to the council in explanation of the plumber's actions, but I never received a reply. Hopefully he received the recognition he deserved for putting his own feelings and thoughts aside for the benefit of someone in dire need of his skills when many others would have found it difficult if not impossible. I was thankful that of all the plumbers that were on call that Sunday night it was him, when any plumber could have been forgiven for not wanting to work in such a distressing and contaminated area. I was beginning to realise more and more that these apparently lucky times that could easily be called coincidence when the best possible outcomes are achieved could not all be so!

Firefighters have to employ coping mechanisms for all the terrible things they see and have to deal with. It gives them the best chance of avoiding or lessening the possibilities of serious mental illnesses like the post-traumatic stress that affected many London firefighters following their attendance at the King's Cross railway station incident in London which had many fatalities. It is not a job, as many seem to think, where they sit down all day drinking tea and playing snooker, but one where they continually train and keep their skills in place with hi-tech equipment to be used in dangerous and difficult circumstances where they could themselves end up dead or seriously injured. When you need them there is no better service than the British Fire Service and their professional skills, ability and willingness to do the unpleasant jobs should not be allowed to be eroded. In a world where we regularly see distressing and difficult incidents, King's Cross, although unique, is far from uncommon in the circumstances of the high loss of life where all the emergency services put themselves on the line by going in when almost everybody else is coming out.

21

The White Dove of Peace

After the healing session with Lisa I was invited to 'sit' in her 'closed meditation circle' of invited guests. Closed circles are considered to be a faster way to 'develop' than the 'open (to all) circle' I was still attending at the spiritual centre. They have to cater for a wider range of understanding from novices like me to the more experienced, as well as the fluctuating numbers and the frequent change of 'sitters'. If you sit in a closed circle there is an expectation that you will commit each week, unless circumstance will not allow for it, whereas the open circle places little if any expectations. Whether they are closed or open circles, their aim is to achieve personal and group development through the experience of meditation and discussion by the increased energy that a group of like-minded people can supply. When you attend either you are said to be 'sitting in circle'.

Lisa had already explained to me a little more about 'spirit guides' and 'doorkeepers' and the difference between the two. I learnt that we can have many spirit guides who can change at times in our life to suit specific aspects of our journey to facilitate spiritual growth and that they can be with us for varying amounts of time. Doorkeepers on the other hand, are spirit guides who stay with us for the duration of our incarnation as an overall influence and we will only have the one, from whom we will be likely to be the essence of in character.

Lisa had seen clairvoyantly my doorkeeper or spirit guide although she did not specify him as one or the other. He was described as a Native American Indian who was very tall with broad shoulders and quite serious. Many years later I was lucky enough to be given further proof of him and his name on two separate occasions by two people who did not know each other, one of whom confirmed him as my doorkeeper called 'Running Bear' who was a member of the Blackfeet tribe who lived on the borders of America and Canada in his previous incarnation.

For a while I had continued attending both meditation circles until I found it too great a commitment and decided just to attend Lisa's, but before I did I was to experience an event which would help to remove much of my doubts around the authenticity of clairvoyance that had enabled two members of the open circle to 'see' a man in a RAF uniform and a woman in a nurse's uniform at my very first meditation.

I had met Iain from Durham Fire and Rescue Service at the first residential course I ever attended at the Fire Service College in Moreton-in-Marsh, Gloucestershire. Iain and I were both leading firefighters then and were selected to attend the six-week 'Junior Officers Course' along with twenty eight others from different fire brigades across the UK.

On the first morning I had arrived early at the lecture room and Iain had come in much later and sat next to me, something we did for much of the six weeks. I suppose the first inkling I had that Iain was different was later that first day when I next opened my course notes and discovered a large but creative doodle on one of the pages and Iain smiled at me. He was always joking and messing around and by the end of the course my notes were full of his cartoon doodles, many of which I would not find until years later when preparing for on-duty lectures at fire stations.

Most firefighters adored being in the Fire Brigade, but Iain loved it more than most. His other passion was lorries, Fire Brigade ones preferably, but any would do and on his days off he would always be driving the biggest lorry he legally could for a friend who had a haulage business. Over the thirteen years we knew each other he would regularly volunteer to deliver to the Bristol area and he would stay with me overnight. I always felt quite embarrassed by the chaos he cause by parking his huge lorries outside my house overnight, but he would just laugh it off as a man proud to be a driver.

On one memorable day he convinced me to go out with him multi-dropping in the Bristol area when, to my further embarrassment, he managed to get the lorry stuck under a low bridge on a major commuter route, which caused traffic chaos.

I was a single man at the time of Iain's sudden death in 2001. I had been out on a Saturday night and returned home at two in the morning to an answer machine message from his wife asking me to call, whatever time it was. Iain had died from a massive heart attack that afternoon whilst helping to trim a friend's tree. Three days later I was getting ready to go to the Wednesday meditation circle at the spiritual centre when I had an unexpected phone call from Lisa. She had been meditating and had been shown (clairvoyantly) the 'white dove of peace' with a message that it had come from someone called Iain – she didn't know Iain and didn't know he had passed away! Up to that point I had never experienced anything other than peace and calm in my meditations but that night I saw a white dove flying around in the sky above me. Was that clairvoyance, was it my imagination? I had no idea but it had already been explained to me that the two are linked and that is how it is achieved, especially in the early stages of developing clairvoyance. Whatever it was, I assumed it to be because of Lisa's phone call and the only thing that mattered to me was that I saw something that I hadn't consciously been thinking about.

As usual, at the end of the meditation, the circle leader went around to each one of us in turn and when it reached the man sat next to me I was amazed when he gesticulated with his hand and said he had seen a white dove flying around the area above my head. I hadn't spoken to him or sat next to him before and that was the first time since I had been going that he had spoken about seeing something. My doubts were immediately silenced but as a constant cynic they wouldn't take long to return.

I shared my own vision to the group and also explained the circumstances of Iain's death and Lisa's phone call. I can no longer remember the group leader's explanation but it made no difference; this was much too powerful an event to be dismissed as a coincidence because of Lisa's telephone call, so again my interest was being cemented by real life events. Although there was a marked difference between the 'astral planing' I was said to have experienced with Lisa, it was still an invitation to trust that there is something else out there in all our lives that is communicating with us.

Iain's funeral in Spennymoor, County Durham, was massive. I had no idea that he was so popular as just about the entire Durham Fire and Rescue Service, including civilian staff, turned out to line the street from the fire station to the church, all people whose heart and soul Iain had touched. Iain had lovingly restored a vintage turntable ladder aerial fire appliance and his coffin, adorned with his brigade cap and uniform, was carried on it at the front of the cortege.

Nearly everyone had a story to tell of Iain's kindness and generosity, including me when I recalled how he had insisted upon getting onto my roof in the middle of a massive rain storm to fix a leak before having to drive the six hours home; and we laughed when I told the story of him getting his lorry stuck under a bridge and having to have the lorry tyres deflated before it could be pulled clear by a recovery truck; he had never told anyone that story.

I stayed at Iain and Sharon's house the evening of the funeral and a tearful Sharon told me the story of their last weeks together.

Iain had – for as long as Sharon could remember – always wanted to travel by train to Whitby Bay. Completely out of the blue Iain had arranged it and they spent a wonderful day together there. He had also bought a lovely oil painting of fairies and elves playing in a garden which was so out of character for him and had hung it on the lounge wall. Sharon was convinced that on some level Iain knew he was about to pass away, and with the many similar stories I have heard since I have no doubts that on some level he did and it was not coincidence.

Our young families had become good friends and we would visit each other on many occasions over the course of our thirteen years of friendship when I became proud to have known Iain and equally proud to have maintained contact with his wife and children, Philip, Simon and Rebecca, all of whom have followed in his footsteps as firefighters. God bless you my friend, the Earth Angel.

22

Spirit Rescue

As well as going to my 'home' spiritual centre I began to try others and I became increasingly hooked on this very different journey it was offering me. It was a particularly happy time for me and, despite still having girlfriends, I succeeded in being more honest with myself, and them, and didn't always 'jump in' quite so deep. There were many reasons for that; first and foremost I had begun to see that I was the common denominator for all the relationship failures and I tried hard to stop blaming others by taking personal responsibility – although I hardly knew what that really meant then; and secondly, I would stop lying to myself and others about my true feelings and was even more determined to abide by my earlier decision to not stay in a relationship unless I was genuinely certain. Easy to say, not so easy to do, but at least the intention was good.

Meditating at Lisa's was a revelation, but it took me a while to settle as I felt out of my depth and doubted much of what the other members were describing as their experiences. For months my experiences were limited to seeing colours, but I was increasingly feeling more at home with my new friends, most of whom were experienced spiritual mediums, until one evening when I had my own sensational experience. I could see, and this was definitely not my imagination, a very tall man dressed in a distinctive smart brown pin-striped suit with shirt and tie that would have been from an earlier era, probably the fifties. I had no idea who he was, but he 'stayed with me' in my vision, and I was excited that I could see him as clearly as I had 'seen' the lady and the man picking flowers in the fields of flowers.

Lisa drew the circle to a close and asked us all to bring our attention back into the room. She was obviously aware that I had seen something because unusually she came to me first. Being the quiet sceptic who had secretly questioned the regular visions of others made me feel privately embarrassed as I explained what I had seen. Lisa asked me who and what the man wanted and because I didn't know she asked me to close my eyes and make contact again. This 'going back into it' as Lisa called it, was the first time I had ever been asked to do it, but much to my surprise the man was still there so I mentally asked him what he wanted. Although I didn't hear a direct voice I somehow seemed to know what he was communicating and that he had been drawn to the circle by the light emanating from it.

Lisa, who said she could see what I could, explained that he was the energy of a man who at the time of his passing had not made a complete transition. She then coached and supported me through the process of linking through our 'spirit guides' until I saw an elegant and beautiful lady. She was very tall and stood with her arms open in a loving and welcoming gesture within her own brilliant white light that shone from behind her. I have never again since seen such a bright light. Again I seemed to somehow know that she had been waiting for the man to return and she was there to assist him 'across', if he was in agreement to go. I could feel his uncertainty and reluctance, so maybe I was the ideal person for him, but he eventually moved towards her and as he did I experienced a surge of energy going through my body and felt very emotional. And then it was finished, and it was to be yet another experience that would seem to have been a solitary one that I would not be allowed to forget.

Lisa explained that the energy of the man was stuck and was what many have come to identify as a ghost, but what I had learnt to identify as a spirit. Since that time I have had time to examine and piece together the different vocabulary used in association within spirituality and the use of ghost(s) in particular, is one that I feel is an unfortunate and misleading description of a spiritual energy simply because of the often scary connotations attached to it. The reality of that, so far as I have experienced, is far away from the truth, but the end result seems to be one of frightening people away from anything termed spiritual and a wonderful opportunity to understand life on a different level.

Whatever the man and the woman were, ghosts or spirit beings, they were definitely not human, despite appearing to be. That incident would become a breakthrough night for me by helping to assuage my healthy scepticism, and now I am used to working with the energies of spirit I can honestly say there is no other feeling like it that I have come across.

At work my new understanding added a new dimension when dealing with the many fatalities and when our work was finished I would find a quiet place to say a silent prayer for the energy of the human life ended to return home. I was amazed at the feelings I felt as a response; on one occasion I experienced a 'whooshing' sensation around me and on others a lesser, but still distinctive feeling of what I have come to call 'a rush of energy' around my body, but the most common feeling was the same tingling sensation down my neck and into my spine that I had experienced when my son was staying with me many years before and we were visited by a former occupier of the house who had passed away. It's what many call a truth chill, a description which I think is pretty apt.

This new world that I still did not fully understand was opening up for me and it would be an understatement to say I was really enjoying it. Although it added a new dimension to my life, sadly it made little, if any, difference to the one that continued to cause chaos in relationships. Had I been able to transfer my new-found inner contentment, peace and growing understanding to my relationships, my life would have been perfect. But I have learnt that life is not perfect, and it never can be when experienced through the eyes of an honest ignorance, because I now see our lives are our classrooms, where opportunities for growth and understanding are continually placed in front of us along with the teachers as fellow humans on Earth to help us. Our teachers are often seen as our enemies or at best those we have bad or good relationships with. Life of course does not always make it easy for us to recognise difficult situations as opportunities; they are often camouflaged by different circumstances to ensure our continued participation and to reinforce our understanding of each lesson. They invite us to discover who we are by offering us what we need to find out in slightly different ways that are essential to our continued and hopefully ultimate learning, through the repetition of Groundhog Days.

23

Spirit, Soul or Ghosts

Since I first walked into Belmont Road Spiritual Centre – called a church by its governing body, the Spiritualist National Union (SNU), I have realised that many people seem to be extremely cautious and even frightened of anything with a spiritual connection, let alone that it is a church, and I am not entirely sure why. One possible reason has become clearer since I began sharing my experiences with people who are interested in how I found the answers to my own search for happiness, because when I get to the bit about being led into a spiritual church, they seem to lose interest and walk away as soon as possible with mutterings of 'witches, broomsticks and ghosts that are evil and to be avoided'. But that is so far from the truth of my experience; indeed I have found great comfort in the relaxed and loving way that most of these organised spiritual churches/centres operate with a non-specific religious format and freedom from the normal church dogma, simply because their core beliefs encourages personal growth through personal responsibility.

Perhaps it is the 'orthodox' church and their leaders who have something to fear in trying to keep their flock together and with the number of people who seem to be becoming disillusioned with religion as it is now, it is hardly surprising. My own experiences of the Christian Church I was born into has been far from encouraging and joyful as the leaders I have come across, when sharing my excitement of finding myself, have literally turned their back and walked away as quickly as possible as if I was contaminated.

So why do some people connect spiritual churches with ghosts in particular and as being somehow evil? Maybe it is because of the handed down attitudes of our parents and conveniently confirmed by definitions of words such as spirit, spiritual, spiritualism and ghost, because they are quite revealing.

Spirit is defined as *'the principle of conscious life; the vital principle in humans, animating the body or mediating between body and soul'*. The only thing about that I see as being remotely challenging is the word 'soul', but only because it seems to mean something different for each of us, with a variety of interpretations.

Soul is defined as *'the principle of life, feeling, thought and actions in humans, regarded as a distinct entity separate from the body, and commonly held to be separable in existence from the body; the spiritual part of humans as distinct from the physical part'*, which can be hard to grasp – as all things spiritual seem to be – but nothing to be concerned about either.

Spiritual is defined as *'relating to the spirit or soul, as distinguished from the physical nature'*, so bringing the spirit and soul together, but in another definition it goes further and adds the word ghost: *'having to do with the soul which is the spirit, the part of someone which is not of the body'* or with **'ghosts'**, which is *'the spirit of a dead person'*.

Ghost, as well as being defined as the spirit of a dead person, is also defined as *'the soul of a dead person, a disembodied spirit imagined, usually as a vague, shadowy or evanescent form, as wandering among or haunting living persons'*. So here ghost becomes the soul of a dead person and a disembodied spirit and usually imagined as being a vague, shadowy or evanescent form and wandering among or haunting living persons. Is it any wonder that the term ghost can cause so many of us problems?

Spiritualism is defined as *'the belief or doctrine that the spirits of the dead, surviving after mortal life, can and do communicate with the living, especially through a person (a medium) particularly susceptible to their influence'*.

My personal belief is in the existence of a part of us that is a spirit and/or a soul and I feel that most people would find that plausible and acceptable, but although the use of the term 'ghost' does not concern me, I can see how it concerns others, especially when its use and understanding has been prejudged by virtue of our learnt behaviour as frightening and to be avoided.

As I was never brought up or taught anything about spiritual, spirit or a soul or ghosts they do not concern or bother me. In fact, my introduction to spirituality in particular has shown me how beautiful a concept it is. But the word ghost is different, it has long been associated with being scary and frightening, which continues to be reinforced time after time in films, television and books and I believe that is what has perpetuated the fear that is the main cause of the reluctance by many to explore spirituality, which is, after all, *'the quality or fact of being spiritual'*.

There is a synonym for the definition of spiritual that does not use the word ghost at all and uses words like unworldly, immaterial, otherworldly, heavenly, divine, holy, sacred, religious and ecclesiastical, none of which are ever portrayed as scary and frightening and as such have no appeal for writers and film makers. We should stop attaching fear to ghosts!

The groundswell of opinion away from the traditional church is in my opinion being caused by trying to confine personal thinking to shape us into their mould and way of thinking so that we conform. My own Christian belief was offered to me as that of my parents, not as devout or obsessive Christians, but it was there, planted gently and subtly within me as an unquestioning child, and I am pleased with that because it has led me to where I am today. But it has never inspired or encouraged me to explore further, no matter how disillusioned and confused I became about life. Why is that? In part it is because much of it doesn't resonate with me, but it is also about its own need to reinforce what I see as a limiting message of exclusivity and an entrenched belief that promises everything, but at the expense of other religious or non-religious beliefs. I have come to accept all beliefs when used to promote a wide encompassing arm of a community that promotes love, including where necessary tough love, to everyone and everything rather than competition and isolation. Being spiritually aware has given me that by encouraging me to be free thinking with an emphasis on personal development.

My beliefs are quite simple; there is a continuation of life in some way after what we have come to call death, and the worship necessary for this belief is to accept that we are all equal and that we are all here to experience life; to learn to love ourselves and in doing so to learn to accept and love all others, no matter what their beliefs are. As we strive to achieve that understanding and harmony, we are all supported by some sort of life force and it doesn't matter what we choose to call it or whether we believe it exists.

I believe keeping an open mind and living life without fear holds the key to a greater understanding in our lives. After all, we are all spiritual! There is nothing outrageous in that, it's just simply a fact that we are!

Two years after first reading *The Alchemist*, *The Celestine Prophecy* and *Conversations with God* and entering a spiritual environment, books were to play another important part in my development when I was told about a series of books featuring a 'magnetic being' called Kryon, channelled by an American called Lee Carroll. There is a Kryon website where all the books and channellings are free to read and download or can be purchased in their original book form if you choose.

One book, titled *The Parables of Kryon*, contains a wonderful parable called *WO and the Rooms of Lesson*, which inspired me more than any other book ever has. Reading the parable never ceases to inspire me with words full of unconditional love flowing through them all.

The story itself encapsulates everything I have come to believe about living life as a human being with free will and with God and angel guides who watch over us to help if needed but without interfering. It is both moving and for me enlightening and empowering.

24

Earth Angel

I was happy and content in my new house and I was enjoying my time being single with female friends that were just that. As I always seemed to be happiest on my own, with none of the complications that relationships always seemed to bring to my life, I began to wonder if this was my intended life pathway. If it was then I had been getting it hopelessly wrong. But that was all about to change as, without a second thought, I began another relationship, this time with someone who was like-minded and spiritually aware, which lifted my hopes that she could be 'the one'. As was normal for me she was 'all that I had ever hoped for' and that was helped by not living together permanently. I was happy spending one night in the week and each weekend at her house when her two children, of eleven and nine, would be with their father.

Having my own space suited me, but the downside was that I never felt certain of her love and much of the negative side of the relationship was caused by my insecurities and jealousies, but despite that, or maybe because of that, we got on really well and I remained happy.

We first met at a 'singles club' evening and met again, unplanned, two weeks later at a weekend away organised by the singles club in Torquay when the main event was a Saturday evening fancy dress party with the theme of 'uniforms'. I had resisted the opportunity to wear my Fire Brigade uniform and chose to go as a 'cub', which although at the time seemed like a good choice, made me feel quite vulnerable when we all met in the bar area at the start of the dance. The obvious way for me to overcome that was to drink as much alcohol as quickly as possible to give me confidence, which I dutifully did.

The Cubs is an organisation for young children and the uniform consisted of short grey trousers, grey full-length socks with a green garter, a woollen green jumper with a cub emblem, a yellow neckerchief with a leather toggle to keep it tight around the neck and a green cap with emblem. I bought it in a school uniform shop where, after just a few minutes, I noticed I was being watched by the staff while working my way around the shop looking at uniforms for cub scouts, scouts, brownies and girl guides. What I was looking for was whatever uniform had the biggest size available and not what would look best, which was none of them for a 52-year-old man! Eventually, a staff member asked if she could help and when I explained, her relief was obvious as she helped me. I was probably lucky not to get arrested.

At the party we talked, we danced, and with too much alcohol our relationship began. As always it felt great to be 'in love' again, but over the eighteen months that we were together there were incidents towards the end that puzzled me and, despite our good living arrangements, I gradually began to have doubts. One such incident was on another weekend away at a ballroom dancing event with my two brothers and their wives. We were out shopping on the Saturday morning and had all agreed to meet up for lunch at one o'clock. For some reason, and despite my increasing frustrations and protests, she insisted on continually going into 'just one more shop' and when we eventually turned up two hours late they had all left and returned to the hotel. That same evening we all agreed to meet at eight o'clock for pre-dinner drinks. We were allocated to sit together on a table with six others, but three changes of outfits later, having missed pre-dinner drinks, we ate alone as we arrived at our table an hour and thirty minutes late.

Despite never getting an explanation I accepted it as better than the alternative of being without her, but it had 'sown a seed of doubt' as thinking back over our time together other, less dramatic, but nevertheless puzzling incidents began to take on a different meaning as I realised there was something within her character that was driving this type of behaviour. It eventually 'came to a head' some time later when I received a call from her saying that she had been involved in a car accident with no personal injuries, but a little shaken. I was off duty and said I was on my way down to support her, but she absolutely insisted I should not as she was ok. That was fine until the Friday night when I would normally have gone to spend the weekend with her and she asked me not to because she was spending the night out with her ex-husband, having a meal and discussing issues around the children's welfare, something I had absolutely no problem with. The excuses continued for another week until she volunteered, when questioned over the phone, that she had in fact not spent an evening with her husband, but with friends. I finished the relationship.

My friends, who had 'coincidentally' booked a holiday to Spain and had wanted me to go, as I always had before being in this relationship, and aware of the situation persuaded me to book a later flight to join them, which was due to leave in the early hours of Sunday morning. She called me on the Saturday night and after a long conversation I agreed to meet her at her house to discuss our relationship. Despite not being given a satisfactory explanation I agreed to give it another go and I returned home to collect my things for what remained of the weekend, happy to miss the flight. On my way back to her place my daughter, also aware of what was happening, rang me to see how it had gone (she was looking after my dog Spot for the week). She did not try to hide her surprise when I told her I was returning to spend the remainder of the weekend and the relationship was back on. She said, *"Well, so long as you're happy Dad, that's all that matters"*.

I was parked up in a lay-by and thought about that comment and decided that actually I wasn't happy and hadn't been for some time. I carried onto her house and explained that I had changed my mind again and returned home too late to make the flight from Birmingham. I collected Spot the dog the next day and stayed at home for the week. As always it would be a tough time of adjusting for me when I would question myself and my part in the relationship and I would find it hard not to want to run back to her. Although I did not understand the dynamics of what was going on then, I do now; the more she withdrew the attention that I saw as love, the more insecure I became and the more I chased. If only I had been aware of the issues around being lacking in self-worth, things might have been different, but I also believe that life goes on exactly as it is supposed to until it is time to change, when we will be given the opportunities to understand through learning and be different.

My Fire Brigade life remained stable and happy with very little change until 2002 when, due to a brigade reorganisation, I was moved to manage Kingswood Fire Station in the north of our brigade area. There were just thirty-two personnel at Kingswood compared to the ninety-eight at Temple Back and thus proportionally less personnel problems to deal with. Despite my initial reluctance and negative reaction of feeling like I was being 'put out to grass', the station offered a much gentler pace of life and with a reduced workload and less responsibility it turned out to be a pleasure.

One of my happiest memories at Kingswood was a very unusual one when I was completing a fire risk safety assessment at the home of a recently retired couple.

As we sat together the lady smiled and made the statement, *"You're an Earth Angel aren't you"*; it was not a question. I was completely taken aback, not least because I had never heard of 'Earth Angels' before. When I asked why she had said it she just shrugged her shoulders. I explained that I had recently become interested in all things spiritual and she smiled that knowing smile that people do. I took the comment as a compliment and have never forgotten it.

Home fire risk assessments were something that all the fire brigades in the country had started to do as one of the many new community-based initiatives designed to 'get the fire safety message out' to all households. During the house visits we would look at any obvious dangers from fire and give advice. At the time the biggest risk of fire to households were from the use of candles for cosmetic purposes, although the unattended chip pan and the careless disposal of smoking materials were a close second. The crews – and then later specialist teams – would fit free battery-operated smoke alarms if they were required.

We were also taking the fire safety message out to schools in our communities in a much bigger way than we ever had before and what better way could there be to reinforce the message than arriving at the schools in a beautiful shiny red fire engine, when the children and teachers could talk to firefighters and use some of the equipment, especially squirting water around. The hope was (and the evidence shows it is working) that children would take the fire safety message home to their parents to teach them and, when they themselves become parents, their own children in the future.

25

Healing

Andrew and I were the only men in Lisa's circle and we quickly became good friends. Not because we were men, but something deeper that is hard to quantify and my best explanation is the possibility of a past life connection. Since seeing the white dove of peace and the man in the pin-striped suit that completed his transition from being human on Earth to a spirit being in the afterlife, my meditations had been less than remarkable, until one evening when I saw myself very clearly, as clearly as if I was watching a video recording of myself, in medieval times as a jousting knight on horseback. What made it even more remarkable was Andrew explaining he had experienced the same vision, but on a different horse.

Lisa explained that it was to do with a previous incarnation and that Andrew and I had had many of them together. The joint experiences continued over many weeks until they stopped completely.

It was Andrew who told me about a local lady called Nadia who ran courses on Reiki healing and suggested it may be good for me. As healing is one of the cornerstones of a spiritual belief, and I had already experienced my own amazing healing experience from Lisa, I didn't need a second invitation. I contacted Nadia early in 2003, two-and-a-half years before my retirement, and once again the timing was perfect as she was about to run one of her twice yearly two-day courses and there was one spare place!

Nadia explained that there were three parts to the Reiki training and each one had to be done in sequence; Parts One and Two could be done by attendance at her group courses, but Part Three, which many people call 'the Reiki Master', could only be achieved over the course of a whole year by sitting in on other

Part One and Two courses and 'shadowing' her teachings, rather like an apprenticeship.

There were six of us on the two-day course, the other five were females. The first day started with a lengthy and emotional group discussion and it was clear that we were all searching for answers to what life was all about. We were given a history of how Reiki began and a demonstration of the 'hands on healing' using special symbols. There were group meditations on both days, but on the second day we sat in a semi-circle, specifically to be individually 'attuned' to the Reiki energy by Nadia. The joyous and happy feeling of that meditation felt wonderful.

The particular system of Reiki that Nadia teaches is called the 'Usui' system and is said to have been founded in the 1800s by a Dr Mikao Usui who was President of Doshisha University in Kyoto, Japan. He was also a Christian minister. The story of Reiki, we were told, was traditionally an oral story and passed on from teacher to student by word of mouth.

The symbols that Dr Usui was said to have discovered and 'promised to commit to memory' have been passed down the line to all Reiki masters in turn to be used for healing and teaching and it was these symbols that we were attuned with during our final meditation at the end of the course. There is a protective secrecy and mystery around these symbols in order to restrict their use to those who have been 'attuned' and considered 'ready'. We were only allowed to see them and memorise them for use during the Part Two Reiki course (which I completed two years later in March 2005).

Reiki masters alone are the only ones who can officially teach Reiki and Nadia was very protective of her knowledge and lineage and, although I do respect the tradition and the power of the symbols, it does remind me of religion and the use of ritual. Despite that, the symbols can now be found quite easily, with the bare minimum of research, without being trained, but my experience is that using the symbols alone is of little use without the teachings and understanding of life that you can get whilst participating in the course.

Whether Reiki healing energies would work without the healer being attuned to the symbols is a matter of opinion, but I believe they would if you have the right intention and are an empathetic and caring person. The power and capabilities of the mind are endless and what is known as the 'placebo effect' has been proved to work, but Reiki is more about healing yourself first so that, having become more balanced and harmonious with yourself and the planet, students of healing are able to pass that understanding on. Attunements, meditations and group support while training in the Reiki energies, all help with understanding ourselves and work on the same principle as the compulsory counselling students training to be personal counsellors must undergo, when it is rightly believed, and I agree, that we, as humans, will be more effective as counsellors and healers when dealing with the emotional baggage of clients having dealt with our own first.

Although there is very little understanding of how healing works, other than the fact it undoubtedly does, there has been some research carried out in the 1980s by Dr Robert Becker and Dr John Zimmerman when Reiki is practised. Their work studied brainwave patterns between practitioner and receiver that become synchronised and enter the alpha state, and changes in the practitioner's hands when the bio-magnetic field were said to become at least 100 times greater than usual as evidence of how healing is effective.

26

Saved by Angel Bridgette

With my retirement approaching fast, the next year of my Fire Brigade life and exploration of everything spiritual were combining beautifully to enhance and inform my life, which was very good. I stayed clear of any long-term relationships, which was also very encouraging, and that led me to believe that, at last, I was learning and maybe I was just better on my own. Life could not have been any better. But not for long as Groundhog Day was about to return, not with its usual gentle reminders of doing the same old things to encourage otherwise, but with consequences deserving of what would turn out to be another stupid decision as I embarked on what would turn out to be, by a mile, the craziest yet of all my relationships. Not for the first time in my life, I would eventually question how I could be so rational and successful at work and be the total opposite in relationships?

It was Friday evening and 'party time' at one of our regular single club haunts when I met another woman who I would become instantly besotted with – the first being the woman I left my wife for. Once again, fuelled by alcohol, I began a chase that I so wish I had lost – albeit I believe I was never meant to. It would prove to be the storm of all storms that my puzzling personal life had created as one crazy irrational decision followed another; she played me perfectly by not obviously chasing me as I became increasingly more determined to win her love, making a nonsense of my belief that I had grown.

The chase started with an acknowledgement and a smile as she sidled up to me at the bar, we danced, briefly, and she walked away. I found her again, but she was drawing many other admirers and we never danced again; other than the dance that life provides to fulfil its commitments. I was desperate, she looked amazing. I had never seen her before and soon became fearful I may never again, so I waited and watched with the odd casual patrol that was far from it, one that an expert at reconnaissance would have laughed at as amateurish, and at relationships that is what I was – if it is in fact possible to be professional with affairs of the heart. Then she disappeared and I panicked. But I need not have worried as she re-appeared at my side just as the evening was drawing to a close. I grasped the moment like a poisoned chalice and asked if she would like to meet up some time and, with a dismissive and casual air of apparent disinterest, she said, *"Give me a ring"*... *"I don't have your number."* She gave it, verbally, and walked away. There was no repeating the number, no offer to write it down or waiting to find a pen, just a look back to say *'If it's meant to be, you'll remember'*. I recited that number over and over in my head, fearful of asking the few who remained for a pen lest I became confused and forgot the number. When I finally felt confident it was memorised I asked a friendly bar staff for a pen and paper. I cherished that beer mat as all he could find. Oh how I hoped I had remembered it correctly as 'meant to be' and oh how I would eventually wish I hadn't been mesmerised.

We were together for nearly 18 months, twelve of them living together, before my eyes gradually opened. Significantly, her name was also Jane and so she became Jane number three. Three is a powerful spiritual number! In Doreen Virtue's *Angel Numbers* book it says, *'The ascended masters (such as Jesus) are near. They've responded to your prayers and want to help you.'* It would take me a decade of spiritual development before I began to understand how the relationship could possibly have been part of the answer to my drunken prayer nearly five years earlier, but it was, or so I believe.

Later that week, having made the call and arrangements to meet up, I was out with a group of friends, including my mentor Lisa, to watch her husband play in his popular band at a local pub. It was packed and I was struggling to hear a man who was 'apparently' a friend of Lisa's. I had never met him before. He had appeared at my side and was trying to explain that he was a working spiritual medium and after one failed attempt I heard him say that he had to tell me that I had a lack of self-worth. I was shocked by the bluntness and replied with my honest ignorance that I did not. He assured me that it was my spirit guide who had communicated the message and he was just the messenger. The conversation only stopped when I went to the outside toilet, but I was both bemused and amused when he appeared next to me at the urinal and continued. So there we were, stood next to each other at a urinal, discussing my apparent lack of self-worth. It would have been perfect for a sitcom if it wasn't so odd, but the message was delivered and, although I had heard the expression 'self-worth' before, I didn't really understand what it meant and dismissed it accordingly.

We didn't talk again and I have never seen him since. Sometimes I have wondered if he was actually a real person or some sort of Earth Angel, but real or not the message intrigued me. It would be a couple of years later that I realised he, or whoever it was that delivered the message, was right. But I didn't have to wait that long for it to sabotage my life again.

Jane was also spiritually aware, as the comment 'if it's meant to be it will be' indicated and, despite our relationship being far from easy, it moved quickly and within five months I decided we should buy a house together. I would have done almost anything to secure her love of me, which I was still far from being certain of. My 'ideal' house sold quickly and, having found our 'ideal' house, I applied for another mortgage. As we sat in front of the financial advisor at the estate agents I was advised about each option available for the mortgage, and hence ownership of the house. The consequences of each were carefully and clearly explained. With only the slightest of hesitations I chose it to be in joint names. Once again my inner voice was screaming NO, but once again I chose to ignore it, not wishing to 'lose her approval' by showing that I doubted our love and trust for each other.

As we left the office and having said very little before, she said that whatever happened in our relationship it was my house and my money, and if we should ever split up she would not want any of it. We did, and she did and demanded all of her legal entitlement, which for me was substantial.

Prior to living together fully our personal circumstances had ensured we had only been able to live together at weekends, but buying a house and living together for the first time quickly became a worry. My children visited less and less, finding it extremely difficult to be around her and in truth I didn't find it much easier, but I was still determined to embrace 'our love' in my fairy tale and I asked her to marry me. We became engaged, set a date and chose a venue whilst all the time being fully aware of my retirement, which would have been nine months later. It didn't take long for my niggling doubts to grow into a real worry.

That had started with the dubious loss of her engagement ring while she was walking home alone after an argument when it had 'slipped' from her finger at the time of a fall on uneven ground. By comparison that paled into insignificance when she first tried to take her own life. I did all the right things to help, after all I was trained for crisis, but she wouldn't discuss the event or seek help; those concerns deepened with her second attempt and I became increasingly dismayed and frustrated with the lack of any ongoing support from the health professionals who were by then involved; it was clear they neither had the staff, nor the time, to do anything but 'firefight' each case as it came in.

In desperation I contacted a recently retired 'specialist' counsellor whose contact details had been given to me by the appropriately named 'crash team' (who were puzzlingly not available in the evenings after 1800 or weekends) to 'get me off their back'. He agreed to see her privately for an assessment and I was called in at the end of the session when, in front of us both, he said that he was prepared to help, but I should realise that Jane was 'mentally ill' and it would take a lot of hard work and commitment over a long period of time. Jane accepted all that was said without challenge or comment, which surprised me, but was encouraging.

That was to be the second time in my life that someone had looked at me with that serious intent in their eyes whilst delivering what would turn out to be a very important message; John, the spiritual minister from Australia being the first. But there could not have been a bigger divide between the positive invite to go to a spiritual church and this one that was in effect a warning; I got the message!

Over the first weeks of her weekly counselling sessions Jane would bring work home and I believed everything was going well until she began to ask for my advice on what certain things meant and somehow I ended up doing the work with her. This was before I had learnt the difference between enabling and disabling help, and love or tough love, but despite that I believed she was making a genuine effort to overcome whatever it was that was causing her erratic and concerning behaviour.

The third suicide attempt and refusing to return to counselling was the last straw. I had had enough of all the lies and deceit and with my eyes fully opened to the reality of the situation, especially with our impending marriage and my retirement, I decided I had to end the relationship, but not until the right opportunity came up which I knew couldn't be far off; I was right!

Everything came to a head one morning before I left for work when I reminded her that I would be home a few hours late because I was going to pop into a retirement evening on my way home. She stormed out of the house in a temper and didn't come back. I sat on the side of the bed with my head in my hands as a battle raged within me, trying to understand and make sense of my struggles and conflicting feelings, but I knew there could be no more next times... if I could find the courage. I needed help and I turned to my favourite angel cards – Doreen Virtue's *Messages from your Angels, What Your Angels Want You to Know*. I shuffled the pack until one fell out – I have always believed that if there are angels and they really want to help one will eventually fall out, although most people trust a simple 'cut' of the deck.

The card that fell out was what I would come to call 'The Bridgette card' which states: *'Caution is warranted. Look deeper into this situation before proceeding further.'* The additional message within the accompanying book states: *'You have asked for Heaven's guidance, and it is given. This situation isn't right for you. Some vital information has been concealed, so you will need to dig deeper and ask more questions of those involved. Trust your gut feelings, since that is how I communicate with you.'*

My sceptical and cowardly nature demanded more proof, after all the card could have meant have caution in ending the relationship, so I shuffled again and the same card fell out. I was amazed. I shuffled for the third time – not so much because I wanted more confirmation of what I knew I had to do, but because I was trying to find some courage and a small part of me still wanted her to love me. I was, needless to say, completely dumbfounded when the same card fell out for a third time.

I am not making this up; this book is not a work of fiction; everything has happened as I have described it. But I know many of you will still doubt it because if it hadn't happened to me I would have been coming up with all sorts of reasons why it had happened, from not putting the card back properly or having bent the card in some way. But these shuffles were not short shuffles, sometimes they would go on for minutes before the card fell out and I doubt even a trained magician could produce that sort of result without the sleight of hand that must take years to master.

I analysed the words from the book again *'ask more questions of those involved'*, but I had done that so many times only to be greeted with a wall of silence or a change of subject; and as for the *'vital information that had been concealed'*, that would not come to light until much later when I found small bottles of vodka, some empty, others partly empty. They had been hidden all over the garage, confirming my fears of alcoholism and giving lies to my belief that had been satisfied with her words each evening that it was 'six o'clock and the bar was open'. There were so many mysteries that would remain forever unsolved!

I went to work; it would turn out to be a very long day of my calls being unanswered.

I was determined to go to the retirement for an hour and I shared my concerns with my friend Steve. He said he hadn't wanted to say anything before, but had felt from the very beginning that something wasn't right. He tried to get me to have a few beers and stay at his house overnight, but I chose to go home, determined to do what I knew I had to do. The house was empty and with no note of explanation I decided to have one more shuffle of the angel cards. Out fell the Bridgette card again! I know it sounds unbelievable, four shuffles of the pack in one day, the same card fell out four times. Not once did another card fall out. I eventually went to bed at 11pm and she came home hours after that and when I asked her where she had been she wouldn't say.

In the morning I told her it was over. She was calm and said she didn't blame me and asked me if I would move out for a couple of weeks while she found somewhere to live, adding that it was my house and she wouldn't cause any trouble; if only life was that simple!

I moved in with Steve and, once again in my life, despite knowing it was the right decision and that I really had no choice, I was an emotional wreck. Two weeks later she demanded more money than I had already offered in 'compensation' before she would leave, but my renewed offer of £5,000 was still not enough for her. Legal advice had confirmed her entitlement to half the equity (£55,000) and after days of self-recrimination and missing my dog – who I had allowed to stay following her offer to take care of him in the belief I would soon move back in – I put the house up for sale and rented a small house on my own which was available for immediate occupation.

It was two weeks before Christmas when I finally collected my dog, knowing she wouldn't be there. I was devastated by his condition that made it clear he had not been well treated. Thankfully he soon recovered in our new home.

Much to my children's relief and that of many others, I cancelled the wedding and would live in the rented house for just over a very emotional and difficult year, during which I began to rebuild my life.

Over the year the house was for sale I had accepted three offers, all close to the asking price, but frustratingly each one collapsed just before completion, all for different reasons. I had been depressed myself to begin with and spent a lot of time feeling sorry for myself and being 'the victim' while trying to understand why I had been so unaware of the reality that everyone else could see coming. Although it had been frustrating that the house was not selling, once it did over a year later it became very obvious why and the reason reinforced the trust in another spiritual catchphrase, 'that everything in life happens for a reason'.

In the meantime everyone at Kingswood Fire Station was very supportive of me, but I soon learnt that by replaying and updating the story as it evolved I was just 'keeping it alive' and stopping myself from truly moving forward at the same time. But one day I did move forward, and I don't really know why it happened. Maybe it was a triumph for the constant drip feed of messages that encourages 'being positive' from the spiritual events that I had returned to, having largely stopped going during the ill-fated relationship, but whatever it was it worked as one day something just 'clicked' within me and I made a positive decision to stop talking about it and to get on with my life, with an acceptance that what will be will be and all the worrying about money in the world was not going to change anything. To think like that was new to me and it felt empowering, and with a spring in my step life became good again as I began to 'walk my talk' instead of giving it lip service.

27

Taking my Breath Away

'Getting on with life' meant my life just about returned to normal; my small end of terrace house was cosy and Spot and I were happy. My resolve was tested when, on Valentine's Day, I received a tempting text from her, but after a wobbly evening home alone I managed to resist anything but the polite reply I had sent. My retirement was four months away.

Sally was a member of Lisa's meditation circle and we had become good friends. We were sat upstairs having coffee at a mind, body and spirit event in Chipping Sodbury Town Hall when an attractive woman appeared at the head of the stairs and began walking towards us. She was stunning and it was much more than the fur coat she was wearing that made me look twice; my heart was beating so fast it felt like it would jump out of my chest as I stole what I thought were innocent glances. Once again I was mesmerised by a woman I considered beautiful. She stopped in front of us and said hello to Sally. We were introduced, her name was Jane! It was obvious they hadn't seen each other for a while and, after catching up with Sally, Jane said a few things to me, including that she could feel my *'heart hurting'* and if I ever felt in the need of healing, to give her a ring as she was a Reiki healer. I didn't hesitate when I took the offered business card.

Although my heart was still thumping wildly in my chest I knew it wasn't what she had meant and that she had probably picked up on my emotions still raw from the breakup. I didn't have to ask Sally if she was married because she said 'yes', anticipating the question. It was to provide a good test of my new values of not getting involved with any woman who was not free to do so; and of course neither was I, with unfinished business and emotional trauma to rid myself of.

I completed Part Two of the Reiki course with Nadia, which included more personal development through the sharing of experiences and having to memorise the Reiki symbols for future use. We were all 'attuned' for a second time during the final meditation on the second and last day of the course, when once again I was to feel a tremendous peace and calm that washed over me that I wished could last forever. Finishing Part Two meant we could expand from the restrictions of being a Reiki One practitioner and healing of the self, members of the family and close friends of the previous year.

During that year I had sampled many other types of healing, of which metamorphic, spiritual and trance were just a few and each of them were excellent in their own way. I became increasingly ravenous for anything and everything spiritual as I continued to attend any event I could, including, Sunday services and Tuesday guilds at my spiritual church, development courses with crystals and the use and importance of colour and music.

One such course was a one-day development course by a medium called Dave Viney and before we started he placed dozens of crystals on a table in front of us. I was hardly able to take my eyes off one of them as he talked for the first thirty minutes. It wasn't just because the small white crystals I was attracted to were attached to a large black rock which made it the biggest sample on the table, it was more than that, but I couldn't have explained why then. Now I have experienced similar feelings on many other occasions and have come to trust that if I am attracted to something it is because I am meant to be for reasons that will usually unfold later.

Our first exercise was to go to the table and select the crystal we felt drawn to. Still determined to test my scepticism, I decided to wait until the other fourteen had chosen first and then picked it up with a smile and returned to my chair. On closer examination the small crystals attached to the rock were black and white and I began to feel very different whilst sat holding it. Dave came to me first and told me that he knew I would choose the big one because we had the same spirit guide and he had picked it up in a forest while on holiday in an area of Canada where 'our' spirit guide had lived.

He asked me if I knew the name of my spirit guide, which at that time I didn't. 'Running Bear', he explained, was a Native American Indian and part of the Blackfeet tribe who lived in an area around Alberta in Canada and Montana in the United States of America. I felt honoured to have such information because very few people know the name of their spirit guides, and with it my scepticism briefly disappeared as I felt somehow special, and not just because my guide was the same as Dave the Medium's.

Despite my positive intentions to move on I would still have bad times when life was a struggle; I would especially miss the lovely house I had been living in and there were many occasions when I illogically considered going back. It was during one of these spells of depression that I decided to call the other Jane, Reiki Jane as she would come to be known, to arrange a healing treatment in her therapy room attached to her home. I can't deny that the feeling I had when first seeing Jane had lingered in me and that my choice of healer was as much about being drawn to her as the healing. I was not disappointed as I found her no less attractive and as a bonus the healing turned out to be excellent.

It was interesting to experience how Jane had adapted the style of Reiki we had both been taught for her own use, and although the end result of feeling calm and peaceful was the same, I left with a short message from 'reading' a chosen 'Ascended Master's Angel Card'. The second session two months later was very different; the approach was basically the same, but during the healing she started to talk about events that had happened to me in a 'past life' and, in particular, a stabbing in my chest that I had received during a battle as a knight on horseback when I was killed. This was the second reference I had received about my involvement with a 'past life' and it linked in perfectly with what I had experienced, on horseback as a knight, when meditating at Lisa's. Jane explained how she felt it was affecting how I was able to live in this life as she placed her hands over (not touching, shame!) my chest and began waving them around in the air.

I felt absolutely nothing as I walked away, wondering what the heck had gone on, but that had changed by the next day when I woke feeling very sore around my chest area. As I had done nothing physical the previous day that would explain what felt like I had played a bruising game of rugby; it didn't take me long to make the connection to Jane's healing; there was no other explanation other than the power of her healing the day before!

28

Can it all be Coincidence?

With my retirement from the Fire Brigade almost upon me, I started to think about my future. It would have been possible to extend my career for up to five more years until I was sixty, but the thought of continuing to pay pension contributions each month, with no corresponding increase in my final pension, made up my mind, it was time for a change no matter how much I loved my job.

As with all things over time, the fire service had changed and not all for the better; having been taught a different way I was challenging a lot of the changes, especially those specific to health and safety and risk assessments. On joining thirty years earlier, the then old-school firemen had said they 'felt sorry for me', because the job I was going into then was not the same as when they had joined thirty years earlier. Well they were right and they were wrong, and I would be wrong to have said it as well, although there were times when I was tempted as new recruits buzzed with the same excitement as I had. Nothing ever stays the same and neither should it, which is the analogy I use to live my life now; *WO* in my favourite Kryon parable, *WO and the Rooms of Lesson*, had missed many opportunities because he was frightened of the future and the unknown and that had inspired my own thinking about following the limiting beliefs of others on different journeys to different destinations.

Having to start formally risk assessing incidents on our arrival and before we could instigate the chosen mode of attack meant that many officers had become risk averse and, in my opinion, a lesser, albeit safer, service to the public they serve was the outcome. It was not that we were the 'gung ho' types of leaders and firefighters so often portrayed in films by sending crews into severe and rapidly worsening fire conditions, because we weren't. We were well trained to make decisions from the experiences gained and by always taking opportunities to learn from the experience of others. The result of that was that we had learnt to risk assess naturally without the formality of announcing it as proof that we had given it some thought, but my fears of having to delay sending firefighters into buildings to perform rescues with the potential for the unnecessary loss of life were unfounded as it was done by a simple radio message declaring that the incident was either offensive or defensive; in other words we're going in or we're staying out.

There were a number of factors that influence young officers becoming risk averse; the success in fire safety and community awareness had reduced the numbers of fires to learn from and hard-won skills were being lost; another was the knock-on effect from equality and fairness policies that were inadvertently reducing an emphasis on practical skills and ability to think on your feet in favour of reliability and a neutrality of attitude; another was the decision to assess suitability for promotion by candidates only having to show competence in the command and control of 'table top' exercises with imaginary fires and videos used to provide very little realism or any variance of circumstance; in my opinion that has led to a culture of 'the fear of making a mistake'. As with all things in life there is a balance.

I had made mistakes and often could have done better, but I have always made sure I have learnt from them and I guess I was either fortunate or experienced enough – or maybe both – that they didn't cause death or injury. I actually believe my attitude developed into a progressive one as a result of my early difficulties in a new work place, which were caused by my lack of experience, and because of that I had tried to ensure competence through experience before seeking promotion.

One of the most interesting incidents I attended was a 'once in a lifetime experience' of multi-rescues from a severe and developing fire when I panicked, but was calmed and led by the supreme coolness of an experienced sub-officer called George. I was an inexperienced leading fireman in my early days at Temple Back Station when we were turned out to a 'persons reported' incident at about 0200hrs. We approached the fire along a long straight road and we could see the intense fire from some way back as acrid smoke poured out of a ground-floor window, threatening the residents who were leaning out of every window on the first, second, third and fourth floors as it billowed up the front of the house. I was in the rear of the same appliance as the OIC and, as we approached the almost unbelievable scene, instead of taking the shortest route against the one way system, which would have kept the incident and the road in full view and been quicker, he instructed the driver to follow the one way system out of view of the residents waiting to be rescued.

He explained his thought process later; the positives were that it avoided any chance of a head-on crash with vehicles coming around the bend on the one way system, and it gave him a chance to think; the negatives were the longer travel time and the residents panic may have been increased enough to encourage them to jump or climb down. He got it right. Nobody jumped.

We pitched every ladder we carried – six in total – with me unsure of my role and running around like a headless chicken. Every person was systematically rescued as the severe fire on the ground floor was being fought. The only funny moment was when a gentleman on the top floor was gesticulating for one of us to catch his prized Spanish guitar that he was intending to drop for one of us to catch. It smashed into smithereens on the pavement below as we all side-stepped out of its way to avoid injury. Funny for us but not for him! At least he was alive. Materials can be replaced; bodies can't, well not yet anyway!

I did calm down and, getting my head together, I went to look around the back of the house as what we thought was the final rescue was being performed at the front. To my amazement there was one man waving for help from the fourth-floor window and I shouted at him to stay calm while we positioned our thirty-metre turntable ladder (TL) appliance (they're called aerial appliances now), the longest and only ladder that would reach him. The experienced operator of the TL positioned the vehicle facing up the very steep gradient and extended the ladder for a firefighter to climb up and assist the man to safety. Two things; on the ground we realised the man was deaf and the TL operator told me that the safety rules for the TL did not even come close to permitting its use on that steep a gradient. Many younger and less experienced operators would have declined on that basis; that's experience and knowing your equipment to take an informed risk to save a life despite breaking the rules. I feel like there's a lesson for living life in there somewhere.

The experience of everyone that day combined with calm but clear leadership was a key factor in a successful job. I learnt from the experience and gained massive respect for George who never ever mentioned my headless chicken roll, but I knew he knew and he knew I knew. There are things you cannot learn from text books or by just talking about.

Having made up my mind to retire I was sat up in bed on a Friday off with my early morning cup of tea, considering my options. I had been less than proactive in thinking about my future as a retired fifty-five-year old with a good pension, until a week earlier when a colleague had asked me what I was going to do. He suggested that I would make a good counsellor because, in his opinion, and others, I was a good listener and had often been helpful in what I had said; I thought it rather ironic that I was apparently able to be of help to others while still making a complete mess of my own life! So I asked for a 'sign' that counselling was a good option for me, although there weren't any others at that point. (Asking for a sign was something I had started to do since my introduction to spirituality.)

I began my breakfast routine with Spot the dog having to wait patiently for his walk that would normally come first on a work day. As I was running low on my daily nutritional supplements I called Marion, the friend who supplied them; she said it was ok to collect them that morning, adding that it was a coincidence that I had called because she had been thinking about me earlier that morning. She said she would tell me why when I arrived. Having already forgotten that I had asked for a sign I arrived at Marion's and she explained how she was training to be a counsellor and that morning, just before I rang, her assignment had been returned in the post, having been marked by her tutor. While she was reading the comments she had the thought that I would make a good counsellor! Marion had always been a good listener for my problems so knew me well and because of that she added it would be good for me.

Having asked for a sign I had received one within three hours. Yes it could have been a coincidence, but I don't believe that at all. There had been just too many incidents to be all coincidence. No, someone or something was listening and watching over me

There were various organisations in the Bristol area that offered counselling courses, but the one that I was attracted to was with the University of Bristol. As it happened, or maybe it was just another coincidence, they had a three-day 'Introduction to Counselling' course that was available about that time in May 2005, and although I did not officially retire until the end of June I had worked my last day. The course was actually a prerequisite for the full course and I would be assessed during it by the university staff as being suitable or not; I was. I applied and was accepted on the two-year counselling skills course that would start later that year in September 2005. The two-year counselling skills course was also a prerequisite for the continuing two-year diploma course for anyone wishing to continue and complete the whole four-year course to full qualification. I was informed that, should I be successful over the first two years and I was deemed acceptable following interview for the diploma, it was just a formality that I would be accepted subject to any extenuating circumstances – unfortunately there was going to be one and it affected me.

A year after I retired, the rules on retirement in the Fire Brigade changed and, had I stayed until then, I would have been very tempted to remain in the job to be re-employed under a revised new contract, with no additional pension contributions, having already taken the lump sum part of my pension and abated my monthly payment until I finally 'retired' again. The whole process is termed 'abating', and I am so glad I didn't have the option, because there is no doubt in my mind that, had I stayed, the very important next stage of my life's journey would have also been abated; perfect timing again.

29

Transition

If June the thirtieth, two thousand and five, was an ending, then July the first was an ideal time to contemplate new beginnings, and it didn't fail to deliver on my growing expectations of my life that had been enriched and encouraged by my deepening spiritual understanding. Within two years my understanding of who I was and why would be answered and my life would completely change.

Many of my colleagues on retirement had taken new jobs allied to fire safety, but I had no plans other than the counselling training that would prove to be the next important step forward of the many taken since my search for answers had begun five years earlier; once again the timing couldn't have been any more perfect than if I had planned it, and that was what I was coming to expect, but, as a continuing but lessening sceptic, still needed convincing of!

The four-year course was divided into two equal parts of two years each. The first two were focused on learning the basic counselling skills and personal development; the second two, the 'diploma' part of the course, would focus on a chosen counselling technique. My first reaction to the necessity for personal development was that it would be a waste of time. I was ok; I just hadn't found the right partner! How wrong and naive must I have been in being so unaware as to believe I was free from personal baggage after continually questioning my life since the battle of my marriage and leaving for another woman, and how, and why, could I have been still so entrenched in my own ignorance when my personal life continued to be a shambles some twenty-five years later? No. To believe I was perfect – which in effect was saying my partners were not – was so far from the truth as to be laughable. Even my heartfelt plea on first talking to Lisa when I pronounced *'I was such a simple man who wanted simple things'* and to *'just be happy and content'* had not produced the greater personal awareness I needed to change the fundamentals of my life in relationships. No, I was not ok, but I was inching towards a solution.

We had the same teacher for the whole of the first year and I really enjoyed practising the basic counselling skills in groups of three when we would take turns to role play as counsellor, client and observer. From the start we were encouraged as the client to use real-life day to day personal issues as part of our personal development, but those that weren't ready, for whatever reason, were allowed to use made-up scenarios with the expectation that, in time, they would; if they couldn't – and we are not talking about deep and heavy stuff here – they were politely asked to leave the course. All the skills we were shown and practised were important, they included general discussions on issues such as being judgemental and forgiveness etc., but the one that seemed to be the foundation of all the others was 'effective listening', which is not as easy as it sounds. This course hand-out sums it up so well:

LISTENING

When I ask you to listen to me and you start giving me advice, you have not done what I asked.

When I ask you to listen and you begin to tell me why I shouldn't feel that way, you are trampling on my feelings.

When I asked you to listen and you feel you have to do something to solve my problems, you have failed me, strange as that may seem.

When you do something for me that I can and need to do for myself, you contribute to my fear and inadequacy. I can do for myself. I am not helpless. Maybe discouraged and faltering, but not helpless!

But when you accept as a simple fact that I do feel what I feel, no matter how irrational, then I can stop trying to convince you and get about this business of understanding what is behind this irrational feeling.

Listen! All I asked was that you will listen, not talk or do – just listen. If you want to talk, wait a minute for your turn... and I'll listen to you.

Life was good and interesting. The house, which was still occupied by my ex at that stage, was refusing to sell, but the contact between us had lessened and I had long since accepted the mess I had created for myself. Yes, there were times when I would slide back into blame and question my actions while trying to make sense of it all, but even those times were becoming less frequent as I gradually moved on as much as I ever could with unfinished business. That changed in a moment for no better reason than my desire to get on with my life outweighed feeling sorry for myself. Time is a great healer, but is better still when combined with a positive intention and attitude.

Six months after I retired and part way through the first year of the counselling course I received an unexpected telephone call from Jane Three saying she wanted to move on and for me to make her an offer to vacate the house. I was taken completely by surprise and to say I was shocked would be an understatement. Had I vetted the call, as I normally would have, I may not have even answered it, but without my reading glasses I did and, during those immediate seconds after, I was desperately trying to think on my feet as to how I should respond. I had been over the figures so many times in my head, but they never improved and I had already resigned myself to the fact that she would be legally entitled to about £55,000 when the house sold. I had been laughed at for offering £5,000 to 'make life easier' when I first left so I doubled it. We were making and refusing offers like it was

Monopoly money and eventually agreed on £25,000, subject to the house ownership being transferred into my sole name. I took the house off the market and once all the legal work was completed six weeks later, I moved back into my house in February 2006.

Karma is the Buddhist belief that someone's destiny is as determined by their actions in a previous life and was something I had heard a lot about over the previous years. During the following months my thoughts returned to the time of my leaving when I was gripped by fear through uncertainty and worry, but with the outcome settled and plenty of time to think differently about the unexpected turn of events, I began to reconsider why I had got into the mess and acted so irrationally in the first place. At that time I was still unaware of my own imperfections but, even if I had been, karma would still have been a real probability. Why? Well for one thing it fitted my profile of having someone, or in this case, something else to blame, and secondly it made me feel better. What it didn't fit with was my still sceptical nature about beliefs that come without solid proof and of course there are many other unprovable ideological philosophies attached to alien beliefs that I was coming across in what I call my transitional period.

What I was less sceptical about was that once again it felt like I was being given an opportunity through a seemingly never-ending supply of similar experiences, with ever-increasing extremes of circumstance, to learn about myself, and at that time I was in exactly the right place with the right teaching to realise them. Whatever the driving force in my life was, it was making me feel that I was being pulled along, for reasons unknown, to a destination that I was meant to arrive at some time in the future. But my evidence was purely anecdotal and it would remain as a fragile proof that left only one avenue of travel, to trust life. What wasn't fragile was the solid evidence I was soon to receive from my counselling training that would change my understanding of who I was and why, completely.

Although at that time I considered the decision to pay up as a brave one, the fact of the matter was that I had little choice because I wanted to close the door on that foolish chapter of my life and move on. But isn't that exactly what being brave is? I have no doubt that other persons in the same situation would act differently and 'fight for a moral justice' and I see that as being right for their circumstances and brave too; it could also be seen as being 'stubborn' and 'intransigent', but everything we do is subjective and we have to make decisions based on who we are at the time; it is only as we come to know ourselves better that we can trust ourselves better.

In trusting life, and not becoming a victim of it, there will still be times when it feels like it is getting worse, and being able to let go will be tested to the limit and be hard to maintain. I believe times of uncertainty such as this are caused by life realigning and adjusting itself on the road to getting better. There is a saying: 'Life sometimes has to get worse to get better.' More and more I believed that everything in life happens for a reason.

To do nothing when we know we should, as opposed to being uncertain, will go against the flow of a life that is encouraging us along a predestined path and in effect we will be handing over control of our own life to someone else, just as I had done with Jane Three. Uncertainty can be overcome in all sorts of ways but meditation, being in nature and asking for help, will help to hear that inner voice of guidance I believe we all have. Whilst I know that a life that is about the experience can rarely be that simple, it has become apparent to me that achieving a greater understanding of life comes with accepting that there is something bigger involved, which is trying to teach, guide, show and lead us through an ideology of acceptance and trust when we have to let go of many of our preconceived ideas; part of that for me, no matter how flimsy, is to take into account timing, karma, and soul and human life purpose, for ourselves and for others.

I believe when we trust in our life as a journey, we will always be assisted on. If you make a decision that you later regret, like I did, then do something about it and move on no matter how long you take to get there, because it is always 'better late than never'. And although we should continually be wary about going back into old relationships and the same situations, it does demonstrate that we still have something else to learn or complete.

I spent months redecorating the house and enjoying the freedom my retirement was giving me. The counselling course was going well and, having stopped going regularly to my spiritual centre because of the hassle it caused in the relationship, I began to go again and I found the comfort of old familiar ways and friendships reassuring.

On the evening of my first return, I was asked if I would be going to a week-long workshop on 'Spiritual Development' that had been advertised on the notice board and due to start the following day. I rang the number when I arrived home and, due to a last minute cancellation, there was one free place.

The workshop began with introductions and we were given the timetable for a well-structured week with a full programme of personal development, most of it hands on and practical. Two of the subjects, Karma and Crystals, were delivered through lectures by guest speakers and my confidence grew each day as we practised the art of clairvoyance on each other. Over the week we all became good friends but there was one person in particular that I really clicked with; she was bubbly, vibrant, and attractive. Her name was Jane!

Towards the end of the week Jane had announced that she was studying to become a hypnotherapist and was looking for people to become 'case studies'. It would entail being available regularly for a couple of hours one night a week for six weeks. Although I was particularly interested in the therapy that Jane had assured me would be good for my personal development, the thought of female company was equally as appealing. As Jane was working locally to where I lived we arranged that she would come to my house one evening a week on her way home from work.

This was a good time in my life; I enjoyed Jane's company and being a case study, both of which were good for my personal growth and spiritual understanding; I think it would be fair to say we became friends.

One thing I tried really hard not to do was to get romantically involved because I had only been on my own for about six months and I was keen to avoid another Groundhog Day – a good friend used to tell me, 'You can't build new relationships on old loves'. That wasn't easy as the temptation grew with each of our six winter evenings when, having completed the hypnotherapy session, we would sit cosily in front of the log fire discussing spiritual philosophies. I could sense a growing frustration at my apparent lack of interest in allowing the friendship to develop further.

Our planned time together finished with no specific plans to meet again other than the normal follow-up to be arranged in the months ahead, which Jane did by inviting me to her house and offering to cook me a meal as a thank you.

I did consider not going, not because I didn't want to, but because I knew I was close to giving in, but I accepted and I did; which for me was a partial triumph, but only because alcohol did not play a part!

We became boyfriend and girlfriend and at some stage we became partners (I have never been able to work out when that transition takes place despite all the practice I have had). Life seemed to be pulling me along nicely with what I saw as 'perfect timing', encouraging me to believe that once again it was 'all meant to be and we would be together forever'... Here we go again!

Although I loved the area I had moved back to I decided to sell the house. I changed estate agency and was surprised when I was quoted £30,000 more than it had previously been on the market for. My sceptical nature convinced me that this was just the normal selling agent practice of price inflation to get the business, only to be knocked down for all sorts of lame excuses when it didn't sell, but I was wrong, because it sold within two weeks and for just under the asking price, which meant I recouped the £25,000, and the legal fees, I had paid out to regain ownership.

It's hard to imagine the perfect timing as coincidence and once again, encouraged by what seemed to be, meant to be, Jane and I discussed where I would live. We both nervously agreed that I would move in with her.

It was my daughter who pointed out that this Jane was the fourth of significance in my life and I often laugh at the irony of believing everything in life is for a reason and trying to come up with one; I know Jane is a popular name, but even so it seemed a bit ridiculous, or was it? Was life trying to tell me something, maybe even giving me a clue through repeating patterns – Groundhog Day is a possibility, as is karma, or could it have been just a super coincidence? Maybe none of those, but chosen deliberately as being humorous before incarnating, which is my favourite.

Not long after I had moved in, my son was posted abroad with the RAF. One of the communication systems in place to keep service personnel in touch with family and friends by the armed forces is called the 'E bluey', which is rather like sending an email but better. Jane was the fastest 'touch typist' I have ever seen and, having watched me struggle, offered to type as I dictated. This would provide us with many happy and amusing moments when I would read it over before sending, only to find Jane had added many funny anecdotes during my frequent pauses for thought.

The trouble was, she also kindly offered to type up my counselling assignments for submission, which concerned me because it was awkward and embarrassing as I discussed many crazy decisions and the heartaches I had caused in relationships. I nervously accepted and, whilst the first two assessments were awkward, having also touched on the early days of our relationship, the final end of Year Two assessment was extremely embarrassing for me and, despite numerous subtle attempts at trying to convince Jane I wanted to type it myself, she insisted.

30

Who am I and Why? The Bigger Question

The first year of the counselling course had already begun to explain how my life circumstances were shaping my decision-making processes and, having started the second and moved in with Jane, I once again had high hopes for the future. I had also begun to understand how, as a unique individual, that if I had been shaped by my childhood in a less than 'perfect' way, then so must everyone else have been by theirs. And from that I concluded, rightly or wrongly, that none of us can ever be perfect except in the context of our own journeys and in the eyes of God, or any other higher power you may believe in, where we must achieve being humanly perfect with every breath we take. For me, somebody who had for so long thought I was reasonably perfect, that was quite a momentous realisation.

Everything felt like it was coming together. My life, that had so often seemed to be shrouded in a darkness of unknowing, had started to become clearer with each 'light bulb' moment and there were many. I was adding new knowledge to my life from the understanding taken from looking at my past experiences from a very different perspective, and it was developing into the key that would unlock the answers to what had become a purpose in its own right, to find the answer to the biggest question of all, *'Who am I and why am I who I am?'*

In the second year of counselling training I learnt about self-worth and self-esteem, the effect of parenting and the importance of birth order and much more. At the same time my spiritual awareness was growing from the Reiki healing and development courses that were a revelation to me. I listened and learnt from the refreshingly inspiring teachings and philosophies of others, some of whom had found different answers to the same questions on their own journeys forward from the darkness into the light of knowing and who shared their knowledge freely, with enthusiasm and a refreshing love that I have found so typical of so many of the spiritually aware. But not all; some guard their knowledge secretly as if it wields some sort of power. I believe it wields a locked door!

The human and the spiritual seemed to be integrating perfectly in common purpose as one complemented and depended on the other as one, which of course I believe they are, but for some reason so often seem like they are not. If only the light bulb moments could illuminate everything clearly to see the whole picture, but of course they can't for surely life would not seem worth living if we knew everything in advance. So I would have to be content with the glimmers of light to give titbits of information that would tantalise my beliefs rather than the brightness of certainty that would ease my doubts.

I wanted so much more as I devoured and interrogated all I heard, but in particular I wanted to know if I had failed in life with my false promises of undying love and being together forever in just about every relationship I had. I wanted to know if I could truly be to blame when I did not know what I was doing, what I call an honest ignorance, but what I wanted more than anything else was confirmation that I had chosen my life circumstances! Because if I had, then so must have everyone else and failure and blame would be a human trait born from our chosen imperfections, and my relationships, our relationships, had been agreed in some sort of 'soul contract' and as humans for *a reason, a season or a lifetime* of growth and enlightenment and to fulfil karmic and other agreements from past lives. Is that just a spiritually inspired dream?. Am I making realities out of maybes?. Is there a better solution other than randomly chosen lives?

I would also have loved to support each and every one of all of those I had relationships with in the ways I had promised, and from the perspective of spiritual choices I have a small hope that I did, but as a human I couldn't and that is all that matters to us when we are feeling the emotions and pain of hurt. What I did know for certain was that something was driving me on and I couldn't stand still, or give the space and time to understand about the friendship and the commitments that would have seen me through both my challenges and celebrations, my laughter and my tears, because I was being nudged along to help me to achieve what was meant to be for me and to hopefully find the true love within. And when, not if, I found that true love within, it would help me to harmonise the wholeness of who I was and was becoming in a sacred re-union with my chosen and ultimate soul mate; a soul mate who had been somewhere else on a different journey waiting to find their own love within. I wanted to reunite with the feeling of loving and being loved back that I was so desperate for, and of course to confirm that I had arrived at my destination as the same place I had left many, many, years before.

With everything that was happening to me my mind was an explosion of thinking. I was thinking about everything, my childhood and how it had not been, my adolescent years that were an embarrassment, my unexpected but successful career as a firefighter, my failed marriage, and the hurt I caused to my wife and the damage I had caused to my two children, that above all else I loved unconditionally and wholeheartedly.

My mother and father had never showed me anything that I can remember that leads me to believe that they were unhappy. But neither did they show me anything that would lead me to believe they were happy either. Sticking with it and learning to exist together is what I suspect they did. Exactly what I see many couples doing now and something I had also done and was doing. That behaviour of 'accepting one's lot' and 'getting on with it' was much more prevalent in society then and probably one of the values I had brought with me as a learnt behaviour that made it so hard to walk away from my marriage, and all the other relationships. When I did eventually walk away my children have told me that they were the first children in their school (that they knew about) whose parents had separated and were treated almost like celebrities. They also remember that everyone's reaction was one of shock and disbelief because as husband and wife and as parents, we were seen as a happy family and the perfect couple.

No child likes to think of, or indeed looks for their parents' relationship as being anything other than perfect because to do so would be to challenge the belief that life is anything but perfect.

One thing I have learnt and believe in, is that a breakdown in a relationship should not be called a failure and nor is it weak. Failure for me was leaving for another, not for leaving; but of course I didn't see it like that then! To carry on with the arguments and unhappiness in the relationship would have been to deny myself, and as importantly my wife, the chance of true love. A true love that is not a dream and does exist; I have the proof. But of course I didn't know that then either!

The argument from many a parent that they stay in a relationship for the well-being of their children because to separate would 'damage' them is often used as an excuse and justification for not being brave enough, just as I did; and yet unbeknown to myself they were constant witness to our never-ending battles and were already being shaped by it. What would have been worse, to be shaped by continuous disharmony or having two loving parents living separate lives in harmony? If a separation is done in the 'right way', if there is ever such a thing, and the children are not used as pawns or as weapons to exact revenge, they will grow up to be as well-balanced as they would have been as a result of learning from two parents who stay together for 'the children's sake', and often for their own convenience. Either set of circumstances are equally as damaging to children and lead to them learning behaviours that become their norm, which without insight, understanding and treatment will be carried forward into their own lives for the pattern to repeat.

Whether staying or leaving an unhappy relationship is weak or strong can only be decided by the individual and the problem is that most of us do not have the understanding or the 'tools' to do anything about it. What everyone does have is a voice to speak their truth, and that is as good a place to start exploring as anywhere. I did not use my voice in the best way possible during relationship counselling and now I will never know if the outcome could have been any different, but I have also learnt to believe that it is not relevant in a life that is about the experience.

When I told my parents that I was leaving my wife, my father responded by telling me that he and Mum had not always found it easy and 'You've made your bed so lie in it'. Whilst I accept that was fine for them, and probably for many others as well, I see that as living a lie and not being true. Only as individuals can we decide on a course of action and I have come to believe that, for whatever reason, I was nudged and prompted out of my marriage just at the time I had made a determined effort to stay. Although alcohol was a major factor in my adultery at the beginning, I was never once tempted to return, which, for me, is an indicator that it was all 'meant to be'. Had I stayed I would have withered like a flower without water.

That doesn't mean I do not respect all those who decide to 'stay put' and 'fight' to keep their relationship together, for whatever reason they feel is right for them, because I do and that must also be 'meant to be' and equally as hard.

31

Counselling: The Person-centred Approach

The second year of the counselling course remained one day a week for the four terms, and was different only in content and that we had a specialist tutor for each term. In that respect we had already chosen our individual preferences to suit our needs from a range of subjects. There were many to choose from; I discarded counselling in the workplace and briefly considered bereavement counselling, but my overwhelming need was to understand myself and because of that I chose to attend the 'Personal Development Group' in the hope it would continue to inform my personal growth; I was not disappointed.

We had already been introduced to the 'person-centred' approach to counselling in Year One. We were told that it had evolved from the work of Carl Rogers and others and it had resonated with me from the very beginning; not just because it is said to be a part of the humanistic approach to counselling *'a set of ideas about, or interest in, ethics and mankind, not including religious beliefs'*, nor its belief that *'...we are all capable of realising our potential in a process of development and continuous change'*, but simply because it 'talked' to me in a way I seemed to understand, the same way that the book *Conversations with God* had done years earlier; both seemed familiar.

The person-centred approach talks of the 'self-concept', which is the awareness of ourselves that begins at birth when our separation from the 'significant others' in our lives begins, and the idea of the 'me and I' begins to emerge within us. **It says that the real self lies within us all**, and that was exactly what I was searching for in my search for 'who I was and why'. It goes on to say that *'...if we are lucky the self-concept and the urge to grow will develop and reach maximum potential in tandem rather than in conflict. If we are not lucky then conflict will grow and is usually* *between the growth of the self (me) and the needs of significant others around the person'*. Personally, I would not see this conflict as lucky or not lucky, but essential as a consequence of our chosen life choices to facilitate our life purpose, but that is a personal opinion based on my belief in spirituality.

The government of the day, worried about the growth in mental health issues, had chosen a system of counselling called Cognitive Behaviour Therapy (CBT) and rolled out a programme that made it available through the National Health Service (NHS). CBT is a 'quick fix' counselling option delivered to the client over six sessions and the main difference between CBT and person-centred counselling is how the change in a person is achieved.

Whilst the person-centred approach believes that *'if we, in counselling, experience the warmth that the therapy is designed to encourage, we can find our own way to grow and understand who we are'*, CBT has the belief that *'a person can be helped to change their lives by being given constructive programmes to follow which, in essence, rewards positive behaviour and ignores negative behaviour, no matter what the original cause was for the unwanted behaviour'*.

My preference for the person-centred approach is simply because CBT can leave the deep underlying cause(s) locked away, relatively undisturbed in the *'mercurial filing cabinet'*, and clients are taught coping mechanisms to keep them there. Whilst that works for many, it doesn't for me because, having battled for much of my life to understand the cause of my problems, I wanted rid of them, at least as much of them as I possibly could.

Whilst any counselling is best delivered by trained professionals, I believe that we are all capable of the personal growth that will reduce the need for prolonged counselling by getting to the core of who we are and why. What we need is a curiosity about life, and thus ourselves, and to trust that everything is meant to be; with perseverance and a positive intention we can succeed.

That our lives have become complicated is not in doubt, but we can unpick them to reveal the simplicity that can be so rewarding by choosing to live in a balanced and harmonic way through a holistic approach, and in doing so can lessen our dependency and reliance on others. After I asked for help I began, through a series of opportunities, to understand what was happening to me. Those opportunities were offered as introductions to see life from a different perspective, which included meditation and so-called alternative therapies like healing, as well as those deemed somehow more acceptable, like counselling, that are considered 'mainstream'.

Although my choices weren't always fruitful they were never damaging, except maybe to my pocket, but what they all did was to open my eyes to an alternative way of life and the change that could bring about, which was crucial to the success of my 'soul searching'; or as I would now prefer to say 'the search for the purity of my soul'.

Having said that, I know from personal experience that identifying what is causing us to be unhappy or unfulfilled in our lives can be extremely difficult as we get lost in a bombardment of new technologies and sold lifestyles that are not always good for us. As 'subdued' sentient beings they make staying in touch with ourselves and noticing opportunities difficult as they compete against our natural instincts. That is why, in my opinion in any case, it is so much easier to feel comfortable and accepted in life by being a follower rather than a pioneer or a free spirit, and why we seem to have lost the ability to be unique; surely anything in life that is worth having is worth fighting for. I believe that the peace and calm that can deliver the happiness and fulfilment that so many of us crave and cannot find, can seem like an unattainable dream, but it's not and it's never too late to change and wake up to the power within us all.

Change for me has been far from easy, but it has been worth fighting for. There have been many uncomfortable times when I was tempted to keep my disappointments and embarrassments shut away and pretend I was perfect, but I couldn't, because I wasn't and I wanted to be real; I wanted to understand the truth of who I was, partly for the justification of my actions yes, but mainly as a way of understanding and freeing myself from the guilt I felt by learning how to forgive myself.

Many people raise their eyebrows at the mention of childhood issues with a 'here we go again, always blaming the childhood', and there is an element of truth in that also, not for the obvious reasons, but for the less obvious ones of having the potential to become a victim of our life circumstances; rather than using it to propel us forward to do something about it. The truth of the matter is, if we want and need to ask for help then we must be prepared to change and our childhood holds the key to many, if not all, of the answers. It does not necessarily mean we have been intentionally mistreated or unloved as children, in fact it is usually the very opposite, with good-intentioned parents just doing their best; but with that best being informed by the circumstances of their own parents, and compounded by a world that has become increasingly difficult to understand, everything combines easily to increasingly inform our frustrating lives and discourage the potential to be different.

I began to understand that and much more because the person-centred approach had begun to do its job and was dovetailing nicely with everything that my so-called spiritual teachings had opened me up to, but it was also about to be taken to another level. If the person-centred approach was the foundation of what had helped me in counselling training, then what I was about to be introduced to next, Transactional Analysis (TA), would build my understanding to a level high above my confusions and expectations to become the 'icing on the cake' of the two-year course and would change the understanding of my life completely!

Transactional Analysis (TA)

Transactional Analysis is a counselling system that is broadly speaking based on the relationship between the parent and the child and is made up of four main types of analysis:

Analysis of individual personality and ego;

Transactional analysis of what people do and say to each other;

Analysis of **game playing** with ulterior transactions leading to a pay-off;

Analysis of our **'life script'** and the specific 'life dramas' that people compulsively play out.

Although there is so much more to TA than what I will link my apparently chaotic life to here, I will concentrate on the idea that we will all write a personal **life script** based on the messages and experiences of our childhood by the age of seven, and to an increasingly lesser degree thereafter into adolescence. The idea that we would then live out, albeit subconsciously, that life script, made so much sense to me, and it soon became clear that my chaotic life was the result of my own life script that had been composed, learnt and stored in my subconscious mind, formulated from the messages and experiences of not feeling loved in those formative years.

One of the basic concepts of the 'life script' analysis that really resonated with me was something called 'strokes'. A stroke, in TA, is seen as encouragement and praise and being made to feel valued; it is a 'well done' and a 'pat on the back'. I see strokes as being shown and feeling loved, which includes the concept of tough love.

The more I understood about strokes the more I began to understand how the lack of them had affected my whole life by spawning my lack of self-worth and low self-esteem, and importantly I was able to see a recent situation, with Jane, which quite clearly demonstrated that and how it was manifesting in my behaviour.

We were sitting together watching the television and Jane was busy using her laptop computer. I was getting more and more agitated by the continuous tapping of the keys as she typed away, communicating with her friends on a social network site. At that time I had no awareness or understanding of why I was feeling so agitated, just that I was and couldn't stop myself.

I began to fidget around and sigh, which was louder each time with an ever-increasing exaggeration of body shifting until Jane eventually stopped typing, looked at me and asked if her typing was annoying me and if I wanted her to stop?

I lied and said no and to carry on.

"Are you sure?"

"Yes I'm sure!"

"I'll tell you what, I'll stop anyway."

I remember feeling so embarrassed at my actions and not just because I never even had the courage to tell the truth.

So what had happened? I know now that what I was feeling, and ultimately my reaction to it, came from within and was triggered from a memory stored in my subconscious mind and learnt from a time in my childhood when I felt I was being ignored, or in TA's terms 'not feeling recognised'. The tapping of the keyboard, whilst annoying, was just a symptom of the larger issue. How I reacted came from the memory stored within my subconscious mind of how I had learnt to overcome those feelings of being ignored.

Strokes, or love, are gained when we, as human beings, especially babies and children up to and including the age of seven, and to an increasingly lesser degree thereafter into adolescence, receive the recognition of being alive and present, which is a basic need.

Strokes can be verbal or physical and as importantly positive or negative.

Positive strokes can be compliments, praise, encouragements, and physical or verbal expressions of love and affection.

Negative strokes are the opposite, including being ignored, criticism, rejection, being put down and being told to be quiet etc.

If we do not receive positive strokes, and thus the feeling of being loved through the recognition of being alive and present, we will naturally accept a negative stroke instead because of our absolute need to be recognised in any way we can achieve it. We do not know we are doing this; all we are doing is striving to be recognised and we will accept whatever is on offer as better than nothing.

My recollection of my early years was that positive strokes were either non-existent or scarce, but I can remember the negative ones from which I learnt the negative behaviours associated with them. In my case this was the sulking and crying I employed while clinging to my mother in a vain and futile attempt to gain the feeling of being recognised through positive strokes and love. What I eventually gained was a continual reinforcement of the negative strokes of being ignored, caused by my mother's frustrated and angry reaction when she would tell me to stop crying and to get out from under her feet.

Those learnt negative behaviours have become part of me through my composed life script and are stored within me as a subconscious memory which I will 'play out' naturally in my life whenever I feel I am not being recognised by being ignored. Once those negative behaviours have been recognised and understood as such, they can be changed, but more about that later.

It is important to say I am no expert on Transactional Analysis and my own personal understanding of that particular part of it was gained through being able to link it with my own circumstances that dovetailed perfectly with my spiritual beliefs of lives chosen for a purpose.

We can learn negative behaviours through the most innocent and unintended of behaviours of which there are many variations and combinations available from our unique life circumstances. That learning starts from the minute we are born and will continue through our childhood and formative years to be stored in our subconscious minds as our 'learnt behaviour'. It can range from being totally negative to its polar opposite of being totally positive and anywhere in-between. How we behave in life will depend on the actual circumstances that our learnt behaviours have been learnt from, and that can range from an absolute lack of feeling loved, that then leads to a lack of belief and self-confidence when we don't feel good enough or worthy, to being super confident and lovable. It is because there are many variations of personal circumstances available to shape our life script that we need the skills of professional counsellors to identify those that may or may not be affecting us as individuals.

My mother and father in later years would tell others with a smile full of frustrations, but in the jokey way that I have also mastered, what a miserable whining child I was and, in fairness to them I was, and that has continued in an adapted way as an adult. That my understanding now has gone a long way to changing that has inspired me to continue when it would have been so much easier to stand still, but I can't because I like the new me as someone who is positively happier and smiles more.

We all have messages from our parents that we unknowingly remember when we are older; they innocently ring around inside our heads, influencing us at significant times. Mostly we don't recognise that they are affecting us and will remain unidentified as significant until we have the understanding to reveal them. What are yours? Mine were both from my mother: 'big boys don't cry' and 'stop pestering me and get out from under my feet', while 'encouraging' me to be more like my brothers and to go out and play. Both of these were negative strokes delivered with an angry tone which continued well into adolescence as she became angry with me for just about everything I did. There were two that stand out: masturbating, and being marched into my younger brother's bedroom to observe his badly swollen and scarred face after being beaten up in a fight and challenged as to 'why I had not looked after him', when I was neither present, nor brave enough if I had been.

Nobody is born with a lack of confidence or as a whining 'miserable' child. Whining was my solution for seeking the love and attention I so desperately needed.

Ten years on from that time, and completely out of the blue, I would be given the most probable reason why I seemed to have been treated so differently from my brothers and another opportunity to stop being the victim of my life's circumstances.

Kath was a friend of my partner at that time. She was staying with us overnight on her birthday and she had asked if her friend Paulina, who neither of us had met before, could stay as well. It was entirely possible that Kath, who I didn't know that well, had passed information about me to Paulina, but she assured me after that she hadn't, and I think it extremely unlikely she knew enough about me to any depth anyway. The three of them had spent the night apart from me and, unbeknown to me, until I walked in on them in our kitchen, Paulina was giving my partner a healing treatment so I quickly left. Later I was given details by my partner as to how fantastic it had been. As they were getting ready to leave Paulina unexpectedly said my mother was 'around me' and asked if I would also like some healing. During the next remarkable fifteen minutes she described my mother extremely accurately with more than enough proof that Mum was communicating with me through her as I became very emotional with 'truth' chills running through my body. Paulina explained how Mum was saying sorry for the way she had treated me, which in itself was not remarkable, having been told the same by many mediums over the years, the difference on this occasion was an explanation why. Mum, she said, had been suffering from what we now understand as post-natal depression and 'couldn't bond with me on any level'. Writing it down seems such a simple thing and does not do justice to the enormity of the impact it had, and would continue to have, on me as the implications started to sink in. To say it was a relief would be an understatement. It made perfect sense when nothing else ever had by explaining so much, especially the stark differences between my experiences of an unhappy childhood and my two happy brothers who felt the polar opposite.

It certainly wouldn't have helped that I was born four days after Christmas Day at a time when my dad would have expected Mum to get back to normal, with News Year's Eve fast approaching. Who was going to make all the preparations for the inevitable party with his circle of drinking friends and work colleagues? Mum of course; Mum always did everything and nothing would have come between him and his celebration drink and being looked after. Post-natal depression was not an illness that was recognised then and I would suspect there would have been little or no allowance for Mum to rest. How hard that must have been, trying to cope with me as a born at home baby, and an older brother, with a husband who would not recognise the phrase 'hands on father'.

In the book *TA Today* by Ian Stewart and Vann Joines, they summarise life script as:

'Each of us in childhood writes a life story for himself or herself. This story has a beginning, middle and an end. We write the basic plot in our infant years, before we are old enough to talk more than a few words. Later on in childhood, we add more detail to the story. Most of it has been written by the age of seven. We may revise it further during adolescence.

As grown-ups, we are usually no longer aware of the life story we have written for ourselves. Yet we are likely to live it out faithfully.

Without being aware of it, we are likely to set up our lives so that

we move towards the final scene we decided upon as infants.
This unaware life story is known in TA as the life script.'

Subconscious mind

Life scripts are held within us as subconscious learnt behaviours. So what is our subconscious mind? Sigmund Freud (1856-1939) in 1925 used the metaphor of the *'mystic writing pad'* to help us understand the workings of it and today we would recognise the *'mystic writing pad'* as still being on sale as a *'magic slate'*. When we write or draw upon a magic slate, an image will appear because we are pressing against a layer of greaseproof paper that is behind a cellophane layer and a thin wax tablet. When we lift up and separate the cellophane and grease proof paper layers the contact is broken and the image disappears so we can start again with an apparently clean slate. But, although the previously drawn images have disappeared, there will be traces left behind on the wax tablet that are not visible to the naked eye, but are nevertheless there to 'affect' the newer images in a way that is not obvious. Freud suggests these newer images are our conscious mind and the detail left behind from the previous images stay within our subconscious mind as a memory that 'affects' us in a way that we are unaware of.

I had certainly been unaware of my own subconscious memories that had helped to create my life script, but it was still alive and working within me. When it works, which it nearly always does (I am an expert at it), I feel really embarrassed and pathetic. I felt I was being ignored by Jane; I sulked by sighing loudly and moving my body position to ensure I was noticed; she did and she reacted by asking me if I was ok; I lied and said yes, but she still stopped. I had successfully used my subconscious life script and learnt behaviours to get recognition and attention. What it did not do was to make me feel loved or like I had been given a stroke; what it did do was to make me feel inadequate in some way, which of course I was.

My journey, since asking for help, had led me to discover a spiritual side to life that dovetailed perfectly with the counselling course to reveal who I was and why. Without them I doubt I would have discovered my lack of positive strokes as the cause of a well-disguised and hidden lack of self-worth and self-esteem, both of which have been at the core of my lifetime of issues. Because I was not shown how to love I did not know how to love, which was the reason why I had never felt good enough. Incidents like giving the wrong answer at school in front of the class having plucked up the courage and confidence to speak for the first time, and then feeling so embarrassed, was just one of the incidents that have reinforced those issues. And it soon dawned on me that the message received in a bar many years earlier, from a man I never knew or saw again, when I denied in honest ignorance that I had a lack of self-worth, would be proved to be correct

When we look in a mirror we see what others see, a normal human being – so far as any human can be normal – what they don't see and we often don't understand is who we are deep within our subconscious mind where the 'lurking monster' of self-doubt lives.

Self-esteem is the sense of one's own value or worth and if you have not learnt self-worth, or to value yourself, then you will have a low self-esteem; it's how you feel about yourself and if it's not good, you will – subconsciously – not like yourself, the result of which will be that you cannot be real or behave confidently without some sort of a mask to hide behind. One of my masks was my Fire Brigade uniform; another was the use of alcohol. If, as a child, I had been shown love and affection with positive strokes I would have demonstrated confidence and felt beautiful and worth loving; because I had not I developed, or maybe survived, with negative strokes and as beautiful, or not, as I may have looked on the outside, my lack of self-worth from within would tell me otherwise. Hence the phrase 'beauty is only skin deep', and some people being seen as 'beautiful inside and out'.

216

To live life in a happy and fulfilling way we have to value and feel worthy of who we are and in general we will have had to be shown that as a child. Issues with self-worth and self-esteem can be caused in the most simple and innocent of ways and, despite being largely unintentional, are at the centre of most of our relationship difficulties because it is how we regard ourselves and how we are regarded. You cannot see a lack of self-worth in yourself, it can't be held or touched and it will probably remain hidden until we try to understand why our lives are not what we would hope for. I took years to understand that and that I was picking my partners because of it. Not their fault, nobody's fault. The only fault is that we will probably never know unless we seek counselling, but even then my experiences have been that the core issues are not explained in a way that is understandable. My belief is that I have discovered the 'real me' by asking for help and being given the answers because I was meant to, but others will say I stumbled across them and that was a coincidence. You decide, because I already have.

At that time I still had a long way to go to get anywhere near to loving myself, let alone liking myself, enough to change my continuing sulking behaviour and my impossible search for love as an adult was not obvious then. What I have come to realise is just how strong within me the ability to extract attention was and how, in particular, sulking can be disguised in so many ingenious ways.

Not so many months after Jane had typed up my assignment, which included the laptop sulking incident, that to her credit she had never mentioned, another was about to surface, which again I seemed powerless to stop. It has always been a puzzle to me why, having thought I fully understood the mechanics of my sulking and linking it to a lack of self-worth, it continued. What I understand now is that these learnt behaviours are linked to our emotions and are stored in layers within our physical and emotional bodies. At times of stress, illness or generally being out of balance we are less likely to be able to keep them under control, but, if we understand such things, it can be seen as an opportunity to peel off a layer of inappropriate learnt behaviour and their associated emotions, or at least to reduce their impact. Rather like peeling a layer off of an onion. That analogy in itself highlights wonderfully the difference between the person-centred approach to counselling, when the intention is to keep peeling away the layers of learnt behaviours and emotions until the real self is reached, or CBT, which teaches us how to control them and keep them locked away.

Jane was helping a client with a human resource issue and he had come to our home on a Friday to prepare for an industrial tribunal. Although it was only supposed to take the day, something I had no problem with at all because I also enjoyed helping people whenever I could, they had not quite finished and there was little choice but to return the next day. He was extremely considerate to us both, expressing concern about taking up our time on a weekend; he even declined our sincere offer to stay with us rather than a local hotel.

As the second day went on and it appeared they were no nearer to finishing, and despite Jane saying it would only take a couple more hours, I began to get annoyed and frustrated. Even with my recent 'laptop' sulking issue, which should have still been fresh and uppermost in my mind, and my understanding of life scripts and how they store our lack of self-worth for situations when we do not feel loved, it gradually began to rise from somewhere deep inside of me and began to work to gain attention and play games at the same time. Of course, the somewhere deep inside of me was my subconscious mind and the arguments it was promoting were buzzing around in my head as I tried desperately to be an adult, but I couldn't and they all led to just one conclusion: 'I had been alone most of the week when Jane was in work and why should I be deprived of her attention at the weekend?' I had also felt this growing agitation the previous day and had just managed to control it, but by midday Saturday, I lost it and an unstoppable tidal wave of inappropriate learnt behaviour spilled out.

I sulked, not too obviously so that I would embarrass myself in front of the client, I wasn't that stupid! No, my solution was to remove myself from the house and to punish Jane for the lack of attention. I assured her with a treacherous smile that I was just going out for a few hours, but it began to develop into something much more extreme as I thought about where I would go. The answer was of course Weymouth, the seaside resort I had spent so many holidays at as a child, and it was only a two-hour drive away. How ironic! How ridiculous!

I was of course kidding myself that I was 'just going for something to do'. No, I was sulking for attention and 'game playing' at the same time. It worked, it always did, and when Jane had finished she tried to ring me, but I hadn't finished punishing her for 'ignoring me' and my game playing was far from satisfied, removing myself was not enough. I ignored her calls.

She was concerned when I eventually answered my phone, but I was calm and an expert in my execution of this type of adapted sulking and its partner, 'the games people play'. After all, I had had lots of practice since I was very young! When I eventually returned home in the early evening I felt very embarrassed at my actions, but wouldn't admit to any wrongdoing. But I knew. I always did! We always do! And so did Jane.

Because I was so personally involved with TA and how it so obviously explained so much about the shambles of my personal life, I chose to use it as the subject of my final assignment at the end of the first two years. That meant Jane would be typing and reading about my two latest and craziest actions that involved the laptop incident, and my popping out for a few hours that developed into a day trip to the seaside. I had no choice but to come clean about its contents and we did discuss it. To her credit she never made any judgements or observations then either, she just left me with my own very personal struggles.

32

Self-analysis

Having successfully completed the first two years of the four-year counselling course, I had high hopes of putting all I had learnt about myself into practice. Jane and I, despite knowing all my stuff, seemed to be getting on well and we travelled together across the continent.

There is absolutely no doubt that the counselling course had been pivotal in guiding my journey forward since asking God for help. It was to be a time of deep introspection and I was excited by my discoveries as I set about my life with a new vigour. As well as Transactional Analysis and the person-centred approach, both of which explained why I had buried what happy childhood times I did have and gave me hope for the future, we were introduced to the effect of birth order. Most of us can recognise the only child syndrome of not finding it easy to share, but I was not that, I was the middle child of three who struggled to find my own identity and seriously believed I was an adopted orphan. We are said to be resentful with a negative outlook, the most envious and the least bold. My older brother, the first born, fits the profile of being confident, conscientious and achievement orientated while my younger brother, third and last in the order was the 'baby of the family' and can be predicted, amongst other things, to expect others to take responsibility and can be a lonely outsider.

There was a gradual realisation that, because I hadn't felt loved as a child, I couldn't possibly know what true love felt like. I had innocently substituted the feelings of what I thought being 'in love' felt like, which was based on the needs that satisfied my longing to be recognised and thus loved. Accordingly, I would accept the love of partners who had their own needs that complemented my own well enough for the expectancy of a lifetime of togetherness, but in truth could only ever be far less as my false feelings could not be sustained. The process of learning that true love could not exist alone in a physical or emotional attraction, a sexual compatibility or as someone 'to save' – who was more than likely trying to save me at the same time, began to explain why I had experienced a trail of failed relationships and caused chaos in the process. I am unsure whether the periods out of relationships and staying single 'because it was easier' was life's way of trying to show me something, but if it was I didn't see it, as girlfriends continued to arrive. They were either carefully chosen or purely opportunist, both of which would minimise the possibility of rejection, as was my use of surreptitious glances and a smile to 'test the water' from across rooms before I would approach and make my move. They had to be good looking and look good to make me feel better about myself and able to draw compliments and admiring glances from friends and colleagues; I believe the modern expression is 'arm candy'. Some of them had wonderfully bubbly personalities and could light up a room, something I never considered myself as being capable of, but would benefit from as the ripples spread out from the centre of their personality. These realisations were breathing new life into old ways and I began to think differently, but I had also begun to gently question my relationship with Jane; I knew the signs well, but there was no rush as I made sure! The want and need to be real, and truer, and not just hitch a ride through life by playing safe was never far away, no matter what I had learnt of myself. I needed to find my own identity to inform my own journey of discovery instead of being drawn into that of others. It was no longer possible to mask my lacking with the uniform of the 'brave firefighter' that had always made me feel good about myself because I had retired. Jane was working long hours and with plenty of time to think and analyse, that's exactly what I did, especially about my childhood.

As we grow as a person into adulthood we unknowingly begin to move away from what we have learnt and identified with as a child, but if like me you are searching for love, we take the child with us in our adult body, where only adult behaviour is expected and tolerated and we have to adapt.

My childhood was shaped by parents who only knew how to love as they had been shown and shaped by their own limiting circumstance as children, something I don't believe they, and indeed the vast majority of us, would ever challenge. Their attitude was one of equipping their three boys to be tough enough to be able to take care of themselves in a world experienced through the agony and toughness of wars when family, friends and colleagues were lost. Neither of my two brothers, so far as I am aware, unless they wear their own masks and have greater levels of tolerance and acceptance than I, seem to have had the same issues as me, so I have come to accept that my mother and I had a different relationship. And it was entirely likely that the difference was the post-natal depression. One of its many symptoms is the possibility of becoming hostile and indifferent to your baby, something which, if it were true, I couldn't have recognised at an early age as anything but normal. What I do remember was the lack of any warmth or feelings of friendliness and generosity, and although it did not seem overtly hostile at the time it would explain my lack of self-worth when nothing else would seem to.

The lack of communication in sexual education and an unfortunate and traumatic introduction to it while enjoying my first real kiss when I thought I was dying, or at best bleeding heavily, was reinforced by my mother's angry, fierce and forceful confrontational warning to stop messing up the bed sheets by masturbating. Freud would have a field day with that, but you don't have to be clever to see how it inhibited my ability to have a good and loving sexual relationship for many years. And maybe that was just as well as it curtailed my sexual activity to far less than it might have been, and again, I can see how and why that was meant to be also.

No matter what the truth of that time, it has left me longing and pining, even now when I have tried to forget and forgive, for the closeness to a mother that I see in so many others that I will never know. And whilst I accept that I have chosen parents and circumstances it only serves to foster another battle within me as I remain true to the ways of a middle child by feeling resentful and envious, with a legacy of forever having to contend with a bent towards a negative outlook. Whether I am the least bold of my brothers is irrelevant now because I am as bold as life will allow me to be.

Once I started to understand some of the basics of human behaviour, the similarities between my mother and my wife were much easier to see. I had tried in all sorts of ways to please her, but it didn't make any difference. My wife was similar in some ways to her strong and strict father, as was I; he was a qualified plumber, me as a carpenter, but in other ways we were miles apart. I was extremely attracted to my wife and yet there was always an incongruence in our relationship; her learnt behaviour versus mine. I began to see, and believe, that we had 'picked' each other because we were comfortable with each other in a subconscious way and not in the way of our conscious day to day living as we both searched for our own identities through the eyes of our childhoods.

But ultimately it wasn't enough and I left my wife because I wanted to love and feel loved back. Now I know she loved me in the only way she knew how in the way of my mother, so that was never going to happen until I learnt to love myself and then of course I would be different!

33

Spirit Guides and Doorkeepers

Having successfully completed the first two years of the counselling course, by demonstrating competency in the use of counselling skills in a final videotaped practical assessment and passing the final written assessment, all with very positive feedback, I had fulfilled all that I needed to progress to the two-year diploma part of the course and, subject to a successful interview, would start the following year.

Our group had been forewarned that the previous year's diploma selection process had been postponed due to staff shortages and the reality of that was twice the normal number of candidates would be seeking the same number of places, but somehow I had never thought it would affect me.

The University of Bristol's solution was to implement, with immediate effect, a recent proposal for consideration from the British Associations of Counselling Professionals (BACP) that qualification for the diploma courses would require all candidates to have a university degree in another subject, which, subject to agreement, would be implemented over a five-year period. As I didn't have any GCE passes from school, let alone a degree, I was immediately discounted and the assurances given from two years previously would count for nothing. When I challenged that decision, it was eventually suggested I should apply anyway 'to see what happens'.

I had a pretty good idea what would happen, and after giving it a lot of thought I decided that even if I applied I would, in all probability and unsurprisingly, not be successful and I could do without the rejection. In truth it wasn't a difficult decision, even though I was disappointed not to be able to continue my education and achieve something I hadn't at school, because my gut feeling was telling me that I had achieved all I needed to and I decided to 'let it go, move on and trust life' by practising what I had begun to 'preach'.

Trusting and surrendering to life was something that I was beginning to see as very powerful, with my own anecdotal evidence supporting the idea that if something is meant to be it will be. My growing belief, that there is a reason for everything in life, encouraged me to feel that the feeling of 'swimming against the tide' was part of life's way of encouraging me to look at the whole picture and to let it go despite being more than able and willing to fight my corner. Knowing when to fight for something and when to let it go is not easy, and in this case the sense of injustice could easily have got in the way, but I wanted to hold my own power and not be dictated to by someone else's problems.

Part of my reasoning was in the belief that I had all that I needed from the course in the way of personal development and another, the desire, having just retired from thirty years of regular employment and working to the clock, was not to be shackled by working as a personal counsellor. Letting go is not always that easy to trust, but with the passage of time since that particular decision, and a similar one made two years earlier, when selling the house in a relationship separation as part of the settlement when I stood to lose what was for me a huge amount of money; both have been proved to be absolutely the correct decisions.

So many of us end up living an honest lie because we do not really know ourselves and thus cannot really be true to ourselves until we do. We make decisions based on the fear of the unknown and being alone; we ignore the quiet voice of reason that is trying to help us achieve our life purpose as intended because we want to feel safe by conforming and being part of something familiar. We often do not trust ourselves enough as being good enough – lacking in self-worth – and continually strive to prove in an often misguided way that we are. This is why it is so important to know who we are and why we are who we are. Because within that inner knowing, waiting to be nurtured and released by the calming influence of a peaceful self-awareness, there is a route to happiness and fulfilment.

The Arthur Findley College at Stansted on the edge of London is considered by many to be the HQ for the UK spiritual movement; I do not, I believe it to be within each of us as a potential should we need it, although I do accept it is a great place of teaching for onward development.

They had advertised an open day and, as I had never been before, Jane and I decided to go. It was during the time when I was devouring anything with a spiritual connotation. One of the many demonstrations was to be on something called 'trance healing', which I had not heard about before. It was explained that trance is an altered sense of awareness and uses a different type of energy, and we watched as the tutor selected a volunteer patient from the audience and then 'with help from his spirit guides' healed a very obvious 'turn' in the gentlemen's eye. The healer demonstrated how he could go in and out of the state of trance at different stages, which enabled him to explain what he, and his spirit guide(s), was doing and why. Although there was nothing visible to my eye to prove the tutor was in any sort of trance other than having his eyes closed at times, there was no doubting the end result and the delight of the volunteer. I also felt very excited by what I had witnessed.

Jane was a member of a closed meditation circle and I was invited to join. It would be my second closed circle, the first being Lisa's six years earlier, and the first to offer me my own experience of trance.

I learnt that there are many different levels to trance, with some trance mediums claiming to have a level of connection with their spirit guides where they have no idea what they are saying or doing because they are completely 'taken over', while others are fully aware, albeit not entirely in control. I became fascinated by trance.

Not long after, I was watching another amazing demonstration of 'deep trance mediumship' by Angie Cruger from Cornwall. This involved Angie connecting with the energies of a spirit communicator called Richard, who was Welsh and had tragically died in his twenties, as he talked through her in fluent Welsh, a language she assured us after that she could not speak. Following that I attended one of Angie's trance courses in Ebbw Vale, Wales, where each of us would be given the opportunity to 'sit in trance'. This involved sitting in front of the rest of the group of ten others and being as relaxed as possible to allow the spirit guides to step as close into your energy field (aura) as they could. Almost as soon as I started I could feel an extreme heat next to the right-hand side of my body and then my heartbeat started to increase. I must confess to being a little anxious to the changes that I could feel in my body, but I could hear Angie at all times guiding me through it and assuring me that I was ok. Angie was also encouraging me to speak, but I couldn't and with my heartbeat getting stronger and much more pronounced my concerns were increasing as she eventually guided me out of the trance state. I was so disappointed not to have spoken, but Angie was extremely pleased with my attempt.

Life remained extremely good, I was enjoying the freedom retirement had brought and I continued to devour everything spiritual. Since being told my spirit guide's name and tribe some two years earlier I had done some research on both and, although I have never been able to find any reference to confirm Running Bear's existence, I was able find some information on the Blackfeet tribe of Native American Indians who had a reservation and museum in a town called Browning, Montana, USA. Jane and I planned a three-week holiday to America, which would encompass a visit to Browning before going on into Canada and the Rockies, something I had always wanted to do long before my spiritual involvement. Whilst there I hoped to get some sort of feeling, but the Blackfeet tribe museum was closed and the Browning reservation generally made me feel very uncomfortable and we moved on within an hour of arriving.

The Blackfeet tribe of Native American Indians originally occupied territory that breached what is now the border between America and Canada and they are divided into three groups: the Northern Blackfeet or Siksika; the Kainah or Blood; and the Piegan. As a whole they are known as The Siksika and they occupied territory from the North Saskatchewan River in Canada to the Missouri River in Montana. We never had the time or the resources to explore any of that area and we passed through Canada far too quickly, but one day, when the area of Lake Louise is not covered in snow drifts bigger than I could ever imagine, I hope to return to both countries and explore properly.

While we were in America we met up with a British couple whose contact details we had been given from friends in the UK; they had been in America for some time. We had lunch together and I was surprised when Mick explained he was a deep trance medium and Sylvie, his wife, always worked by his side to provide energy and facilitate the recording of the events. Mick and Sylvia returned to live in the UK a year later and we met again after watching Mick's impressive deep trance demonstration, which was just one of many that were drawing large audiences. Jane and I decided to have private readings. They were advertised as 'Akashic record' readings, which are said to be a record of our soul's journey, past, present and future, and it was during this 'reading', nearly two years after originally being told that Running Bear was my spirit guide, that I would receive another confirmation of his name from Mick while in a state of deep trance with his spirit guide, albeit he was referred to as 'bear comes running' or 'bear', as he offered to be called and that he was my 'doorkeeper' as opposed to the 'spirit guide' I had assumed.

Native American Indians are well-known for loving and respecting a nature that they relied upon for survival and I do not see it as coincidence that the only time I ever felt comfortable as a child was when playing in the woods behind our house. Running Bear has been seen by many clairvoyant mediums and they all describe him similarly as huge with very broad shoulders.

Amongst a whole lot of information that was recorded onto a CD there were two pieces that stood out above all the rest; the first was that between incarnations my soul was a member of a 'soul group' called Cajjunie and the second that the purpose of my soul group was to *'oversee death and witness some of the worst atrocities that man had committed towards his fellow man'*. Soul groups are talked about a lot at spiritual gatherings, but again nothing can be proved. However, although the information that I was given about Cajjunie as 'one of the smallest of all the soul groups in the universe' with 'forty thousand members' does not particularly resonate with me, other than I often consider myself to be a loner; its purpose of overseeing death and injury definitely does and I find that interesting.

That one piece of information alone has helped me enormously by giving me a possible reason why, when being surrounded by death, I have rarely found it problematical and why I had felt so little emotion at the time of my mother and father's deaths. I used to think that was because of my perceived lack of love between us and that still may be the case, but in that instance, and ever since, I have felt so much better about myself and it felt like another piece of my life's jigsaw had been found to assist my growing understanding of who I was.

Of course I have often wondered if I was just making all this information fit, but whether I was or not, and it certainly doesn't feel like I was, it was definitely helping me to find myself and the love I had become so desperate for.

34

Psychic Surgery

My introduction to 'psychic surgery' as another modality came at a weekend healing event in Somerset. We had just arrived and began exploring the large site that included a huge marquee packed with therapists, clairvoyants, healers, psychic artists and many others offering their services or products. As we entered the marquee people were taking their seats around a large stage to watch a demonstration of psychic surgery by a young man called Gary Mannion. We watched the thirty-minute demonstration in amazement as he invited a lady, with a severe shoulder injury, on to the stage and cured her.

He started by explaining that he worked with a healer from the spirit world called Abraham and for the purpose of the demonstration he would be asking someone from the audience with an injured shoulder to volunteer to be demonstrated upon. At least twenty people from a two hundred strong audience volunteered their shoulder injury, but Gary was very specific about the type of injury that would be ideal for the growing audience to witness and, by a process of elimination about the type of injury and the debilitating effect it would be having, he whittled it down to a middle-aged lady. She was invited onto the stage and sat facing the audience; it was very clear that when asked by Gary to lift her left arm in the air she was in a lot of pain and could only manage to raise it level with her chest. She explained that she had been receiving treatment from the National Health Service for many years, until recently when she was told there was nothing further they could do for her and she would have to live with it; that meant being unable to perform basic tasks like towelling herself dry after a shower and pulling on a jumper.

Gary stood slightly to one side and behind her as he explained through the microphone, looped around his head and taped near his mouth, that he was going to use the tips of his 'pointy' fingers as a sort of implement around the shoulder area while talking to us the audience. He explained that he would very rarely, if at all, look at the shoulder while working, as his way of ensuring that he didn't allow his human curiosity to take over and interfere with his healing guide(s), Abraham and his helpers. They, he explained, would take over his body by merging their energies in a similar way to what I had witnessed at Stansted in the trance healing demo when the 'turn' in the eye had been cured, but only to a level required for the healing to be effective whilst not affecting his ability to control the functioning of his own body.

He stopped talking to us at certain times during the session to allow us to clearly hear the cracking noises picked up by his microphone and coming from within the lady's shoulder. She said she felt no pain, just very slight pinprick-like sensations and after about fifteen minutes he asked her to stand up and raise her left arm as high as she could. She cried with joy as she was able to raise her arm fully above her head with no pain or discomfort.

It was my first introduction to this sort of healing and it was a remarkable demonstration of what psychic surgery is capable of. From my point of view, being able to see the demonstration of a very real physical healing also makes the link between the human energy and a spiritual energy quite clear and leaves little to doubt about its authenticity, unlike my own very personal spiritual experience at Lisa's years earlier of people I knew to be humanly dead that were talking to me as I flew through the air in what I have come to see as astral planing/projection. What we all witnessed that day was hard to doubt or explain away, although there will be those without similar personal experiences to mine who will undoubtedly try to do so.

The queue to talk with Gary after the demonstration for very obvious reasons grew very quickly and we returned later to talk with him on his 'stand' where he was working with the six others he was teaching. He explained his vision of setting up healing centres all around the UK and his willingness to travel and teach to achieve this. We arranged to meet up with him in London some weeks later where we could watch another of his demonstrations and spend time with him as we were very interested in becoming a part of his plans.

Once again Gary asked for a volunteer to demonstrate on, but this time his options were limited by the lower attendance. I had two injuries that I could choose from; a damaged and swollen left knee, which I had had trouble bending for many years following football injuries that had been compounded by continuous kneeling on building sites as a carpenter, or bone degradation in both my hips that had been recently diagnosed by x-ray as needing imminent replacement surgery and one of which was causing a worsening groin pain. I volunteered my knee injury, which was causing me problems by just sitting in the audience, and I was happy to be selected. I explained my left knee, and specifically the cartilage, had been operated on following a football injury many years previously and I had damaged it further when I had stumbled and fallen backwards from the top of a stepladder, out of a first-floor sliding sash window opening of the Victorian house that I had removed for renovation.

I was so lucky not to have suffered a serious injury that day as my fall was broken and then deflected by a large open sunshade umbrella on the patio below, which I rolled off and was turned upright to land on a plastic chair, that duly collapsed under me and from which I had ended up sitting uncomfortably on the patio with my already inflexible knee flexed back beneath me. My dog, Spot, came bounding down the garden, thinking I was playing and licked my face as I tried to push the still working electric heat lamp off my arm where it was burning me. My elderly overweight neighbour who had witnessed my fall defied his size by jumping a stone wall that would have won him a gold medal at the Olympic high jump and tried to pull me to my feet, but my Fire Brigade training had taught me to get up under my own steam when I was ready.

Gary's treatment on my knee, which I could only detect by the heat coming from his hands, was performed and commentated on in much the same way as in Somerset many weeks earlier, but unlike then, when the lady demonstrated the difference, mine was only obvious to me as I sat back down and bent my knee with a 75% improvement and no stiffness or discomfort, even when I stood up later. That improvement stands good to this day.

The bone degradation in my hips had only come to light because six months previously I had been invited as an over-fifty to attend a government pilot scheme to investigate hips.

Later that weekend, and pushing my luck, I was able to ask Gary for psychic surgery on my hips, which he did and also informed me he had 'instructed my brain to grow replacement bone in my hips'. My first reaction was to doubt that as being possible and with the pain not causing me too much trouble I forgot all about it. Two months later it suddenly dawned on me that the pains had disappeared and I had developed a craving for milk, which I had started to drink by the glass full, something I had not done since childhood and had not connected with his treatment. I can only assume that my body needed the extra calcium to be found in milk because the worn bones were growing. At the time of writing, some nine years later, one hip has been replaced in 2014 and the other is still not giving me any problems despite being very active as a walker.

Meeting Gary and watching his demonstrations had stirred my memory about a book that I had been given almost a year before. The book was called *The Surgeon of the Rusty Knife* by Brian Fuller and was the life story of a very famous Brazilian psychic surgeon called Arigo. It is a fascinating story, full of many witnessed accounts of miraculous healings. Arigo had no medical knowledge or knowhow, and yet, working with the spirit world, they facilitated remarkable improvements and cures from the terminally ill to problems with eyes. As Arigo's fame spread across the world he would become inundated with people seeking help, until he was mysteriously killed in an accident!

Despite my healthy scepticism I have no doubts about the authenticity of the healings I have witnessed and been subject too. That the spirit world are trying to show each of us through various types of contacts and unexplainable events that there is something in our world and universe that is not completely within our ability to fully grasp is also not in doubt in my mind. If we could just believe and trust or at least keep an open mind, then I believe our world would be a better place to live in, and not just because of the healing potential, but because of the love it generates.

There is an entrenched suspicion from a substantial percentage of human beings which seems to be perpetuated in the media generally and by many religious organisations, that these 'alternative therapies or modalities' are, at best, used by charlatans to gain power, fortune and fame and at its worst are evil and to be avoided at all cost.

And yet it is both ironic and wonderful that when some of these total sceptics or their loved ones become terminally ill or sick, and medical science can do no more for them, they search out many of these alternative therapies out of desperation and a last hope. I just wish that it was more acceptable in our societies and more people, who for whatever reason are sceptical and sometimes scared of it, could seek out its benefits; especially the healing available from Reiki and spiritual healers who, in healing emotions, can promote a physical well-being as well. I would never suggest that people do not go to their doctors when they are injured or unwell, but healing as a complementary therapy to mainstream medicine should not be ignored.

Of course, psychic surgery and healing is not always successful on a human level to everyone who uses it, and the sceptics will jump on that and say that if it is coming from the spirit world or other non-worldly source of power then surely it should always be successful. There are probably many reasons why that is not the case, which is outside of my level of understanding, although I do see karma, life purpose and continued abuse of the body by lifestyle choices as possibilities.

For another wonderful example of what healing can achieve, but this time self-healing with the balancing and harmonisation of the mind, body and soul, read *The Journey* by Brandon Bays; it is an amazing and inspirational story.

35

Psychic Art and the Death of Spotdog

At that same healing weekend event in Somerset, Jane and I were 'introduced' to the work of a psychic artist called Patrick Gamble, who was also at work in the huge marquee. We watched in fascination as he painted a beautiful work of art for a client sat at his side seeking confirmation or introduction of spirit guides, or family members passed if they should not be the same, seemingly lost in his own world and oblivious to all the many whom surrounded him. I was almost desperate for a portrait of Running Bear, but with the whole day, and those to follow, fully booked out we wandered off with his business card to explore so many other interesting aspects of the so-called spiritual world and called days later to arrange appointments for us both in his art studio the following week.

I went in first and Patrick explained that he could, with the help of his spirit guides, only paint who was 'with me' at the time of the sitting and it may not be who I was hoping for. I wasn't hoping for anything, I was praying for a portrait of Running Bear, but that's not what I got. Yes, I was disappointed, but not completely surprised once I had time to consider the outcome from the perspective of my belief that the spirit world will not automatically fulfil needs, because they can see the bigger picture of the future. To supply on demand would only have served to encourage my expectations and place too much importance and dependency on those who support us from the afterlife, rather than living my life in the moment and trusting what was produced as exactly what I needed at the time and meant to be for what can be a multitude of reasons. And mine, on that particular day was, I believe, not to get too hooked into symbols and ritual and to lead my life as a human without expectations other than those that will fulfil the adage that 'all good things come to those who wait'.

The portrait was beautiful, but I did not recognise the man who Patrick suggested was a family member from a previous generation. Without a name I call him Joe Bloggs and many clairvoyants had already described 'seeing' him around me, and as one of my spirit guides I honour him for supporting me on my journey as a work in progress.

Jane on the other hand, having no expectations at all, was far from disappointed with her magnificent portrait of a beautiful Native American Indian squaw and in that one act my lessons of 'being careful what you wish for' were reinforced through my disappointments and envy. Jane, knowing how disappointed I was, remained dignified and considerate of my feelings that day!

I did eventually get my portrait of Running Bear many years later from another psychic artist called Margaret who had become a friend. Margaret was a quiet, unassuming lady who kept her work mostly to herself; she had no natural artistic ability, but had been woken from resting one afternoon at her home and encouraged to go to her art room and paint a picture for me. Having been 'taken over' by her own spirit guide she produced the most amazing and original portrait with accompanying words of encouragement and she arrived unexpectedly at Belmont Road Spiritual Centre weeks later, fearful of my reaction to the quality and accuracy, due to her lack of confidence, to present it to me. She needn't have worried on either count, with those able to see Running Bear clairvoyantly, vouching for its accuracy. I have since had it framed and added the words reproduced below to the border.

'When I was drawing this portrait I saw the Fool Tarot card. To my understanding this card means being poised on the edge of change; leaving the safety zone takes courage; need to jump in at the deep end and be open to new experiences and opportunities.

This guide has great strength and commands attention and is a leader in his tribe. He will help to strengthen your spiritual beliefs and deepen your faith. Walk into the sunshine out of the shadows. Look at Mother Earth, how she continuously sheds and renews herself; be adaptable to change; embrace it. Go forward without fear, be stubborn. Stand your ground and be positive. Embrace the lessons and knowledge coming to you and learn from the mistakes you make as you walk your path.'

February 2009.

Jane and I had many good times together, including travelling to see family in Australia and New Zealand, but no matter how much I tried, once again I was unable to control and hold back the growing feeling that our relationship wasn't enough for me. For a few months my indecisions were pretty much as they had always been at these times, but after much toing and froing, from making it work to being determined to do the right thing, I did.

What tipped the balance was the loss of my faithful dog Spot who had a stroke and I had to make one of the most agonising and terrible decisions of my life to end his. It was October 21st 2007 and he was thirteen. His eyesight had been steadily worsening for about six months, but the vet could find no obvious reason why, although he did suggest a tumour on the brain as a possibility. As he was still a very active and lively Welsh Border Collie I decided to do nothing but monitor him rather than put him through an exploratory operation without any guarantees of success. His very obviously worsening eyesight was becoming more of a problem as he was unable to see me if he ventured too far. He could still hear me calling him back and it was often amusing, watching him running in my general direction in the wide open spaces and veering off in slightly the wrong direction, but he loved being out and that never changed, until one sunny Sunday afternoon when Jane and I arrived back home and his normal enthusiastic welcome and rush into the garden was somewhat muted. He uncharacteristically struggled out of the door and slumped down in the middle of the lawn where there was no shade from the bright sunshine and had hardly moved minutes later when I checked on him. His eyes were rolling and he was dribbling and when I called him to follow me back into the house he stayed motionless and looked at me in a forlorn way.

I carried him inside the house and called the emergency vet, who advised me to bring him in. I carried him to the car and awkwardly laid him on the back seat in preference to the boot of the estate car where he would normally jump into. I feared the worse as I talked to him and carried him for the last time and laid him on the treatment table.

The vet's diagnosis was a stroke, possibly caused by a brain tumour, but I was so upset I was having a job to assimilate all the options and possibilities as she asked me to decide what to do. I asked many questions and repeated them every time she came back into the room, having given me some time alone with him 'to decide'. I wanted her to change her mind and tell me that after treatment he would be better in the morning, but she was very patient as she reframed the same reply each of the four times she returned: 'There were no guarantees of a recovery or a good quality of life, even if he did survive the night.' I agonised over the decision I already knew had to be made. I guess I wanted her, the vet, the professional to make the decision, but quite rightly she wouldn't and was very patient each time I tried to encourage one out of her; what she didn't say was actually the clearest indication of what she wanted too, but her professionalism forbade that too. The decision had to be mine, but how could I choose to lose my faithful companion, my best and most unconditional friend who had become more than a dog because he had been by my side through every one of my experiences in the last thirteen years; listening to me with no judgements and by default becoming party to my unsettling decisions. He had even experienced my drunken prayer to a God that I now wished would save him, and I did ask, but I knew he wouldn't because his time was up and I believe he knew why. Finally, with nowhere else to go with my own arguments and exhausted, I knelt down on the floor and with my face next to his and stroking him... no, not stroking him... loving him, I looked into his beaten eyes through the moistness of my own and whispered, *"Ok Spotdog, we have been through so much together, but if it's time for you to go please give me a sign."*

Unlike me he didn't hesitate, but struggled to lift his head just high enough to look me in my eyes and lick me once on my face. I knew that was it.

The vet returned and I reluctantly said I didn't want him to suffer anymore. I held his head in my hands and stayed as close to him as I could. The lethal injection was already prepared, which only gave me slight comfort that I had made the right decision. Almost immediately, and much quicker than I had thought it would, Spot's head became heavy. I was shocked at the speed, but would later take some comfort from it as the vet and her assistant confirmed what I already knew, that he had gone.

Unable to control my emotions I ran out of the surgery and screamed louder and cried uncontrollably like I had never done before, until I could cry no more. It was a solitary and isolated place in the country, rather apt really, as for the first time in my life I couldn't have cared less who heard me or what they thought as my outpouring of grief continued.

Spot had returned the 'tough love' almost immediately by showing me that I could feel the emotions of the loss of someone close to me; that I could love my dog but not a human was a fact that was not lost on me, but that was for later as the grief consumed me.

This was only to be the second time in my life that a death had affected me, and in writing this now, a decade later, I have cried again and again at the loss of my unconditional best friend. Proof, if ever I needed it, of how we store the energies of emotion within us. Jane's support during all this time was invaluable as she waited in the car to drive me home, but it didn't stop me reliving the guilt I had felt since moving in with Jane and her cat that terrorised Spot everyday by not allowing him into the lounge.

Women are generally much better than men at releasing emotions because we are usually taught that big boys don't cry, which is most definitely not a good thing to do.

The British seem to have a very reserved attitude to grief which is not prevalent in many other cultures. Towards the end of my career I had attended a serious house fire when a mother and her two children had tragically died. It had affected each and every one of us who attended that day badly. I remained at the incident for many hours with a colleague, investigating the cause of the fire and gathering information for the report that would be needed for the coroner's court. The family were Asian and as the extended family arrived they gathered together to support each other in a loud emotional outpouring of grief through tears and wailing, which could be clearly heard and occasionally witnessed from an adjacent property. It continued for the whole time we were there – at least two hours – and I suspect well after. I admired a culture which is informed and openly confident enough to display their grief that must have had huge healing benefits in helping to lessen the terrible effects of grief in the days, months and years to come, because clearly it could not help to assuage the immediate grief of losing three family members.

The consequences of this fierce fire were both devastating and upsetting and I cannot even begin to imagine what it must feel like to lose your own child, let alone two and a wife at the same time.

Life without Spot was not the same. I found it awkward to walk on my own in the countryside and woodland that I so enjoyed and where inspiration would often come to me, and I was finding it harder and harder to fill my time in a satisfying or rewarding way.

Fear in our society has created a suspicious nature when females encounter lone males in isolated places and who can blame them? So to avoid the awkwardness and questioning looks I confined my walking to built-up or crowded areas or would drive an hour to the nearest beach, where questioning looks are fewer due to the open and exposed nature of the beach. My only desire was to get back into the purity of nature that I so missed.

I was gradually becoming more depressed and I could feel myself shutting down. It is a feeling I had had many times before in my life and knew from experience that I could do nothing about it unless I changed my life.

By then I had started to use my Reiki training as a healer by volunteering once a week at a centre in Bristol for families with children who had life-limiting illnesses. It was called Hop Skip and Jump and carers and the children could go whenever they wanted. The centre offered all types of support and the opportunity to meet others in the same position and, despite the long distance I had to travel, I derived an immense amount of satisfaction from doing it.

It was two months since Spot had died and nearly two-and-a-half years since I had completed my Reiki Two healing course with Nadia. I asked her again if I she would train me as a Reiki master, but her policy of teaching her Reiki master pupils one at a time over a full year hadn't changed, which meant I would still have to wait the three years she had previously informed me of. Although my belief and trust in her 'apprenticeship' method of teaching complemented my own beliefs, born out of my experience of being promoted far too quickly in the Fire Brigade and the struggles that ensued, I was not prepared to wait that long.

The only other Reiki master that I knew was 'Reiki Jane' who I had not seen for quite some time. As it happened, she had a course planned for about a month later, just before Christmas 2007; I would be the third pupil, which according to her was the perfect number to teach. When I arrived I was surprised that I was in fact the only pupil as the other two had dropped out at the last minute. Jane said she had considered cancelling because teaching one person was far from ideal as it hindered the healing practice sessions that were part of the course. Two days later I was qualified as a Reiki master. Two months later I left Jane. Seven months later I was informed by a mutual friend that Reiki Jane had already been separated from her husband months before she trained me, but hadn't told me.

36

The Camino Way

Jane and I had been together for nearly three years and had many really good times. After the decision to leave, many of my friends found it easy to blame the loss of Spot as the reason, but I know it was not.

Without Spot I had more choices of property and I moved into a first-floor flat back in the area where I had last rented the small house; for the first time in my life I didn't have a garden. As usual this was a difficult time for me with lots of self-analysis. I knew it was the right decision, but that had never stopped the doubts rising before and this was no exception. It was an inevitability that the happy memories of my time with Jane would come flooding back and they did as I questioned my decision without the support of my dog.

Hindsight is a wonderful thing... How many times have I said that! Was I at the stage then of understanding that everything in life is meant to be, or is that something that is born out of finding yourself and in particular loving who you find? I sat for hour after hour, reliving the happy times over and over, I had no choice... there weren't any bad or unhappy times except those nagging doubts that it wasn't enough. Would any relationship ever be enough for me? God knows, I hoped!

I reclaimed my old furniture and other possessions from the crammed storage unit, where they had waited patiently for three years, and built another new home out of old memories and comfort zones. My reluctance to be rid of them symbolic of the lack of trust I had in myself and relationships.

It was easy to see what had happened because it had happened before; there was an attraction between us. Jane was attractive, and fulfilled my definition of good looking and looking good. She was intelligent and spiritually aware, driven and dynamic. I was drawn to her but hesitant; she gave me confidence because she was, and I had confidence I wouldn't be rejected because she made that clear. I felt loved and in love with the feeling of being in love; I didn't know anything different. Then I did – the counselling course had ensured that within our time together. Could I change, should I change, did I know how to change? Would I be the same person if I did? The pattern of our life was set, held together by our mutual love of spirituality. We travelled, life was exciting and fun, but it was too late, I knew I could not survive the doubts created so many years before as a child searching for approval. Spot dies. Everything changes and exposes my weakness and the will to fight myself anymore. Jane works long hours because she enjoys it, I am retired and have too much time to think so I leave; determined and hoping to be strong enough to remain that way but my record does not auger well for that.

I filled my days by walking to the library to use the Internet, not willing to invest in the future by having it installed. I returned to the bookshop and read, hoping I guess to find answers again. I wrote poetry and affirmations trying to lift myself. I doubled my one day a week healing at the centre, which helped to fill the void I had created and made me feel a little more worthwhile. I made the decision to walk the Camino Way.

The Camino Way was a pilgrimage that I had read about in the book *The Camino* by Shirley McLaine many years earlier. Although at that time I was fascinated by the story and hoped one day to be able to do my own, I had no idea just how important it would eventually become. Shirley McLaine's account of her walk had included many 'amazing' spiritual experiences and her own struggles to 'find herself' on this famous and popular pilgrimage, although not so famous that I had ever heard of it, so maybe it finds us, when the time is ready.

I searched the Internet, which revealed an organisation called the Confraternity of St James, based in London, who are dedicated to promoting and supporting those who are contemplating the pilgrimage.

I learnt that *camino* – which is Spanish for *'the way'* – is known by its official title of 'The Way of St James', although some call it the Santiago Way. It is said to be a major Christian pilgrimage of which there are many routes to choose from; each route has its own starting point, but they all converge and finish at the Cathedral of Santiago de Compostela, Galicia, Northern Spain. A few of these 'many routes' are considered to be the main ones.

It seemed like a challenge. The timing was perfect and I formulated a plan. I bought all the essential equipment that was considered by the confraternity to be the maximum that could sensibly be carried in a backpack for the 500mile (800km) walk from my chosen starting point of Saint-Jean-Pied-de-Port in France. I loaded all the equipment and other essentials into my first ever backpack, and as advised I emptied it and discarded the borderline stuff, which met the criteria of 'nice to have but not essential'. How good a decision that turned out to be only became obvious on my first day's walking from close to the French border across the Pyrenees and into Roncesvalles, Northern Spain!

I left the UK in late July 2008 but not before one last complication that I could and should have avoided.

It was a week before my flight out of the UK to France when I was approached at the Hop Skip and Jump centre by a lady who I had only met once before at the retirement function of an ex-colleague months earlier. Unbeknown to me she was a good friend of Reiki Jane and after the obligatory small talk she asked me if I knew that Jane had separated from her husband, which I didn't, and offered to arrange a meeting between us, which I declined, explaining my plans for the Camino for the following two months. It had been just over three years since I first met Jane while out with my friend Sally, who she also knew, at a weekend mind, body and spirit event and seven months since I last saw her when she had qualified me to be a Reiki master and sensibly failed to mention that she was separated.

Despite my reluctance and preference to wait, Jay managed to engineer that Jane and I talked before I left, although in truth I didn't take much persuading. After a short telephone conversation we agreed to spend a day walking on Chesil Beach, Dorset, with her dog Natch, on the basis that it would be 'good training for the walk'. Natch didn't actually make it as he had a cut pad on his paw. I picked Jane up on a gloriously sunny day and, unusually for me, I didn't stop talking about spiritual stuff for most of the journey to the car park. Jane said very little; she wasn't given the chance as I talked more than I can ever remember talking to anyone in my life before.

As I was not familiar with the area, Jane suggested we walk an apparently well-known loop across the local hills from the Swannery car park – with stunning views across the English Channel – and return along the shoreline of the gently sloping shingle beach. Halfway along the miles of almost deserted beach we stopped for a rest to cool our feet in the inviting crystal clear waters. Without any shade from the smiling mid-day sun in the cloudless sky I decided to cool off with a swim in my underwear, which would 'dry quickly enough in the sun'; this was very bold for me and also very unlike me. Jane looked at me to see if I was serious, but once I was swimming, couldn't resist the opportunity and we swam together with her modesty preserved by her small black strappy cotton top and underwear. The swim was both refreshing and titillating as we awkwardly manoeuvred around each other trying to avoid the personal contact that I wished for, until, what could have been accidental, we touched and I bravely gave her a hug, trying to hide my normal diffident bashfulness and pretending to be confident.

Lying on the beach drying off we had our first kiss and we were completely alone in every sense of the word. Afterwards Jane said she felt guilty about kissing me because her spirit guide had told her 'quite firmly' not too. But she didn't resist and neither did I. That first kiss, which I had waited a long time for, felt very special, as most first kisses do. We finished the walk and had a meal at the pub close to the car park where I was amused at Jane's concerns and failed attempts in the toilets at hiding her bare face, having washed away her makeup in our unplanned swim, and having brought nothing to replace it; other than her beautiful smile.

That day should have left me on a high as we said our goodbyes and I prepared to fly out the day after the next, but I wasn't, I was shocked as Jane explained to me that she would be having dinner the following Saturday with someone that she had recently been in a relationship with and wasn't sure if it was completely finished. Had I thought about it I would have questioned why she had spent a very romantic day with me when she had unfinished romantic business with another, but more than that, had a day that had been so amazing for me meant so little to her? But I didn't, and maybe that's because I hadn't invested too much of myself into it and hadn't promised her my world of undying love. So far as I was concerned Jane wasn't free and was a good test for my 'new found values' of 'not being with anyone unless they – and I – were free'.

The flight from Bristol to Biarritz and the onward train journey to Saint-Jean-Pied-de-Port turned out to be by far the easiest part of the pilgrimage. I followed the dozen or so people on the same train carrying backpacks to what turned out to be a registration centre in an office staffed by volunteers.

One of the items I had received from the Confraternity of Saint James in London as part of the package was a Camino 'passport', which would be needed as qualification to sleep in the hostels (called aubergés) that I intended to use for my first night in France and the remainder across Northern Spain. No passport, no sleep was the rule in both the local authority-run auberges and the many privately owned ones interspersed along the way. I tried to avoid the more comfortable, and thus the more expensive, of the private ones because somehow it felt alien to the ethos of the pilgrimage.

The passport would be stamped by every accommodation used with its own unique identifying stamp and a minimum amount of them would be required as proof of completion of the walk to qualify for a certificate issued in Santiago; they are also used to ensure that you do not stay in the same locality or hostel for more than one night, unless you have a medical certificate showing you are unable to walk for medical reasons. That rule is in place because of the huge pressure from the numbers of pilgrims, especially in the school holiday period from August to September, which can exceed the bed spaces available; towards the end of my five-week pilgrimage the number of pilgrims began to decrease rapidly from being near to its capacity at the beginning.

Many pilgrims, or peregrinos as they are called in Spain, complete the Camino in yearly stages – not necessarily consecutive – of one or two weeks at a time to coincide with holidays away from work and will still receive their certificate when they eventually reach Santiago.

My Camino passport was a much larger one than the pocket-sized version available had I registered in Saint-Jean-Pied-de-Port, and judging by its quizzical examination on many other occasions, was clearly not the choice of the majority. It was nevertheless stamped by a volunteer and I was given up-to-date changes of circumstances from those printed in my book, and shown to the room of my local authority hostel, one of many in the same street of Saint-Jean-Pied-de-Port, for my first night's sleep.

There were a total of six dormitories in this particular hostel and I was the first to choose from the eight bunk beds in my dormitory. I chose a bottom bunk for ease of access and Sven from Plymouth, who I recognised from the train, joined me in the same dormitory. Pleased to have the comfort of a fellow Brit we agreed to meet up and eat together at a local restaurant later. As I had planned an early 6.30am start I went to bed early at 9pm and was surprised not to be the first. That first night and the following morning were to set the pattern for the remainder of the walk as I settled into a routine of early to bed and early to rise.

I was not the first to leave the full dormitory in the morning and, like those that I had watched through the dimmed light of their torches, I tiptoed quietly around before leaving in the semi darkness. Not showering, or having breakfast, would be a routine abandoned for the first time since I had married as I left Sven sleeping to walk nervously into the unknown, alone with my thoughts. Having investigated the way the night before, I walked towards the beautiful sunrise and, within 30 minutes of leaving, it was high and hot enough to have soaked my special shirt designed to wick away the sweat generated on the gently rising and narrowing lanes lined with picture postcard homes. The higher I reached, the steeper and narrower the lanes became as the houses disappeared to be replaced by fenced fields of lush pasture land full of cows, some with the obligatory bells around their necks to help their owners keep track of their location. Everywhere I looked, the views across the Pyrenees were stunning.

After about two hours of walking I decided to stop at a surprising, but conveniently placed café/bar where I ate while resting for less than was sensible, being keen to reach my day's destination. I left just as Sven strode purposely past and we walked together for a short while, but I was too slow for someone who had already booked his return flight home and had schedules to meet. I had no such restraints, other than my concern that I would be in time to secure a bed at my chosen aubergé, which was actually 'Hobson's choice' because it was the first and only one available at a sensible distance. I paced myself to what I thought was sensible as, older than most but younger than others, allowing a steady flow of my fellow peregrinos to pass and disappear around the many twists and turns of the mountain road ahead; only to re-appear as rush-hour like commuters ahead as an indication there was still a long and winding way to go.

Soon enough I came across Sven sitting on a grass verge with shoes and socks removed and an open first aid pack tending to his blistered and angry looking feet. I waited with him as a friend glad of the rest would, but soon after resuming Sven would pull ahead again. This tortoise and hare routine was to happen three more times as his feet became increasingly more blistered and worryingly for Sven; 'uncomfortable' on this, our first day of walking.

The summit seemed just ahead for hour after hour, but the continually dashed anticipation of hope of reaching the top were somewhat eased by the increasingly stunning views of the mountain range ahead and the sweeping valleys below. On the one hand I was disappointed not to start heading down into Spain as I was so tired from the energy-sapping heat and humidity (it reminded me of the breathing apparatus training we regularly did in the heat and humidity chambers of the fire training buildings where we were pushed to the limit to understand how heat and humidity brings not just exhaustion, but confusion of the mind), whilst on the other hand the views took my breath away and replenished me in a way that made it completely worthwhile.

The summit over the top of the Pyrenees, where the border with Spain was identified by a small sign, was reached when I was least expecting it as I rounded a bend to be faced with a downhill choice, clearly explained by a polite notice. Easiest was the long and winding lane that snaked away into the distance that the majority seemed to be taking, but quicker and harder on the knees was the very steep, unmade woodland path etched out over eons of time by the personal choices of peregrinos able to manage it after a gruelling day competing with the physically draining conditions. The strain on my knees was excruciating and I almost immediately regretted taking the short cut, but after seven and a half hours of walking I joined the long queue on the shaded parts of the lawn hoping for a bed at the converted convent in Roncesvalles.

Many of the earlier arrivals had been given numbered cards to indicate their places in the queue and had gone to find refreshments, but the staff had left before I arrived and I would have to wait to hopefully secure my bed. When the staff eventually returned at 4.30pm the queue had grown substantially and I was glad to have started early and taken the short cut.

This was to be the first of many occasions where I would be sharing a large undivided sleeping space. The dormitory could accommodate 60 people in a long single room with bunk beds down each side. As one of the earlier arrivals, my luck was to be allocated a numbered top bunk at the farthest end from the main entrance and close to the fire exit door. I struggled to climb up to my bunk as there were no ladders, but once there I relaxed and watched the steady allocation of beds, on the opposite side to mine, filling back towards the administration point.

Well after the last bunk was allocated the volunteer staff made room for about thirty additional pilgrims by allowing them to sleep on the floors wherever they could find a space, including the basement cooking and toilet area, nobody was turned away while the doors were still unlocked!

Sven and I found somewhere to eat and then relaxed on our bunks on either side of the room, but for me that soon turned to concern and horror as I watched all the staff leave at 10.30pm, stating they would be back at 6.30am, and heard them lock the main entrance doors. The fire exit door right next to me remained as locked as I had found it on first arrival and with no windows we were locked in as a disaster waiting to happen.

I was worried, why would I not be, this had been my bread and butter for thirty years. I spent a long time assessing how long it would take to force open either of the two doors should there be a fire, but eventually dropped off to sleep with the day's exhaustion triumphing over my thoughts of staying awake just in case. I woke in the morning, before the staff returned, relieved to be still alive and that the silent killer, carbon monoxide had not paid us a visit.

Why would you lock about 90 people inside a fire risk? I presumed it could only be to allow the volunteers to sleep in their own beds, but whatever it was it was crazy and, if not in Spain, illegal in the UK, where not only would the two exit doors for the numbers within the dormitory, let alone the basement, be deemed inadequate, but to then lock them, especially with so many of the pilgrims ignoring the no smoking rule while relaxing on their beds, was negligent at its kindest and stupid at its worst. And to further compound that, there was no fire separation between the massive risk of fire from the basement kitchen and the ground floor, oh... and no fire detection or alarm system either! Not that any of it would have made much difference in the event of a fire or gas leak etc., because no one was getting out of there!

I thanked God that I was one of the many up and waiting by the door and ready to leave before the return of the staff. I again left without showering or eating, but for the very different reasons of being glad to get out of there and head to what would be a three-hour walk to the first available café.

Leaving in the dark and basically on my own as the others scampered off into the darkness was testing, but as with the previous day, and those still to come, I really enjoyed the solitude while never being completely alone for too long.

The downside to leaving early was that it was harder to locate 'The Way' markers that are available along the route all the way to Santiago. They were mostly big yellow directional arrows painted on walls, or anything else that could be utilised, at changes of directions or as confirmations of the right way. In some locations, mainly towns or large communities, the arrows are incorporated into designer type heritage plaques screwed to walls or monuments, but conversely they were sometimes found painted on moveable objects such as refuse bins or marked out by stones or sticks in forests and woodlands forming crude, but essential, arrow shapes on isolated footpaths. By the time I finished the pilgrimage I had learnt to expect many more obscure ways to mark 'The Way', but because I was lost on just two occasions, before finding my way again, I had obviously found the ones I needed to find; a bit like life really.

As early as the third evening I was to have a huge lesson in the belief that I was living my life in a truly spiritual way. It would show the reality that I still had so much to learn, or maybe unlearn would be a better way of looking at it.

Unless you were super fit, hurrying or both, the numbers of hostels available during the first week were limited and, although Sven and I would both get beds in the same auberg\u00e9 for the first three nights, many would not.

I arrived at the hostel and sat next to Sven who was sat on his own amongst a neat line of backpacks with his back against the wall outside the locked entrance door. I suppose it should have been fairly obvious that the backpacks were indicating the places in the queue of the earlier arrivals that had gone off to explore, but even the slightly threatening glares I received as they started to return didn't alert me; that was done by another pilgrim later who made it quite clear. I had no idea that it was an 'accepted practice' and I didn't make the same mistake again. Why Sven hadn't told me I do not know, but my honest ignorance had at least enabled me to get one of the very few beds in a small dormitory at the small auberg\u00e9.

The earliest of the later arriving pilgrims would be offered a mattress for the floor and when they ran out could find any available space. After 'claiming' my bed by unrolling my sleeping bag and placing my backpack onto it, I would complete my end of day walking routine by showering, washing clothes and hanging them out to dry. I would then try to sleep for as long as possible, which wasn't easy with all the noise of fellow pilgrims going through their own routines and discussing their day's walking, before exploring the area.

On my way out of the hostel I was approached by an English lady who I hadn't met before. She explained she was part of a group of ten English-speaking pilgrims who had arrived too late to get a bed or a space on a floor. In line with the policy of most of the local authority-run auberges, the staff would 'move heaven and earth' to accommodate everyone, and as such they had all been offered the use of the outdoor, but covered, open-sided 'racquets court' in the village. This, she explained, wouldn't be available until 9.30pm when the local people had finished using it and *would I possibly have a bedroll, that two members of her group didn't have, to make sleeping on the concrete floor more comfortable*. I lied and said 'no' with my apologetic and genuine smile!

As recommended by the Confraternity of Saint James I had purchased a bedroll, a very expensive best I could buy bedroll from a camping shop in the UK. The assistant had convinced me to buy the best with the advice that if I didn't use it, I could return it for a full refund if it was still in its plastic wrapper, which it was. I met Sven while out looking for somewhere to eat. He had been told about a local bar that offered two sittings and offered a 'peregrinos (pilgrim) supper' – many of the bars and cafés in the towns and villages on the Camino would offer this service and I went on to use them many times and they were always good quality and value – the bar wasn't hard to find in the small village and we were able to book in for the second sitting. While we were eating, two peregrinos came in and started to talk to people at the opposite end of the very long and fully-occupied table that sat about forty. One of them asked those within earshot if anyone had a spare bedroll, I heard, but kept my head down; there were no offers.

Just when I thought I had 'got away' with it a Canadian lady who I had met and walked a short way with earlier that day looked my way and shouted, *"Pete, you have a bedroll don't you?"*

Carrying the bedroll strapped to the outside of my back pack for all to see, I could hardly deny it again, so I cheerfully said 'yes' and felt exceedingly embarrassed as I listened to the story of the uncomfortable racquets hall I already knew whilst pretending I did not!

We agreed to make the arrangements after the meal and even then, while alone with the two people seeking the bedrolls, I tried to discourage them by explaining that I would be leaving early in the morning at 6.30am and would have to have it back by then. The arrangements were made and Sven also offered the use of his.

That night, feeling guilty and disappointed with myself, I wrote six pages in the daily journal I was keeping, exploring and agonising over why, when I professed to be 'so spiritual now', I had lied and denied someone an aid to comfort on the pretext of hoping to get my money back when I was not exactly poor.

When I collected the bedroll the next day I forced myself to overcome my need to stick to my normal morning routine and eventually collected it an hour later than agreed. I hoped that by belatedly finding a small crumb of kindness from within me it would go some way to alleviating the guilt and disgust I felt about my actions. It didn't! And needless to say, neither I, nor anyone else, used the bedroll on the remainder of the pilgrimage and nor has it been used since!

I was to see Sven just twice more, the next time was two days later and then, much to my surprise, on my arrival in Santiago just over four weeks later on the day he was due to fly home. For all his concern about missing his pre-booked flight home and his intensive schedule, he had arrived in Santiago just two days before me.

The only day I did not walk of the thirty was Day Ten, due to tendonitis in my left ankle and a severely blistered toe. Having followed my normal early morning routine that day I had delayed leaving the hostel because I could hardly walk with the pain. After spending an hour in the dining room trying to 'tape up' the blister, having watched another pilgrim doing the same, I conceded that it would be really unwise to walk.

I was thinking about how to find the local medical centre where I could get the treatment and letter I would need to be able to stay in the same town of Santo Domingo de la Calzada for two nights running. I could of course have stayed without the letter by staying in a local hotel as this was a popular holiday location, but I preferred to use the hostels, which seemed to be used solely by pilgrims and felt more in keeping with the challenge. As I was looking on a notice board for the location of a medical centre, a pair of 'angels' in the shape of an Italian couple appeared behind me. They told me they had also stayed in the convent overnight and were also delaying their start due to injury and knew where the medical centre was. Barbara especially could speak enough Spanish and English to get by which was just as well because her partner Merka and I could speak little if any and in my case was limited to buying a coffee or a beer. The Spanish spoken in that Northern Basque region was different to the south, which was why, by my end of the Camino, having not eaten anything other than what I could point to or pick up, I had lost two stones in weight.

Although I was once called an Earth Angel I never knew why. On this occasion it seemed extremely likely that Barbara and Merka were just that, because they were not only so kind and helpful to me, but whenever I saw them they were always surrounded by fellow peregrinos and obviously very popular. Could our meeting have just been another coincidence? Yes it could, did I believe it was? NO.

As it was still quite early in the morning the three of us planned to have a cup of coffee and leave the hostel a little later, but that plan was scuppered by a very officious 'sister' from the convent who ushered us quickly out onto the street with a smile and a wave as she locked the door behind us. This was the first, and the last time, I would stay late in any hostel, and when I thought about it, I could see that they would want to get on with their own busy day before opening again in the mid-afternoon for the new arrivals. After all, this was not a hotel but a convent managed by nuns that had been adapted for pilgrims to rest and sleep. There were to be many other convents that opened their doors for a small fee along the way.

We hobbled together to the medical centre where a doctor diagnosed my tendonitis and sent me in to a very tired looking nurse – who had probably been on duty all night – to clean up the blister, organise the anti-inflammatory drugs and the letter I needed. Despite Barbara explaining what the doctor had said, the nurse refused to clean up the blister, saying I should learn how to do it myself. She did, however, give me good advice about ongoing 'feet management' whilst walking in the blistering daytime temperatures, which together with an Internet search on blisters later that day, meant that once I had rested and taken the very strong tablets, I was able to walk much easier the next and each subsequent day without problems.

My already established routine of stopping at the first convenient café to eat and rest was adapted to apply the advice I had received at the medical centre for changing my sweat-soaked socks for dry ones as often as possible. To achieve that I would often delay my first stop for cafés where I could sit at an outside table in the early morning sunshine and dry my feet for an hour before putting on fresh socks; I used the extra half an hour to rest properly and write my journal. The only justification I had for being in such a hurry was a concern that the additional time could mean I did not get a bed for the night, but I always did and the new routine enriched the whole experience from thereon in.

The whole adventure, and that's what it was, was amazing for a variety of reasons. I began to find out who the real me was by continually being tested both emotionally and physically. There were times I was scared, but also times of great beauty as I witnessed many acts of kindness and amazing scenery. I stopped spiking up my hair with gel for the first time in twenty years, and never returned to it, after my hair became long and annoying and I had the most appalling of haircuts, as I was palmed off with an inexperienced stylist that I communicated with in a confusing mixture of sign language and facial expressions. I laughed and cried inwardly at the sight of my reflection in the window, but what did it matter and to whom? Maybe it was the real me I was looking at with my mask removed, and anyway, what was the point in worrying when I wore a silly but essential sun hat each day?

Daily survival had become more important than my vanity amongst other pilgrims also trying to find themselves by testing themselves to become real; no one knew who I was or what I had done, I was an anonymous human being, which to be honest is all we ever are despite any thoughts of grandeur or superiority. I had already lost the mask of my Fire Brigade uniform and my Jaeger suits and the Camino had stripped what was left of my 'Emperor's new clothes' syndrome that boosted my fragile confidence. I should have felt exposed, but I didn't because all that I was experiencing was the exposing of my low self-worth and esteem for what it was, something learnt that could be changed; it helped to be anonymous.

My new uniform was chosen for practicalities, not vanity, and it gave me confidence only because most of us were dressed the same, after all I had the choice of two shirts, blue or brown, both with functional pockets and one with UV protection; two pairs of shorts, both beige, one deluxe pair which could be turned into trousers by zipping on legs, both with pockets everywhere; sturdy walking boots and flip flops for best, three pairs of walking socks with at least one pair drying at all times on my backpack next to the two water bottles refreshed hourly from village water fountains; 'potable', as opposed to 'non-potable'.

The evening my hair was butchered I sat with all nationalities choking on my evening meal of octopus and Ribera wine, a local delicacy that the guidebook said could not be missed and I oh so wished I had; although it did achieve me forgetting my hair!

The restaurant was packed, mainly with peregrinos; some of us must have been single, or unattached, as some like to say, possibly widowed or divorced, but mostly they were in pairs and probably married, or in bigger groups, but all mingling together with the many that were terminally or seriously ill, which, along with other brushes with death, was a common theme. I was just trying to find myself, which when it came down to it all of us were doing. I never spoke to anyone.

Many of the larger and younger groups were often affiliated to churches and religions. One such group would provide me with one of the most memorable occasions that I had the good fortune to witness – and there were many – as a group of twenty Italian teenagers, with their Catholic priest leader, morphed into a choir from a giggling and excitable band of children and sang during an impromptu and short evening mass in a courtyard just outside of the large auberge we were all staying in. Their singing moved me to tears with its beauty and simplicity and I wanted the moment to last forever, which it has in my memory and heart. I took the opportunity to tell them later in the large shared kitchen, while they were all cooking and sharing their laughter and joy, although the priest had to summon the one teenage girl in the whole group who could speak a little English to translate. They were obviously thrilled with my compliment, which was a small gift in return for what they had given me.

Many groups sang while walking their way along The Camino and whilst sat in a café the next day for my hour's rest the same group passed me by doing just that. As I sat writing my journal it made me stop and it brought a huge smile to my face and it's not very often that happens to me!

An extract from my journal, written on Thursday, 21st August 2008, best describes Day Twenty Two of walking as another memorable day. Although it was not a typical day so far as the terrain went, hence the treat, as I took eight-and-a-half hours to walk twenty-two-and-a-half miles, eight more than the eventual average:

'I began walking at 5.40am with clear skies and a stunning half-moon to light my way. There was nothing normal about the terrain which was a particularly arduous mountain stretch that seemed to go on and on and up and down, mostly with treacherous underfoot conditions along some winding mountain edges. The stunning scenery kept me going and alert despite the extremes of the freezing cold start and baking hot finish, with only occasional breaks in the clear blue skies to shade the sun. I had already decided during my ninety minute break to treat myself and rest my weary body in luxurious accommodation at the end of the day.

Everyone seemed to be struggling on the winding rocky path leading us down to a delightfully refreshing scene of people swimming in the inviting waters of a wide shallow river that divided the town of Molinaseca. Although it was still some distance away the anticipation and the now searing temperature of the mid-afternoon sun made me hurry.

I was breaking all my own rules in rushing and felt a bit awkward as I passed a young lady clearly struggling with the unstable rocky underfoot conditions. According to my guidebook the river water was freezing at all times of the year, but it wasn't stopping many of my fellow peregrinos cooling off in it. I had no intention of swimming and as I wandered across the delightful arched bridge, and, as if on cue, I was approached by a Spanish lady asking if I was looking for a room for the night.

I was shown to the room in an attractive looking terraced property by a gentleman she had summoned.'

This would be the only night I would stay in what they called a private hostel, which was more like a small 'room only' hotel. It had been recently refurbished to a very high standard with a wonderful double bed, clean fresh white bedding and an en-suite power shower and bath. The cost of 45€ was high compared to the 3-4€ of the municipal aubergé and 8-12€ of the better private ones, but as it was to be my one night out of an aubergé across the whole pilgrimage it was well worth it.

Whilst I was still checking in (he still checked and stamped my Camino passport) I was slightly embarrassed when the Danish-speaking girl who I had overtaken was shown in by the lady who had first approached me. The gentleman explained to her that I had just taken the last single room and the only room left was a double at 65€. I did wonder if he had made a mistake as my room was definitely a double as I understand the term. She agreed to have the remaining room but once again, if looks could kill! I would have willingly paid either I was so tired.

The hot water was plentiful and after a hot bath I washed my day's walking clothes. There wasn't an outside washing line so I had to improvise by attaching my clothes to the adapted nylon cord I had carried round with me and hung it out to dry from the window, above the rear yard.

None of the fancy restaurants did a peregrinos supper, I assume because the local authority aubergés were quite a long way further out of town, so I paid a good value 13€ for a three-course meal and a bottle of wine and had my best sleep since starting when I crawled into bed at 9.20pm. If I wanted proof of the previously hard day then it was, unusually, struggling to get out of bed at my usual 5.30am, although I did help myself to the fresh coffee provided in a reception room, eventually leaving an hour later.

It is possible to do small lengths of The Camino as an organised package tour when you walk each day without luggage, which is transported ahead to your next hotel. I saw many groups doing this and, whilst I respect those who have no choice for health reasons, I feel you lose something of the experience of pushing yourself to the limit in an unfamiliar environment out of your comfort zone, although some pilgrims did the ultimate and slept under canvas and the stars each night for free and would have been justified in thinking the same of me. Some peregrinos had dogs; others I saw completed it on horseback with all the complications of stabling or finding secure grazing that that involved. Personal choice should always be respected and I had learnt the hard way not to judge another's choice when I knew nothing of their personal circumstance.

By Day Twenty Seven of walking, the effort had become increasingly draining. It is relentless having to walk day after day and a huge amount of resilience is required, but my spirit was about to be lifted and my weary body rested when, at midday, I passed directly outside of a very different aubergé, where gentle music and the smell of a burning incense stick grabbed my attention.

This aubergé is in a place called Ligonde and was actually called a 'refuge'. I had no intention of stopping until an American teenager called Tyler from California spoke to me from its garden and offered me coffee and food. I didn't take much convincing. Tyler explained that he and his five American colleagues – two boys and two girls – were volunteering for a religious organisation called Agapé, They were on secondment in Spain and from their organisational base in Madrid would spend on average between 1-2 weeks at the refuge, although I was to learn that some stayed much longer. Agapé is a Greek word for unconditional love that I had come across on my counselling course and that's exactly what they were about to demonstrate during my overnight stay.

Tyler and I had an interesting conversation about our respective beliefs and, although I felt he found it hard to accept or understand some of my mine, we did find common ground in our belief of God and Jesus and that our lives are about love. He explained their 'mission' through the practical aspects of running the refuge where guests and staff would eat supper together, which the volunteers would cook; that night it was rice and chicken. I was so taken aback by the ethos and kindness of this group I decided to stop walking for the day and to rest my body. I would not be disappointed for many reasons, the most important of which was that it was a place of very obvious love and so very different to what I had been encountering; I would not be disappointed!

I was the first to accept accommodation for that night so I selected one of the eight beds and rested before exploring the area. Many of the passing peregrinos stopped in fascination to take a look at this unusual set up, which was apparently mentioned in many of the guidebooks, but not mine.

With plenty of time to spare I wandered around the community of Ligonde, treating myself to a couple of midday beers in the local bar and just being what I had come to see as kind to myself when life becomes a bit of a struggle. I had written earlier in my journal for that day *'I have had enough now and want to be at the end'.* I returned to the refuge to relax and sleep off my beers and really enjoyed just hanging around with no targets to meet for the rest of the day.

I remained the only peregrino until 6pm and just as I was beginning to think I might be on my own, others began arriving; there would be ten of us by supper time two hours later. The table was laid and the food just being served when we were joined by an apologetic peregrino bursting through the door who had obviously been rushing. He was welcomed with an honest sincerity and the same warmth that I had been six hours previously and the staff enthusiastically set another place at the long table, promising a mattress would be found to sleep on later as all the beds were taken. The atmosphere was wonderful and a real bonus was having apple crumble for pudding. We all helped clear up and the volunteers then prepared a side room for evening prayers at 10.30pm to which we were all invited but not forced or encouraged in any way. I had decided to go to bed just as there was a knock on the door and four young Korean boys entered. They were also welcomed as warmly as before by the Agapé team and offered food, which they declined. They were found makeshift beds in the prayer room, so the prayers were cancelled, offered the use of the shower facilities and given the herbal tea they preferred.

I wrote in my journal the next day:

'It was so wonderful to see the welcome, no thought of saying they were full (which I had witnessed on many occasions, but only where there was alternative accommodation available). I had wondered why I had stopped there and having witnessed this unconditional love, I realised why. It was beautiful and another lesson for me in kindness and caring even if it means changing your plans. People are more important than prayers and this was to be another reminder about the night I refused to help others until shown how to do so.'

By the end of my pilgrimage at Santiago I had lost the two stones in weight and with the remaining eleven stones spread over my six-foot frame I felt like I looked, tired and haggard. The shear effort of walking between twelve and twenty-two miles a day for thirty days in hot temperatures, up and down mountains and along long dusty paths besides main roads with insufficient fuel in the form of food had taken its toll.

What I had gained was a lot of real confidence and a belief in myself that I could do and achieve anything that I wanted to in life; I had achieved a personal goal with very little help from others, even though I had met many people of different ages and nationalities and formed friendships and a sort of unwritten camaraderie with fellow pilgrims, all of whom had their own very personal reasons for doing The Camino.

The Camino tested me, I had dug deep into the false and materialistic world we all seemed to have inhabited, but had come through the other side, I think, a better human. Much of the learning is instant, but it also has a much deeper and profound way of changing the way I looked at myself and my life that is not realised or understood until much later.

I spent three days in Santiago in a good quality hotel, declining the offer to sleep for free in the local aubergé that was afforded to everyone as a 'well done' gesture for finishing. Sleeping in freshly laundered, crisp white bedding in en-suite accommodation again was much too tempting and, despite its undoubted contribution to my personal growth, I had had enough of crowded dormitories and hoping for bottom bunks as I returned to the comforts that I had come to expect as 'normal' in my life. It encouraged me to think about homelessness and rough sleepers who do not even have the luxury of choice as I came to appreciate what I called my basic and challenging living conditions of the last thirty days. It was far from basic because everything is relative!

Agapé is something we should all adopt and practice, but believe me it is not as easy as it sounds and I won't pretend otherwise. My dog Spot had achieved it effortlessly!

Two of the friends I made from Bavaria, who had started much deeper in France than I had, continued onto Finisterre, which was originally thought to be the end of the world by early pilgrims as they looked out across the expanse of what we now know as the Atlantic Ocean, but most peregrinos stopped at Santiago de Compostela and, even fewer still, turned around to complete the return journey to their starting point.

I was also reunited with the fluent English-speaking José and his six Spanish colleagues at Santiago. They had walked the same route as me and we had crossed paths many times over the thirty days. José gave me a personal tour of the cathedral and showed me all the points of interest, which I would have undoubtedly missed on my own.

I booked my return flights to the UK via Madrid and Alicante where I spent five days relaxing on the Mediterranean, while staying at my friend Steve's villa at La Marina.

37

NLP

Both my children were shocked by how thin I looked on my return from The Camino. I felt rested and pleased to be home.

During the second week of the pilgrimage I received a text message from Reiki Jane, *"nice evening, wrong man"*. My phone, by choice, was for emergencies and the occasional catch up with my children and the message had come through while enjoying my breakfast of bread and cheese bought from a village store earlier; it tasted great. I replied purposely in a perfunctory way with a smile on my face that mirrored the cautious feelings born from a day out that meant a lot to me, but apparently less to Jane.

The pilgrimage was far more than having to overcome the physical and mental effort required to survive day after relentless day. The time spent alone with my thoughts demanded a constant inspection of my life through each solitary step as I relived every crossroad and avenue that had led me to the pilgrimage as a necessity and not just the challenge I had convinced myself of. It is easy to see how you can 'find yourself' on a pilgrimage that is used to hosting so many personal battles. With nowhere to hide and alone with my thoughts, all of life's pretences were stripped away, forcing me to be real; even if you are running away you have to find your way back!

I had met a young Irish girl on The Camino who was walking in the same group that had borrowed my bedroll. She always seemed happy as she flitted around from person to person with that lovely way that always seems so prevalent in the Irish; she had even offered to help me with my first inadequate attempts at repairing my blisters, as someone who had experienced them herself the year before. A week later, as I was leaving my sunny spot outside a café in a small town square, refreshed with clean socks and dry feet, I met her walking alone, looking lost and sad. It was not an easy decision for me to stop and talk, because my routine and regimented attitude to life demanded otherwise, but I did as we found a different table and over coffee for the next hour I met a different girl with her 'mask' removed. She explained she had completed the Camino the year before in the search for answers to a relationship breakup and, having found them, had returned home with a renewed enthusiasm to start her life afresh. She was back for two weeks, hoping for more answers to the same problem with the same man; Groundhog Day again! I may not have been good at sorting out my own similar problems, but I was an 'expert' of sorts with many Groundhog Day experiences of my own to pull from. She left with a spring in the step, determined to trust life and do the right thing through discovering who she really was and why. Life of course will keep on providing opportunities to learn; it's us who do not listen, but we will when we're ready... if we are supposed to!

The first meeting with Reiki Jane since my return went well and we began to see more of each other thereafter. Initially we both had times of uncertainty, the collywobbles was how my mum would have described it, but we were both happy to give each other the space and whatever time was needed. My first and only doubts came in the form of a rising panic after we had spent a night together. It had come out of the blue and was a new feeling for me as I wrestled with my thoughts for hours until Jane woke and I tried to explain to her how I felt. I didn't make a good job of it. Amongst other things we discussed the possibility that it was Jane's own recent day of uncertainty, when she walked away asking for her own space and time, that had brought on my own, but my words must have felt like an ending as she left to go home, which was not my intention, only to panic for a different reason when she had gone as I was overwhelmed by the fear of losing her. I called her within the hour to say I had been clumsy with my words, which patched the wounds. Jane was to have her second wobble a week later, which we also worked through, eventually, but not before I had written the following letter that was never finished or posted:

'Dear Jane,

I need to write this. First of all thank you for the honest decision you have made. I suppose having made it once before it was inevitable that you did again as I try to work through these changes.

To be honest I do not feel it is entirely over. I believe the timing was all wrong. Remember the words you were given by spirit 'not to go too deep with him'; in hindsight kissing you on the beach that day was a mistake, as was the day itself. Our connection is unquestionable. I still feel the same about you now as that day at Chipping Sodbury three years ago when I first saw you.

There are of course two ways to look at this situation now. Firstly to accept that everything that has happened since three years ago is perfect timing and meant to be or that we were never meant to get together in the first place.

I don't believe that and I believe this.

We are meant to spend the rest of our lives together, but at the right time. Had we not gone to Chesil Beach or kissed we would still be apart now and I would be freeing old energies to build new love on good foundations.

My walk through Spain was a catalyst for change, that's why I am struggling now and since being home. You acknowledge this. You were prepared to keep it on a very low, casual, uncommitted level. That is how it would have worked out. I have had no desire to be with anyone else since Chesil Beach. The oddity of the situation would be laughable if it wasn't so sad. I of course did not want you to go or not to see you again, why would I not want to be with someone who has made me feel so different.

I did feel different with you, I did not feel desperate I just really enjoyed being with you. You say you want more in lots of ways but especially communication.'

I think we both knew there could be no more chances, but we didn't need any as something rather special began to emerge between us and, forgetting all about the possibilities of 'Groundhog Day', I was in love again.

Reiki Jane soon became the fifth Jane that I had relationships with as we established a routine of living together at my flat on weekends and Jane returning home to look after her two sons during the week. This was a good routine, satisfying my need for space as I readjusted to my own life.

Our life together has been a wonderful experience ever since and we were married nine years later. We didn't need to be married, we just wanted to be to help seal our very special love. Yes there have been times when we have disagreed, and we have had to learn to compromise and live together, but with what is for me, a refreshingly honest relationship, our friendship has grown into something very special. Somewhere along that timeline I have learnt to love myself and that was essential if I was to accept Jane's considerable capacity to love; and at last, I know what a happy and fulfilling relationship with no doubts and no jealousies feels like, it feels like love as we hold onto each other with our arms wide open. Everything in life is so much easier when done from happiness and with love instead of a need that can never be truly satisfied.

Although I had learnt so much about myself from the counselling course and The Camino, I still needed to change the subconscious learnt behaviours that had caused many, if not all, of my problems in relationships. The opportunity to do so came my way very early on in my relationship with Jane while we were still living apart in the week.

With the ending of my previous relationship came the ending of sitting in the closed meditation circle we had attended together for many years. Consequently, I was grateful to be offered a place on the closed circle that Jane had been running for many years also. I already knew a few of the sitters, but I didn't know Dawn until she came on my second week. As the circle drew to a close, some of the group went home but others, like me, stayed to talk. I was talking to some of those I knew about my recent adventures and in particular how I had become aware that I had a lack of self-worth, but didn't know what to do to change it. Dawn, who was stood to one side and had been listening, spoke up and volunteered that she could help me by using techniques she was learning during her training to become an NLP (Neuro-linguistic programming) practitioner, something I knew nothing about.

We agreed to meet. The first session was to get to know each other and agree a contract for working together within agreed parameters. We talked about my childhood and made further arrangements to meet. The second session confirmed what I already knew, that self-worth and low self-esteem issues were affecting me and Dawn went on to explain, in layman's terms, the mechanics of how my learnt behaviour, as memories from my childhood, had been stored in my subconscious mind as neural pathways. I had never heard of neural pathways before, but according to Dawn's NLP – and my memory of how it works from that day – memories are somehow formed through chemicals that are associated with them, and are stored within our neural pathways, as they travel across them in our brains, to become a set memory of not just the message they are formed by, but as importantly how we learn to deal with the message.

At this point it is worth repeating that the actions that had shaped my learnt behaviour from my childhood, that in turn had informed my life script and 'given birth' to my lack of self-worth and low self-esteem, were formed by the negative memories of those learnt behaviours and stored in my neural pathways from where they would resurface in my life as a subconscious behaviour every time I felt I was being ignored and not receiving positive attention in the form of strokes or love.

Dawn went on to explain how, by forming alternative positive 'memories' in our neural pathways to run alongside and parallel with the original negative ones, we can begin to challenge our negative outlook on life and make them more positive, thus increasing our self-worth and self-esteem. She did this by determining key words from a series of questions about my childhood and then including them in key sentences she encouraged me to determine. They would then become the basis of my hoped-for change as positive messages begin to supersede the negative ones.

My key word was obviously love and my three short sentences were: 'I am loveable', 'I am worth loving' and 'I am worthy of love'. All of which I would have to say repeatedly, out loud, whilst looking into my own eyes through the reflection of a mirror. As I had come to believe that the eyes are the windows to our souls, it made complete sense to me, and with plenty of spare time I followed the instructions meticulously three times a day for many months in my flat. Despite initially finding it very uncomfortable to look into my eyes and say the key phrases with any sincerity, I soon got used to it and actually found it quite liberating, and at times very funny, as I laughed at myself while making faces into the mirror saying 'I love you, I love you' etc.

It is this period of my life in particular, while living most of the week in my flat alone, that enabled me to change the subconsciously learnt message of my stored behaviours and increase my self-worth and start the journey of becoming the real me and not the negative-based learnt behaviour me. Very quickly I began to feel the benefit as I began to feel like I actually 'liked' myself and then to 'love myself', which enabled a genuine love for Jane to flourish as I allowed her to love me back and accept it as lovable.

Dawn had taught me how to get the ball of change rolling and once it was moving it was quite simple to keep it rolling as it gradually gained momentum and increased its speed. The more I loved myself, the easier it was to accept Jane's love; SIMPLE, and all it had taken was fifty-five years!

I had been told so many times that I would know when I met *'the right one'* and whether that would have been the case if Jane had not been with her husband when we first met I will never know. What does 'knowing' mean? And how is it recognised or felt by those who say *'I knew as soon as I saw her or him'*, when it concerns matters of the heart? How do we define the love of another as opposed to the need of 'being in love' when we have never felt it before? What I do know is that I had been transfixed, with my heart beating out of my chest, as Jane emerged at the top of the stairs like a beautiful rainbow. Could that and my disappointments of learning she wasn't free be seen as indicators of being 'meant to be'? I have no idea, but what I do know is that seeing her in her professional capacity of a healing therapist, when I knew of many others, was entirely intentional and unwise and I shouldn't have done it; and nor should I have used the excuse of not wanting to wait for three years to be trained as a Reiki master, especially so because it was at a time when I knew my existing relationship with my then partner, Jane Four, was at risk. I believe my knowing was on a deeper level of understanding than my being human would allow for – although I also believe that it is possible for some humans to achieve that too – and meant to be for when our circumstances were ready.

The reality of having those 'naughty' three or four healing sessions with Jane in the many months that followed our 'chance' meeting was in being told all her marital problems at the end of one of my own treatments. I wanted to say leave him; what I said was all the right things as I 'advised' her on what she could do to rekindle the romance with her husband, after all 'I was an expert of sorts'. I sat at home later and thought about the irony of what had happened with mixed feelings and torn loyalties that I had no right to have, and six weeks later, when I returned for the last time, she thanked me profusely for helping her with her marriage which was *'back on track and rosy again'*. I was ruefully pleased and would have liked to have given her a different sort of a hug to our normally cautious and respectful one as I screamed 'NO' inside.

When Jane trained me alone to become a Reiki master years later she had acted very professionally and never talked about her marriage... or that she had separated from her husband; I didn't talk about or ask for help with my own relationship either. It seems odd now, knowing how we both felt, while tiptoeing around our feelings for two days. Although I was tempting fate with my decisions to be closer to her, it clearly wasn't yet time for either of us then and I have no regrets because she was always great to be around, which is easy to say when we are finally together.

We had no further contact until I had been on my own for about six months and that 'chance' comment by her friend that had made sure I knew she was in fact free. My time alone was important and invaluable for lots of reasons, but I was still surprised to hear on our first meeting following my return that she had in fact been involved in two relationships after her breakup, not just the one I knew about. I was grateful that she hadn't told me everything before I left, not just because it was none of my business, but because it would have been something else to think and worry about.

Does all that mean she had always been the one, or does it mean that I had made her the one by learning from all my experiences and growing up as I began grasping back control of a life that, I believe, had been stolen to order in a childhood shaped so strongly and adequately by negative feelings?

Whether knowing everything that happened between us was meant to be for all the right reasons would qualify as knowing she was the right one from the moment I first saw her, I do not know, but for fairy tale and spiritual purposes I would say yes, but for the romantics amongst us, probably not.

38

Returning Home

The word 'home', that I had used to describe how I felt on my first ever visit to Belmont Road Spiritual Centre, was about to come into significance again after my pilgrimage when I had started to attend the centre more often. One Sunday evening I was welcomed in the usual friendly way, but in particular by two committee members, who seemed more desperate than keen, as they competed to tell me the story of how the president and secretary had 'unexpectedly resigned' over a disagreement and would I be prepared to become president. Having just retired from thirty years of regular work my first reaction was to say 'no', but I said I would consider it.

I returned home and thought about how important the spiritual centre had been in my life. The management side of my Fire Brigade career had equipped me perfectly for the role, with experience in heading committees and making decisions, and this small commitment would give me something worthwhile to do while giving something back.

Being unsure I decided to ask for a 'sign', and as with the previous occasions when I had done the same, I didn't have to wait too long as I walked in for the following Tuesday afternoon guild. The medium taking the service that afternoon was Lorraine who, like Lisa had been many years before her, popular and well-respected 'on the circuit'. I hadn't seen Lorraine for some time, but knew her quite well and, after the perfunctory hellos, she asked, *"Are you going to be president? You should consider it as this place is like home to you."*

I agreed to become the new president – a rather grand title that I was uncomfortable with – subject to meeting the remaining committee members, which I did.

Having been handed my personal set of keys, I spent days piecing together scattered paperwork and gathering the evidence for how it had been managed. What I found was years of paperwork that was patchy and unorganised. But what it also revealed was that we, the committee, were also responsible for the management of a lower ground-floor flat, which had its own entrance via the rear garden, and a first-floor flat, which was accessed through the church front door and up the stairs via a lobby and was far from being the small commitment I had expected. Neither set of occupants were anything to do with the centre, except the committee were in effect their landlord.

The whole of the large Victorian semi-detached building, and not just the spiritual church that occupied the ground floor, was held in trust by the Spiritualist National Union (SNU), whose headquarters and teaching college I had visited on an open day years earlier in Stansted near London. They had been willed the building by its former owner decades earlier to be used solely for spiritual purposes and to be managed locally on a daily basis, to its satisfaction, by its members. The committee's role was to be the voice of its members and to implement the rules and regulations of the SNU by submitting annual audited accounts and records, and to facilitate an annual inspection from their regional management team.

This was a business with a huge health and safety commitment. We appointed a new secretary and treasurer and set about the worrying problem of a serious lack of records, a significant amount of non-compliance with health and safety regulations, substantial rent arrears from the first-floor flat tenants and an exceedingly low rent on the lower ground-floor flat. All of which were rectified within the first year. During the second year we redecorated the centre and upgraded its facilities and completely revamped the, by then, vacant first-floor flat with the help of an official loan from the SNU. We also slightly adjusted the format of the spiritual service to include an increase in the use of modern music that had already been started by the previous president as a replacement for the older style spiritual hymn book, and to refocus the centre as a place to have fun through a more relaxed format. It worked, as attendances gradually increased.

Once again it seemed more than a coincidence that my life skills fitted the needs of the church perfectly, and although it kept me much busier than I had envisaged, I really enjoyed the three and a half years I spent on the committee.

That came to an end in a similar way to the resignations of the previous president and secretary, following a continual battle with some of the good-intentioned, but old-fashioned members, who were so typical of their type in resisting change. In particular there was one strong-minded individual who was influencing certain 'easily led' committee members and causing unrest, which led to lies and deceit with an eventual division of interests.

Despite my request to the individual to stop and join the committee – which was declined – it carried on until my position also became untenable and I resigned. It is an irony that many of the so-called spiritually aware that I have come across, be they committee or others, are far from that, as I had also discovered about myself at times on the Camino. But I was proud of what we as a committee had achieved and, in accord with my new spiritual beliefs and everything happening for a reason, it was time to walk away and move on.

During the three-and-a-half years I was involved with Belmont I had moved out of my flat and bought a new four-bedroomed townhouse (three storeys) close by. That hasty decision was fuelled by the disappointment of a late collapse of another purchase that had dragged on for six months and a desire to move from the flat to a property with a garden. Despite the good financial package that was on offer at that time I did wonder why, whilst living on my own, I had decided to buy such a spacious house.

The answer to that became clearer a year later when Jane's divorce had been finalised and, having sold her marital home, she moved in with her twenty-year-old son Mike and Natch the dog. Mike was able to live more or less independently on the top floor of the town house, which he turned into 'his pad' with an en-suite bedroom and lounge, that gave us all more autonomy and helped us to combine our lives together. It also calmed my concerns from my previous experience of living with my partner's young children fifteen years earlier when I had become disgusted by the way I treated them as innocents in my problems, although as older and wiser Mike would turn out to be a pleasure.

Inspired by a good friend of mine in the Fire Brigade who had owned a beautiful motorhome and, with Jane's love of France and a growing clientele for her spiritual healing there, we decided it would make sense to buy our own motorhome and be in control of our own travel arrangements.

Jane had always had a desire to live in France, but I was not so sure and, although the house was serving its purpose, I was becoming increasingly frustrated with living on a poorly-designed development with car parking issues. When the motorhome was not in use we stored it in a secure compound on the edge of Bristol so that was not a problem, but eventually we agreed that I would sell the house and live away from the hustle and bustle of the city.

Selling the house proved more difficult than I thought, but a year later it sold and, as we could not decide between living in rural UK or France, we decided to place all our furniture and belongings in storage and live in the motorhome until we were certain. Our first adventure was actually not in the motorhome but in Courtyard Cottage, which was owned by friends and was part of a managed complex on the edge of Dartmouth. We were there for five weeks and it was a magical time in the extensive grounds, and not just because it was there that we became engaged. I would often sit and write in the quietness of nature, including the following:

'Wednesday 14th March 2012

Dear Father God,
I wish to manifest the following.
A house to live in the countryside; rural not too isolated, but quiet and near to areas of population.
I would like to try before I buy.
The house should be cosy, comfortable and light and bright.
It should have a minimum of two bedrooms.
It should be able to facilitate my, and Jane's, work for you dear Father God.
It would be similar to Courtyard Cottage in location to the sea and other people.
Please put options before me/us now so we may start to settle.

With Love
Thank you.'

We had always known we would have to move out of Courtyard Cottage at Easter and it was then that we returned to the Bristol area and began living in the motorhome on small registered camp sites. We were absolutely amazed how many other people were doing the same, although most of them while letting out their houses in preference to selling them, which, we soon realised, came with its own problems associated with the need for a permanent address. One couple also owned a property in Florida, but could only live there for six months of the year and so would return to the UK to collect their motorhome and, having stayed on the site for a while, would travel to warmer countries like Spain or Portugal for the remainder of the summer months. Another couple had been travelling extensively across Europe over the previous eight years for months at a time and would only return long enough to plan their next trip. It felt so liberating talking to these travellers and I admired there lifestyle choices of living life to the full.

Jane and I began working more and more together, promoting spiritual development in the UK and across France, and the motorhome proved an invaluable and cosy home to be able to take with us.

We were only sorely tempted to live in France once when we were offered to buy a spacious plot of land on the edge of the Dordogne in a forest development – centred on a lake – with social and leisure facilities, including a fully-equipped gym, indoor swimming pool and restaurants. We knew this area of France well and had many friends and contacts there. The whole project was owned and managed by a Belgian man who had become a good friend and, as we would have been able to tailor the interior design of the bungalow to our own liking, including a swimming pool, patio area, and double garage that would have been ideal for spiritual workshops etc., we were sorely tempted. As well as the reasonable cost, which would have been affordable and well below what you would expect to pay for similar in the UK, the offer was made even more tempting by being offered the adjacent plot as well for the price of the one (they were the last two remaining because they were the closest, but not too close, to the quiet country road).

In the end we decided against it because, as much as we liked France, we also liked the UK and something was telling us that we should remain based in the country that we were both born in.

During our time in the UK we took the opportunity to explore our own country off the 'beaten track', including spending time in particular in West and North Wales, the Lake District, the Yorkshire Moors and Northumberland. The freedom of having, and in our case living, in a motorhome, was wonderful and it could have not been shown more than when we camped up next to an unspoilt and beautiful beach on the Northumbrian coast and next to a public house with restaurant. As we were completely self-contained we were able to stay for over a week, moving just once to fill up the fresh water tank. We shopped locally and walked daily on what felt at times like our own private beach.

As the year moved on into the colder winter months of France, we began to consider how and where we would be best advised to spend the rest of the winter. The choices were quite simple, either head further south to Spain or Portugal where the warmer climates would suit living in the motorhome or return to the UK, put the motorhome back into its rented storage compound and rent a property. We decided to return to the UK and, within hours of making that decision, we were contacted completely out of the blue, by the same friends who had gifted us the use of their cottage in Dartmouth seven months earlier, to ask if we were interested in renting their country cottage in Somerset, which had 'unexpectedly become available'.

We accepted there and then without needing to look at it and there were two reasons for that; firstly our friends, who were quickly becoming our angels, had great taste and we knew it would be wonderful, which it was, and secondly, the timing of the offer could have been nothing short of synchronicity and a sign that it was absolutely meant to be.

The thatched cottage was in a quiet country hamlet with seventeen other properties on an unclassified cul-de-sac road nestled between the edge of the Exmoor National Park and the Quantocks; as you can imagine, the nature was stunningly beautiful. We moved in mid-October 2012 and rented the cottage for a year, before, having fallen in love with it and the lifestyle it offered, asking if we could buy it. Our angels said 'yes' and, despite having to sell the motorhome to afford it, it really was 'a dream come true'.

We were able to walk Jane's dog Natch every day, either in the surrounding countryside or on the beautiful coastline fifteen minutes' drive away, and he probably had the best eighteen months of his life exploring with complete freedom away from the farmers' livestock, before dying unexpectedly of a heart problem.

Everything I had asked for in that letter of manifestation written some seven months before we moved in had been met. Maybe that's a coincidence too, but I know it was not; it was meant to be, as everything in life is.

Jane and I married three years later and despite still occasionally slipping into old learnt behaviours they have gradually receded as my understanding of self-worth, and the integration of a new and positive message to supersede the negativity of the original, has informed a new me by harmonising what's left of my negative subconscious memories with a conscious being that has long since passed over a tipping point to the opposite side, where happiness and fulfilment abounds in my new life with a new script, both of which would have once been beyond my wildest dreams.

PART THREE

WHO WE REALLY ARE

39

Synchronicity and Personal Responsibility

As babies we are born dependent and in need of support and guidance, indeed we would not survive without it. Without realising it we hope to grow out of our childhood dependency and into free-thinking independent individuals who are capable of 'standing on our own two feet'. If we do not grow we will remain 'in dependency' created by our 'need' and will require continuing support; for example, I didn't grow as an emotionally stable person because I didn't feel love as a child. I was loved in the only way my parents knew how in line with their own circumstances. As a result I searched for similar feelings as an adult to those I experienced as a child, but with the added complication of a growing physical body and a distorted expectation from an expanding mind; I had reasonable expectations that I knew what I was doing. I didn't and, unsurprisingly, what I continually found was a temporary fix of conditional love that would evaporate with the initial euphoria of thinking I was 'in love'.

Getting involved with spirituality led me to train as a counsellor and my life changed as I began to understand the reality of my previous decisions, made from the honest ignorance of my own choices, as opposed to decisions for my future that, although still informed by my past, were being made with a growing understanding of personal responsibility as informed by a growing emotional intelligence. As it did so I began to take control of my life, and possibly my destiny.

One of the key elements for my change was recognising a sequence of events that I would have previously identified as coincidences, to see them instead as synchronicity and meant to be. One coincidence now and then would hardly have been noticed in my normal life, but when I looked back over the sequence of events since asking for help I could hardly have missed the series of three self-help books (spiritual by any other name) that I would not have normally read, which had been 'put' in front of me; could it have been coincidental that, whilst reading the third, *Conversations with God*, I would meet an Australian spiritual minister at my brother's having popped in unannounced for a cup of tea?; could it be coincidence that he was reading a book on philosophy and we started to discuss the books we were reading, the result of which was him inviting me to join him at a spiritual church the next day?; could it have been a coincidence years later, when considering what to do when I retired from the brigade, I was led to consider training as a personal counsellor from a 'chance' comment made by a work colleague?; could it be coincidence when days later I asked for a sign from whoever was supporting my journey that it was the best direction for me to take and I was given a direct confirmation within hours?; could it have been coincidence that the counselling training gave me so many of the answers to my drunken prayer as I began to understand who I was and why? Was it really coincidence that Transactional Analysis (TA) – a system of counselling that never mentions spiritual issues in writing – screamed an association at me from its pages to align perfectly with my new belief that we choose our life circumstances for the purpose of enlightenment? Surely all that had happened to me, with one coincidence after the other, has to be more than just chance!

Synchronicity is defined in dictionaries as, *'situations that look like accidents, but are not they are system'* or *'the occurrence of two related things simultaneously without planning'*. Coincidence is defined as, *'a striking occurrence of two or more events at one time apparently by mere chance'*. I like to imagine synchronicity and coincidence as a gentle and all-encompassing life force that encourages and supports us all surreptitiously through the anonymity of God, and implemented by His or Her helpers to enable all that is meant to be, as planned and at the appropriate time, like the weave of a fabric supports the finished cloth.

Looking back over the years before I asked for help I can see the possibility that I had always been helped, I just hadn't noticed. I like to think that whoever was helping me had upped the ante to enable me to act through my growing instincts. But, whatever it was, making the transition from coincidence to synchronicity was important for me because it extended my imagination from thinking that everything unexpected in life must be out of our control and personal responsibility, to being helped and enabled to take control. Most of us never come close to challenging what has become our accepted ways of looking at life and indeed, until my life was in crisis neither did I, but it is so much more than changing our learnt behaviours and following the crowd, it's about rediscovering our pioneering spirit and challenging our societies that have almost become stagnant through dependency.

Take science for example, there is no denying that it has provided us with fantastic progress in so many ways, but at the same time in other ways it has become limiting as we rely and depend on it more and more.

The indigenous peoples and their modern descendants had a science that relied on their knowledge and wisdom of the land and seasons because they had nothing else. They lived simple lives, respecting the land where instincts and community were important and they learnt the hard way how to support themselves while often trusting in unseen gods to bring good fortune. Modern science has 'allowed and encouraged' those hard-earned instincts to gradually desensitise through lack of use, and as a result our lives have become ever more complicated and lazy through dependency and a lack of engagement because it is easy and we can. The only thing we have to learn the hard way is that good fortune does exist within the science of synchronicity.

As we have become 'apparently' more sophisticated and civilised – although I do question who are the wise, savage and uneducated ones – we have come to rely on science and 'good willed' scientists to look after our futures. It is as if we have substituted them as our god or other saviours who will save us from poverty and extinction and pretty much everything else we bring on ourselves. That reliance may yet come at a price as we accept, without question, that modern processes must be good for us and will secure our futures. Becoming dependent and accepting will ultimately erase our wisdom and leave us ever more vulnerable to so-called progress.

Our dependency and trust in a system that seems to bring us progress through comfort has been used to secure obscene profits for big business, often at the expense of others and the planet, with little, if any, regard to the long-term future. As our planet becomes more and more crowded and technological advances makes communication across it as easy, if not easier, than talking to our neighbours across the garden fence, we can watch the damage as it is being created. There is no hiding place or excuses because the evidence that we are stripping Earth of her irreplaceable natural resources is there to be seen. And yet powerful lobbyists that are employed by powerful leaders of ever-increasing global business conglomerates are more determined than ever to deflect our thoughts away from the realities of a profit at all costs mentality by skilfully delivered reassurances that all is well. But the reality is that our planet is not well, and nor are we, and we cannot continue consuming and abusing our Earth; it is like burning our homes to stay warm and we are allowing it to happen because we have lost our voice by trusting in those who shout the loudest and longest.

Apathy and naivety has deflected our awareness of the global environmental issues and how they will affect us in time. We stay safe in our closed and comfortable existences and choose to ignore them by convincing ourselves that it's someone else's problem. Well it is not, it's our problem and we have to begin taking personal responsibility again; what an irony it is that our scientists are trying to find solutions to the damage that science has helped to create in the first place! Earth is not a commodity, it is a living entity.

Our Earth is out of balance; we are out of balance and we are all killing off the 'hand that feeds us'. Even if you are not concerned for yourself, be concerned for your children and your children's children. Try explaining to them, when they enquire, because one day they will and they will say 'why did you allow it to happen?' Above all else let's hope our children are free and brave enough to stand up and enquire through an open mind to develop a belief in a life beyond science and what they are currently taught. We must not let apathy line the pockets of those who have a vested interest in our innocent ignorance by allowing the stripping of our planet; our home! As long as there's a market for precious unsustainable commodities they will continue to be plundered.

Earth is our 'home' and above all else we need her healthy and balanced to supply the oxygen we need to breathe. Without it we cannot live here. And that's not rocket science, but what is, is that our so-called 'space pioneers' have been unable as yet to find another planet as an alternative. Travel in space is no longer science fiction developed for our enjoyment; it is now real life viewing. Can there possibly be another planet like Earth that is so beautiful and perfect for us? Maybe, but we have a responsibility to Planet Earth – what so many refer to as Mother Earth – and the balance she must surely provide in the Universe.

We are occasionally shown the 'fight' by so-called 'eco warriors' who understand and care enough to protect Earth's natural beauty and her integrity – our heritage – but they are often discredited as anti-social and depicted by those with a vested interest as law breakers and trouble makers. Maybe a small proportion of them are, but not the vast majority who care; we all have to wake up to the simple fact that each and every one of us is a guardian of the Earth for our time here. We were passed the baton of care that has been passed since the beginning of time to pass on again; let us not let it crumble in our care.

Centre stage of Earth's physical destruction is our rain forests, which are often described as the heartbeat of our planet and often referred to as the 'lungs of the Earth' and yet they are being uprooted at a phenomenal rate and not replaced. I am no expert on global warming but you don't have to be to understand what an irreplaceable commodity for our survival the rain forests are; we are able to live on Earth as human beings only because of the rain forests, which produce the oxygen and other trace gases we need to breathe, so how long will it be before we will all need life support systems?

Will science keep up or will Earth be left in a position of no longer being able to support life as we know it? Will we have any alternative but to find another planet that will support us, and what if we don't? And even if we do, who will be the first to leave and colonise it? Rather than space travel unfolding as a fascinating challenge for our scientists to provide universal travel and recreational fun with the promise of universal riches, fortune and fame for the financiers, it will gradually take on the greater significance of necessity for our continued existence as we know it now. So who will be the first to go? I wonder, will it be you or your descendants, or will it be those who have the power and wealth which was created by the consumption of our homelands in the first place? Another irony!

We are in a vicious circle of dependency because we do not look at the bigger picture that synchronicity and our instincts are trying to show us. Of course there is an absolute need for a good and loving science used with good and honest intentions, but not a science that is manipulated and used to put profit before the well-being of our planet and her occupants.

Science is also used by those who seek to discredit beliefs such as mine by continually demanding absolute scientific proof. When none is forthcoming it is used to belittle what for me has become the most plausible and believable option in my search to discover the answers to 'who I am and why'. Just because I do not have a level of scientific proof of the possibilities of a loving god, higher power or other life force, and I do not exclusively believe in one religion or another, does not mean I should be belittled in my beliefs of an afterlife of some sort. After all, I do not hear science discrediting the beliefs of mainstream religions.

My beliefs have encouraged me to understand personal responsibility with a freedom of choice that supports my ability to think for myself without dogma and limitations. It would serve us all better if we could start to think slightly differently by not thinking exclusively like a human and a good start would be to take an alternative and more encompassing view that takes into account the unknown universe. If we don't take responsibility for ourselves it will be unlikely we will be able to take a responsibility for our home, planet Earth.

So what better place to start than our bodies? I have long considered my body to be a temple, not in a self-adoring way – although I have often wished I was an Adonis – but in a way that is considerate and respectful for the purpose it was originally designed and has since developed. I know that sounds obvious, but despite being bombarded by information to that effect, many choose to ignore it and then look for help to sort it out. My body is uniquely mine and I am the only one who can take full responsibility for its well-being. Without it functioning correctly, for whatever reason, I will have to adapt my living or, in the worst case scenario, prepare to stop living in this incarnation. I like being human because at this moment I know nothing else!

I haven't always thought like that, it has been a very gradual process and unfortunately in the past I have also been less than sensible in protecting and looking after my own body. Being around death and serious injury begins to focus your mind, but it's not just that either, maturing in other ways has played a part which didn't really start in earnest until I asked for help. It has been a slow process, but it's better late than never and never too late to start!

When I joined the Fire Brigade in 1975 it was considered by some to be tough and macho to go into smoke-filled areas without wearing the breathing apparatus that by then was available to protect the lungs from harm. As the new probationary fireman, the older and more experienced 'smiling' firefighters would enjoy taking me into what I considered heavily smoke-logged areas of fires, bursting with a pride that they were able to breathe comfortably as if it was some sort of badge of honour. I was being initiated into a unique club of foolishness as I coughed and choked while being reassured it was 'just good clean smoke'. Well of course it wasn't, then or now, because all smoke contains, amongst a host of other harmful particles, carbon monoxide, which is rightly labelled the silent killer.

Daily we are surrounded by newly-developed foods and recycled materials of all descriptions developed in laboratories; that has led us to become a 'disposable' society of dangerously toxic modern materials and we should be constantly cautious to protect our bodies from harm in ways that we are only now beginning to fully understand and many ways that we still don't.

Circa 1975, that was the sort of misinformed attitude that many of our manual workers were still regularly subjected to. The 'experienced' firefighters that taught me would have already served up to thirty hard and difficult years fighting fires and of course would have themselves been 'taught' in the same way when they began their own careers. It is obvious that in their earlier careers they would have had significantly less choice in protecting themselves and there were of course arguments at that time that smoke from the natural materials on fire was reasonably clean, but despite an advancement of safety knowledge many of them would still choose to pass on their early experiences of teachings and learnt behaviours as 'the only way' from the 'good old days'. Living in the past is comforting but limiting. Maybe in some way those behaviours were carried forward in the misguided belief that it reflected on how undoubtedly tough firefighting was for them in their earlier years and an indictment to their personal survival in a dangerous job; or maybe it was quite simply what I see in people all the time, a lack of desire, caused by a closed and limiting approach to change what had become their own way of thinking, which had to be the only way and the best way.

It is the same lack of desire to change our learnt behaviours and thinking that most of us take from our parents or other significant persons into adulthood without challenge. Unfortunately, it is a road with the potential to stifle free thinking and reinforces an unquestioning acceptance that someone else will do our thinking for us. That is not good for our own well-being and is not taking personal responsibility.

The introduction of health and safety regulations has rightly changed attitudes to protect a vulnerable workforce, and yet mental health, which is covered by the same regulations, seems to attract much less attention. While self-regulation was introduced to save bureaucracy and red tape for businesses, it has also helped to focus the minds of those it applies to by putting the emphasis back on personal responsibility and that can only be a good thing.

Although a certain amount of stress in life is said to be a good thing, too much can become destructive. That is where meditation and mindfulness can help. I was introduced to meditation on entering a spiritual environment and I have no doubt it has been one of the cornerstones of my increased self-awareness. It accesses the natural inner peace and calmness that lies within us all as our soul, waiting patiently to be 'woken up' and heard through our growing instincts to help with our busy lives and, in my case, complicated relationships. Although meditation is surprisingly called an 'alternative therapy', I call it essential and is not complicated at all, being no more than a quiet time to clear the mind of normal day-to-day chatter; it can be practised on your own, costing nothing but time, and is perfect for personal development.

Meditation was another of the jigsaw pieces that came to me at the right time when I needed it most (when the pupil is ready the teacher will appear)! Getting into it can take a while, so if you do try it, be patient and persevere. The reward for me was that feeling of peace and calm that allowed me to listen to myself and an inner guidance that I call 'accessing the soul'; others call it the 'higher self' or 'inner voice' but it matters not what you choose to call it, it can be the foundation of a balance and harmony within your life that will slowly build into an empire of understanding by unlocking another 'door of opportunity'.

Personal health and keeping our bodies nutritionally healthy is so important. I believe it to be at the very core of our general well-being, which promotes the powerhouse that everything else radiates from. With foods from around the world readily available and information on what our bodies need published in abundance you would think it is easy to be healthy, but it isn't and that is the truth of the matter. Our bodies are intricate, delicately-balanced vessels designed to support our journey of life. It has evolved and adapted over eons of time to our ever-changing planet and nature's foods. If we continue to feed it a balance of natural and preferably organic ingredients and water it has developed with, from choices such as meat, fish, vegetables, salads, fruits, nuts and seeds, it will function at its nutritional optimum. It's what I call 'cave man food', but it has been pushed into the background by scientifically-developed alternatives that have more to do with profit than good health. Good taste is not just what excites your taste buds, it is a choice between healthy eating and manufactured eating.

Our choices of modern foods and drinks are phenomenal, but many of them are developed to become addictive. Yes they are labelled, but who understands them except scientists and others with a vested interest. These so-called modern and contemporary foods are processed and designed for speed – fast foods – and convenience, taste and cost. They contain all sorts of fancy named additives which most of us do not understand. What we are eating is fuelling another battle within our bodies between a natural well-being and a continual fight to remove additives that are not good for us. You only have to look at the increase in food intolerances as an indicator that all is not well.

The food available to us now, especially the so-called fast foods, are not necessarily about good health but good business and profits. However, clever advertising and marketing will try to convince you otherwise. Unfortunately there is no 'user manual' for looking after your body so we have to use our common sense and look at ourselves with a critical and honest eye. Are we really healthy or are we being hoodwinked to believe that we are just because it's easier and convenient? Convenience often means can't be bothered and because everyone else does it, it must be ok. We face a bombardment of choices and are fed biased research and manipulated data to indicate we are eating healthily when all that is really healthy is the bank balance of producers whose purpose is profit at all cost, citing consumer choice as justification. For every report on the unhealthy side effects of processed food and drink there is a contrary one funded by manufacturers with vested interests to preserve their food chain of riches that hide the truth; the lobbyists hard at work once more. That's why I feel it's sensible to stick to the 'cave man' foods that are tried and tested as a lifestyle choice, with just the occasional foray into convenience foods for what it is, a treat of convenience that have been cleverly made to taste so good. Whilst I cannot deny their appeal, I prefer the sweet taste of being healthy more. I wish to preserve my temple for the purpose I have chosen it.

The world we live in is a rapidly changing and evolving one. We are regularly tempted by goods from around the world, which can be ordered online and delivered with astonishing speed. Whereas consumerism used to be more or less local, it is now global and I often wonder how that has affected the local environments of governments and businesses who look to maximise their opportunity for financial growth. Not just from tourism, but in the use of non-sustainable natural resources. Can we be surprised that they now choose to be in control of their own destiny when many of them have experienced years of exploitation from so-called developed nations who have plundered their resources in the name of development, aid and wealth? After all, they are hopefully trying their best, often with limited resources, to improve the quality of their own people's lives.

As technology advances we are increasingly able to recover and use both sustainable and non-sustainable resources, which are being consumed at what I believe to be an alarming rate. Whilst I understand the need for raw materials to promote growth for all nations, I see the notion that any part of planet Earth – either on or under the surface – being consumed as 'eating the hand that feeds us'. To make matters worse it seems so often to be the case that the wealth created and the damage caused is not necessarily used for the benefits of those peoples who live in the affected regions. The motivation instead is often, once again, for profit to satisfy the greed of individuals in governments who are in positions of influence and control. They turn a blind eye with a total disregard for the future of Earth and have comfort in not being alone in believing it to be someone else's problem. There is plenty of financial wealth created on our planet but there is also an equal amount of financial poverty, but whether financially rich or poor there is nothing better than having a clear conscience.

Maybe if we all thought about and considered the consequences of our personal actions it would change attitudes. If there is no market to sell in, the raw materials being consumed to facilitate our own comforts would be left intact. The trouble is it is so easy to pretend it is someone else's problem, but it is not, it is our problem. We are in it together because we share the planet together; it would be great to be able to trust all our global leaders to be responsible for their part of the planet, but will they?

There has to be a better, more balanced way of living for all mankind and that is why I believe in personal responsibility from us all. By doing everything we do with love would be a good start, but it would appear we are more in love with possessions and lavish lifestyles than finding out about our soul's purpose and how that fits in with life as human beings. Whether we have chosen our lives or not, we are destroying our home!

Let us not leave life to chance or compensation and retribution at our deaths.

40

The One, How Do We Know?

Having believed I had found 'the one' on so many occasions before, it would have been surprising had I thought that of Jane on our first meeting, and in any case, seeing life as being about the experience it now seems to me to be largely irrelevant. What I see as qualifying to be 'the one' is the inevitability that we will be together with whom we are supposed to be together with, either for a reason, a season or a life time, as we learn from our chosen experiences to inform, should it be necessary, our subconscious behaviours. The legacy of that search for 'true love' is in the hope for an inner peace and contentment that will fulfil our deepest and innermost desires and an acceptance that we will have no further need to search.

Whatever the experiences of our journey, whether we see them as being good, bad or indifferent, each one will eventually enrich us with its beauty, if not in this lifetime then in another and beyond. We should never give up on life, despite the bitterness and disappointments of dashed hopes in this world, because we will be repeatedly given the opportunity to flower and blossom again. Disappointments, if we can know where and how to look, can show us something of ourselves and will feed our souls as the building blocks of who we hope to become, and by renewing the possibilities of finding the true love within, we can rekindle the light of possibilities for a journey well-chosen in our search for the one.

I see our search for the true love within us all as the longing for a reunification with our missing piece that is held by God through a link to our soul; not a god that seeks qualification through rituals or false promises, but a god who is guardian of our soul and loves us and nurtures us unconditionally through the experience of finding our real selves. And by learning through living, and according to the choices chosen and tailored by our soul before conception, the human purpose will have been fulfilled, as mine has by a knowing that has made me feel whole again.

It was in trying to understand the mysterious veil that is said to divide the physical world of being human and the esoteric world of being spiritual, that I have realised that being a successful human is not just for a select club or a fortunate few, but a world that exists to help us all to see through the so-called shroud that hides the duality of being human and spiritual as a way of finding we have a missing piece. It was within my understanding of how that fits into my own journey that my purpose has been found, but I also understand that it is not necessarily the journey of others, for whom being human alone is enough.

That Jane Five has been found within my search to love myself is not a miracle, but a testament to not giving up, and that was only made possible by understanding and accepting, without solid proof, my journey through the eyes of a spiritual world that dovetails perfectly with my understanding of our human world that I live every minute of every day; one indispensable to the other as a crucial element of my success. Accordingly, Jane has become the one, above all the other Janes, including my first wife who believed that one day someone would 'get the best of me'. And only now, having found the route to my true self and the human love I was missing through a spiritual dimension, have I understood what she meant!

My journey through life is epitomised through the microcosm of my Camino pilgrimage, which changed me by encouraging my growth through the test of simplistic living that demanded I be stripped of all the pretences my subconscious mind had masked and hidden. Jane knew all my history because I had always been honest with her in all our healing sessions together and she became tolerant of me because she knew me, which meant we had a chance to grow together, despite many of her friends warning her off of me as a 'womaniser' but she knew me better than that and trusted me and herself.

Maybe that, alongside the timing and me being readied by my new knowledge and understanding, is also an indicator that she had always been the *'right one'*. Would we have been ok and ready for a relationship together if she had been morally free and not married when we first met? Possibly, but the fact of the matter was that she was in a relationship and thus not available, and as I had begun to learn to trust life and what it places in front of me, it was not meant to be, then. After all, I had learnt the hard way that getting involved in a relationship, when I was not morally free to do so, will cause an increase in the inevitable turmoil of emotions. There is no doubt that I could have done things better in that regard and had I done so it would almost certainly lessened the damage and harm caused. Many people, while accepting I could have done things better, will also insist my actions were wrong, but can anything per se ever really be wrong in life when it is believed to be chosen and part of a bigger picture yet to be seen? Certainly I was a weak-minded person, not fully 'matured' and weakened further by alcohol, which gave me a false confidence to mask my shortcomings. And maybe my life has been full of all these things, being weak, doing the wrong things, making poor decisions, but they are words not experiences that have been lived through! Words have everything to do with being human, but less to do with our spiritual experiences.

If I am to believe, which I do, that we choose our life circumstance specifically to learn from then I could argue that my children must have chosen me as a parent specifically to experience exactly what they had experienced and for that to happen as it did, then I had to meet someone at a time when I was not morally free to do so to help create that experience.

Were my actions wrong or were they meant to be? Have I

allowed my spiritual beliefs to fit my actions to ease my guilt? Maybe, possibly, but who knows for sure? Should I ditch a belief that in all other regards has enlightened me and fulfilled me? Surely it is a good thing to believe in something that has been the prime mover in removing the victim mode that I was undoubtedly stuck in and allowed my life to blossom, or would it have anyway?

Ah yes, many of you will say, your life may be blossoming, but what of your ex-wife and your children, are theirs? Well yes, I believe theirs have, but it is not for me to say or judge, or anyone else's for that matter other than themselves, although we all surely will! Let us all strive to be arbitrators of our own lives and not seek justification of it through the lives of others!

I left my wife for all the supposedly 'wrong reasons' and I accept that and, despite my beliefs, I would change it if I could. But I can't and even if I could where would I be now? What else would have been the catalyst for the change I desperately needed, when I didn't have the courage to leave my children who I loved unconditionally; would I have suddenly found some courage or our relationship miraculously improved?

I have thought long and hard about my beliefs that I have chosen my life as it is, and the alternative that it was not; but if it has not been chosen then how would it work? Were my parents randomly allocated as the next available in a queue as my soul waited to join with a baby already conceived? Do you even believe we have a soul?

Let's take the second possibility first; there was no choice and I was conceived randomly.

My father happened to be a factory worker at that time and my mother already had one son. I was born at home in the south west of England where they lived. My conception may or may not have been planned, but as I had no choice in it, the timing of my birth must have been coincidental and I happened to be born in late

December 1949, four years after the finish of the Second World War. This meant I was born under the astrological star sign of Capricorn and not *'on the cusp'*. Some people believe that your star sign has a bearing on our personality, but whether it has or not, it is only relevant in this scenario because it was chance and not chosen. I was born as a boy because of the way the fertility process played out. I happened to be white because my parents were white and my height and looks were mostly dependent on the genes of my parents and their families as are many, if not all, of my other traits.

Had I been born, by chance, in another country at another time I would have been completely different with totally different circumstances. Would I be the same person I am today, sitting here writing this? No. As it is, my life has been ok and I could say I am who I was randomly born to be. Of course my mother and father would also have been randomly born, and in their case in an era and a society that believed it was not a good thing to be too soft or loving with children. That and the hardships and emotional turmoil of living through a war shaped them as parents. Not surprisingly, they didn't seem or feel particularly loving, although my brothers do not feel the same way. Despite all that, my parents were good-intentioned hard-working people with good honest values. Had I by chance been born to parents who were more outwardly loving with easier personal circumstances I would surely not have struggled with a lack of self-worth and been more confident, but I will never know because there are so many permutations that decide our fate. So basically my parents and their circumstances have helped to make me who I am today and I have just got on with it.

With this possibility I cannot see a purpose to life other than the experience of surviving and living life as best you can while trying to be whatever you deem to be 'successful', but that doesn't stop any of us from trying to understand it and seeing our lives as lucky, unlucky or just how it is.

The other possibility is that I did specifically choose my life for a specific purpose and to achieve that purpose I had chosen my father and mother carefully. My father was chosen as a hard-working factory worker with a solid, if undemonstrative, attitude to life with a charisma that made him extremely popular, a real man's man. My mother had already delivered one son and, although she didn't know it, would have two more, something I did know because I was to be the next. She was a hard-working ex-silver service cook who married and became a housewife who was neither demonstrative nor obviously outwardly loving; her husband had clear boundaries set for their relationship and mostly left the care and upbringing of the children to her, the cave man model! I was born a boy at the family home in the south west of England because that suited the journey of life I wanted to experience; there were other choices available, but this is the one I chose. The timing of my birth in late December 1949, four years after the finish of the Second World War, meant I was born under the astrological star sign of Capricorn and not *on the cusp'*, which suited my personality needs perfectly. My mother would become unwell with post-natal depression after my birth, which would be left untreated and compounded by a husband who would give little, if any, help. He would have a *'just get on with it'* attitude *'while I go out and hunt, gather food and party'*. As a result my mother would be unable to bond with me, which suited my need to be and feel unloved perfectly.

All that was chosen and my life has worked out perfectly; you could say 'I am exactly who I was born to be'.

As I chose all this carefully and left nothing to chance the experience has been exactly as I wanted it to be. Had I chosen differently I would be completely different to the person sitting here writing this now, but I am not and so this must be one of my purposes. I have come to see that my life is not just about surviving but embracing all aspects of it, good or bad, happy or sad, whilst loving myself and everything I am, as much as I can.

I have tried to understand my life and this scenario is the only one that makes real sense of my life.

Whether purpose and success in life matters is dependent on how you understand why and how your life is playing out. But whatever you believe, it doesn't take away the harshness and the beauty of where your choices and decisions have led you. Purpose matters to me because it has helped me to remove the attitude of being the victim and that has been crucial in my search for happiness and fulfilment. I see my life as successful simply because I see it as part of a greater purpose that I have been helped to achieve by something or somebody across the veil of an alternative world, which means it must also be part of the purpose.

41

Making the Change

I remember very little of my life through childhood up to my early teenage years, and my perception up to the age of fifty remained one of being lost, unhappy and unfulfilled with a propensity to be sad; although that has lessened in the last fifteen years it still lurks somewhere within. If I had to sum up my life experiences I would say that the love I was searching for was beyond my capabilities and I was not normal. My younger brother told me recently that he and my older brother had concluded many years earlier that what I was looking for in a woman did not exist. Although I don't feel it would have changed anything had they told me, I have often wondered why they didn't; saying it now gives me the opportunity to say that she does exist and always did as we waited for each other by getting on with our lives and, in my case, learning to love myself.

At the time they were right of course, because I was incapable of being, or having, the 'perfect' partner. There were many reasons why, but they all had one thing in common, my so-called 'inner child', the little boy in me who was still in control and anchoring me in immaturity, although maturity is another word I have come to struggle with when applied to our human lives; can we ever have *full development* or have *perfected condition*? How does that equate to a human being learning about the self on a continuous journey of development?

Of course there are many who would not see my life, or I assume any life, as a journey for development specifically chosen. They will rightly have opinions based on their own lives and have no need to search for such answers, while others see life in snap shots of human time rather than from a journey driven by a spiritual dimension of which our human journey is just a part. I was a snap shot person, unable to see anything but my immediate circumstances until the night I cried for help. It was to be quite some time before I realised someone or something must have been listening and had already responded to what I had come to consider as a lack in me by manoeuvring me into position for the personal growth I so badly needed.

I found myself in a spiritual environment where everything was different, not weird as so many see it, not religious – unless you want it to be – just different. I made new friends and heard of a world I didn't know existed, but a world where I began to grow from a combination of ideas that interested and engaged me like nothing had before. Where the Fire Brigade had been a challenge I knew I had to overcome, this was as a welcoming and warming embrace that didn't feel like an invitation to learn about myself through the ethos of spirituality, but that's what it was.

I learnt how to meditate and about healing, primarily for the self, but for others as well. I was introduced to the concept of personal responsibility and free will and, most importantly for me, despite the fact it had never bothered me before, I began to see death in a very different way. There was of course much more, each a piece of a jigsaw that combined to reveal the possibilities of a bigger picture for a life that had given me so much but so little. What I heard fascinated me but I did not become obsessive as I have seen so many become. The answers to my seemingly shambolic life were delivered in an easy and relaxed way that had been so easy to miss and did for quite some time, but as the momentum of my new way gathered pace, so did my awareness and it gradually integrated into my way of life as my new normal, and as it did so my default position of retreating back to the comfort and familiarity of old ways lessoned in increments equal to the gains to make room.

One of my biggest lessons has been that real and lasting change takes time and a lot of patience, something that I was not good at despite being continually encouraged to achieve almost from my first day in the spiritual environment and mostly ignored.

When I was much further down the road of my new spiritually-aware journey I began to consider whether there had been a 'light bulb moment' when I made the connection that I had been helped, but if there was such a moment I do not recall it as such and I am sure that something that was so momentous would have been at the forefront of my mind. That time is best described as the turning of a dimmer switch that had gradually released me from the darkness of my inherited and honest ignorance by illuminating the way forward on a very different road to the one previously travelled. It was my way rather than the way of others as I learnt to be my own person and, although I never felt like a pioneer, I can see now that in the sense that I felt I had discovered something for and about myself, I probably was.

Had I the understanding to be able to look closely at the events of that time I would have discovered something powerful going on beneath the surface of my shallow and safe life, but at that point I had no need to understand about things that are meant to be and delivered through coincidence by a god who, according to Einstein, was helping while remaining anonymous; understanding that beautiful analogy would be for another day and when I was ready. Being ready means that everything will happen in the fullness of time if it's meant to and we can be patient enough; if we rush life we can leave gaps in the very foundations needed to build a stable but different future, a future which must be better served by the integration of the new with the old ways that are still valued, and can cause instabilities in your life as you wobble around the axis of uncertainty when they are not.

Starting from scratch can never be an option – not for me anyway. How can it be possible to leave behind fifty years of a life shaped by learnt behaviours, whether they were considered appropriate or not, especially when some of it was considered highly successful? And what about the experience of the change itself, something which I believe is as important for the journey as the destination! The simple answer is that parts of our lives cannot be erased like a mistake in a manuscript, and if you think about it, why would you want to? Each part of it has made us who we are and is part of our story, whether we were knowingly or unknowingly aware of our so-called 'imperfections' or not. If we can accept and be proud that we have chosen our journey for the experience we can also be proud that we have survived it and can change it if we are supposed to. My chosen journey had revealed, what I would call late in life, why it had seemed so chaotic and gave me the encouragement and belief that I could make the changes I so desperately needed through understanding. One of those fundamental changes was the belief that my childhood had been an unhappy one, when in fact it had been proved otherwise by my childish drawing of them under the guidance of one of my counselling tutors. That they were real and honest memories was not in doubt but if I needed proof it would have come in the fact that they had secretly informed my own happy times as a parent, teaching and playing with my own children. But the most fundamental change over all else was in the understanding that my life had been secretly shaped by a lack of self-worth, and thus a lacking in love and the desperate search that ensued from it, a job made even harder by the negative outlook on life that came with it. That I could change the message and become more positive was a revelation to me as I began to rebuild my life.

Those were the things that my change was born from and I began to take personal responsibility. Through these realisations I was gradually able to stop blaming my wife, and eventually my childhood, and begin to take personal responsibility. I was able to understand that no matter how much my wife and I had battled there was so much good that had come from our marriage. We had made a family together and built a beautiful home; she had given me tremendous support and encouragement when I decided to change careers; I was introduced to the wonders and freedom of family camping holidays and was eventually thankful for her insistence on being re-introduced to nature through family walks in the woods that had once been my childhood playground, but abandoned as a teenager in favour of alcohol. She was one of my greatest teachers in life as I moved out of primary education into the University of Life.

I also recognised how and why I had learnt to be a good parent and less successfully how to be a husband and that my shortcomings were nobody's fault; they were chosen to fulfil my life experience and I believed they could and would be overcome. And they have been, almost!

If you, like me, are searching for answers in your life and you are puzzled by many of your decisions that seem to continually end in disaster or have failed in some way, despite the hope and optimism of relationships that you thought came with feelings of true love, then issues of self-worth will almost certainly be playing a part.

Whilst at that time I understood and accepted my lack of self-worth, it would not be the immediate saviour I had hoped for – if only life were that simple! The immense power and subtle sway that my lack of self-worth held over my actions and reactions have been so hard to change; it's a bit like changing the direction of a huge ocean-going ship from full speed that frustratingly takes time. I am still surprised even now by the ways in which my lacking in worth has prevented me from being able to love myself fully and I have had to be very patient, while changing direction towards the perfection I have demanded from myself, as the process of becoming real has taken so much longer than I expected.

They say patience is a virtue and it is one that I took a long time to learn. What helped was the understanding that, having asked for help, I was receiving it and so long as I continued to be encouraged by what I saw as a growth in my personal confidence, I would stay on the journey that was directing me steadily forward on the change of direction, no matter how long it would take. What helped was the pledge to myself, that having left my wife for another woman, I would honour that decision by never accepting second best in a relationship, and in doing so I hoped it would go some way towards helping me to justify the regrettable way I had gone about it.

One of the most important aspects of my new life in a spiritually-aware community, where people of all faiths gathered, were the free and open discussions and not being preached at or given subtle ultimatums in the form of threats to my future well-being if I did not conform to a particular set way of beliefs. I felt free to explore by being myself to find myself, whoever I was. The fragile belief in Christianity I had inherited from my parents had neither been adopted with enthusiasm nor challenged in a meaningful way and my intention was not to *throw the baby out with the bath water*, but to try to make sense of my limited teachings and understanding to see if they had any relevance to my new beliefs. What I learnt was that each of our many and varied beliefs are as valid as another's for reasons that are as personal as mine. But what I wanted to know above all else was whether there was a purpose to our lives other than surviving and what, if anything, it had to do with a spiritual and soul purpose, something that Christianity had failed to answer.

The answer of course was in part to be found in linking what I had taken from Transactional Analysis in counselling to my new spiritual beliefs of lives that are chosen and in some way continuous. But that was also throwing up questions of whether, having chosen a life for a purpose, it was ever possible to be right or wrong when making decisions from the honest ignorance of the learnt behaviours chosen from our early lives (I will not kid myself and pretend I was not also looking for answers to make myself feel better and exonerate myself from the regret of leaving my wife).

Being lucky or unlucky was something else I began to question. Could trying to become real, from circumstances that I believed were chosen purposely to shape my human journey of experiences as opportunities to discover who I could become, ever be considered as lucky or unlucky, or is it all meant to be as part of a purposeful journey? Should each of our unique lives at any time on our journeys ever be examined as having been passed or failed and given grades to compare with those of others? And, if yes, how could we even begin to measure our lives as being passed or failed, or successful or not? Surely, I thought, we are born as apprentices to our individual lives on different journeys, so how can we possibly measure or compare our lives to that of others unless we are all here to experience the same opportunities.

As I see it, the only common theme for learning, and with it its greater purpose, is in being human on Earth with the purpose of the enlightenment of our souls. And yet every one of us judges and arbitrates on others as being successful or failing, a vocation for which we are clearly not qualified, but we do anyway as we try to justify our own being. Can anyone on Earth really know what is right or wrong, whether we have passed or failed, whether we are perfect or imperfect or better or worse than others? And yet that's what we all try to do, at least I did, sometimes knowingly, sometimes not, because we are human, with frailties, and we have to survive as we strive to find our place in life and how we fit and compare to the lives of others. But the only way we can do that is to know as best as we can who we are, and that will inevitably take time through change as we move our lives forwards in alternative directions.

I understand now that unless I can learn to forgive, and thus live with myself and the decisions I have made, especially those that I am particularly ashamed of, I will spend the rest of my life looking back, which is not a useful way of moving forward or encouraging growth unless it is to understand and learn; and because of that I am trying hard to forgive myself as an imperfect human trying to perfect my being, and while that doesn't make me feel any better about the hurt I have caused, it has at least released me from spending much of my time wallowing in guilt, and instead has motivated me to try to understand why I made those decisions in the first place, when it was never my intention to hurt anyone; and I am at least proud of that.

It is a fact that many of my decisions were made for what seemed to be the right reasons, but to others would be seen as wrong.

One of those occasions came about when I met a beautiful Irish lady and we spent months crossing the Irish Sea to spend time together whenever we could. Our relationship made my unexplainable love affair with Ireland and everything Irish like a dream come true, but try as I might the love affair with her and Ireland was just that and I couldn't love her in the way that fulfilled my deepest desires for the best, and by default hers. But that didn't stop me from trying, and delaying, for months what I knew to be the right decision as I convinced myself that I had to be sure to avoid going down the same road of emotional upset and feeling like a failure again. I was of course kidding myself and putting off the inevitable, just as I had done so many other times in my life with many other relationships. I knew what I had to do, I always did, but when life is about love, or the search for it, it can never be black or white, especially when the decision is based on a need rather than a desire. To have continued would have devalued everything that I had become and strived for as being true to myself and indirectly to her, but it was easy to convince myself that to give up too early would show a lack of effort. In the end my procrastinations meant I held on for far too long and in doing so gave the impression that all was well when it was not. I have come to know that being true to ourselves is not quite as simple as it seems, as we can only be true to whom we are at the time, and that, in a process of continuous development, changes as we grow. My Irish dream was just that as I eventually let go of the need for love so that I could start the search again! No doubt I have been judged for that too.

During that particular time of introspection it occurred to me that I had drifted through most of my life playing the cards I had been dealt without skill or understanding and believing them to be a full house, but of course they weren't and were never intended to be. That doesn't mean that they didn't matter, but it's why they did.

Just because I now see the way of my life very differently and for a specific reason does not mean that I cannot be terribly disappointed that I could not have been properly in love from the very beginning and saved all those missing years of searching, because I am.

It's hard to imagine any life as 'meant to be', especially mine, having caused so much heartache and pain, to myself and to others. All I can hope for is that they – those who entrusted their hopes to me – are now as content, happy and fulfilled as I have become and that their painful emotional memories have been removed and accepted as they are meant to be; although not knowing whether they are or not will, I feel, leave me with some level of guilt for blaming them for my inadequacies, be it intentional or not.

The day I realised I was the common denominator in all my disasters and vowed to stop blaming others was a momentous day on my journey, but it didn't stop me from feeling and being thought of as a heartbreaker, and it didn't help that my own had also been broken so many times.

I have learnt so much about myself and others on what has become my new way, but I know there is still so much more to learn and understand through the experiences to come.

42

Having Soul?

The cards I held for my marriage were never going to be a winning hand when I was so incomplete and a work in progress. My two wonderful children had shown me that I could love, but in doing so stretched the distance between me and their mother – my wife – until I stacked them in for new ones; only to stack them in as well when I realised love was not lust.

That one decision, to leave my wife for another woman, whether it was a mistake or not, had effectively torn my family apart and would change many lives as I tried unsuccessfully to integrate my 'Saturday access only' children into a new family; it was almost inevitable that it wouldn't work and, once I had made the decision to leave 'the other woman' and be on my own, it felt like a ton weight had been lifted from my shoulders. At that point, and with hindsight, it would have been wise to stay on my own where I seemed to be happiest, but being sensible was something I was not good at then, and within months I had succumbed to what I can see now as an unstoppable force to find love – hindsight of course is a wonderful thing, but it has no part to play in a true assessment of our learning years, or for apportioning blame to decisions that were made from an honest ignorance and with the best of intentions.

My search for true love was inevitably rewarded, it always was, with a succession of girlfriends who came and went with varying degrees of disappointments and self-recrimination. Hardly surprising then, now that I have come to see my life as meant to be, that the pattern would remain the same for all but twenty years – although there was the one exception sandwiched in-between with Dawn who also had two children, albeit much younger than mine, that after an on-off start would last for six years of uncertainty. I was an absolute nightmare to live with and seemingly powerless to be happy. When I finally found the courage to walk away to be on my own the relief and happiness was almost palpable, until three months later when a friend told me he had seen her out and about with friends *'looking more radiant than ever and the life and soul of the party'*. Instantly I became consumed by jealousy and did everything to win her back, and did... eventually, but on her terms. I knew I was jealous but not why, and I was too ashamed to fail again so I reverted to type and convinced myself that everything would be ok. But I needn't have worried because the decision was made for me when, within weeks of moving into our new house, she dumped me and walked away for good; the first time in my life I had ever been dumped. In a matter of months I had gone from liberty to jealousy and from confusion into despair. I guess that was inevitable too.

Dawn was a beautiful lady inside and out, but that hadn't stopped me from continually judging her as not being good enough and, as all those we have the closest of relationships with are, she became another of my greatest teachers by shining a torch on my inadequacies and lighting a new way ahead. I believe our relationship was a karmic relationship, as so many – if not all – surely must be, and thus unavoidable as agreed between two souls as either compensation for actions in previous lives, or simply as soulmates agreeing to help each other in this one. (Many years later again I was to have another, similarly puzzling relationship – that was so out of character even for me – that I would come to see as 'repaying a debt' from a previous incarnation(s) through karma.)

What all this has shown me is that my apparently crazy life, often seen without direction, is in fact a life where I haven't been drifting quite as rudderless as I might have imagined, and my direction, although pre-planned, has been fine-tuned by some sort of life force to keep me on track. Mostly I have become happy to accept that the force must have something to do with an afterlife –

simply because I cannot imagine what else it could be – and although I questioned God, when at one of the lowest points in life, I have never dismissed the possibility that I have a god who is helping me.

It is through my spiritual awakening that I have come to realise that there are many ways to God and that God is personal to us all. Many people, including myself, believe we have a god who 'lives' within us, in what I have come to see as my 'inner temple'. I have also come to believe that my god must have workers who come in many forms, some recognisable, others not. Some of them are given a measure of authenticity because they have been drawn and described by the many who 'see' them; they include ascended masters – of whom Jesus is said to be one; archangels – such as Gabriel and Rafael; Angels – I regularly ask the parking angel for help and there are many others, all waiting to help us; fairies and elementals – who live in nature and help us to be calm and at peace; and other spirits who may or may not be our spirit guides. All of these are said to be available to help and guide us in one way or another, but I also believe that there must be many others who remain anonymous. They are often called aliens or light beings, and the thought of aliens in particular has, wrongly so far as I'm concerned, taken on a sinister meaning that is born from a fear of the unknown and the product of wild imaginations.

Whilst giving names and being able to imagine our helpers from the afterlife makes them easier to accept, it doesn't help to establish whether they have ever been to Earth to live a human incarnation or indeed they exist outside the power of belief at all. For example, I have heard the expression 'Earth Angel' used often, and once it was even inexplicably applied to me, and although I was flattered at the time I could not see how I could be with the state of my life at that time; I was more likely to be a lost angel! Now I look at it differently, and although I am still not certain, I am less uncertain than before; having said that I would never compare myself to the many humans who, so far as I'm concerned, qualify easily as Earth Angels, having chosen journeys with incredible stories of sacrifice and dedication to helping others.

What I do know is that the indigenous peoples, and us as their descendants, have or will one day pass away to the afterlife where I believe they will 'live' in the spirit of who they were as humans in some form or other. They will remain recognisable in our thoughts and imaginations to become acceptable as our 'spirit guides', especially by those who believe in the continuation of life. Although I have never seen him I have had described to me on more than one occasion a spirit guide who works to support me called Running Bear who lived an incarnation as a Native American Indian with the Blackfeet tribe in North America and Canada. He, so I have been told, is in fact my 'doorkeeper', a description of a spirit guide who stays with us for our entire incarnation, rather than one who comes and goes to help at specific times. Whether Running Bear is an angel, archangel or an ascended master as well as my spirit guide or doorkeeper, I have no idea, but does it even matter anyway so long as I believe he is helping me at the level I require? To believe in Running Bear means I must believe we will all become spirit guides or angels etc. in the afterlife.

Whilst I believe we, as humans and clairvoyants in particular, are communicating with the afterlife through the energies of those who have 'passed away', and we are 'shown' images that are representative of the images we are familiar with, there must be many who we cannot be familiar with that are also communicating with us, and that is why I see the afterlife as having the possibilities to be so much more, or less, and completely different to what we have come to believe in through the work of others.

So who is God and what role does God play in our lives? Many people would see my experiences, especially since asking for help, as finding God and that God has been helping me from the very beginning. Whilst I have no real argument with that I still have the desire to search for my own truth and do not yet have the absolute faith that will allow me to accept a god, rather than my god, without question – despite my love for Einstein's assertion that *'coincidence is God's way of remaining anonymous'*, something that fits beautifully with my belief that I have been helped from the beginning of my life and that everything is meant to be.

Almost inevitably, while investigating the afterlife within the limits of my capabilities, what I have found is more questions than answers and whilst my beliefs are biased towards what I can be satisfied with in my own mind, either from the anecdotal evidence gained from my own experiences or from that of others, I have gained some faith and belief in each of us having a soul that links us on a permanent basis to the spirit of us on Earth and in the afterlife. However, the reality of having a soul poses as many questions about authenticity and proof as there are for the existence of a god with helpers, because in whatever form our soul takes, it too remains equally as anonymous and uncertain as Einstein's god.

Soul means something different to everyone and is very often accepted into our lives without too much thought or questioning, despite being unrecognisable, and I have been no different in that respect, but as my curiosity has developed so has my desire to understand where within me my soul, or god for that matter, could reside. And how and why in practical terms it connects me to the afterlife.

I have come to believe that we all have a soul that is part of our lives in some way. I do not prescribe to the thought that some of us can be 'soulless' or that we can 'have soul' just because of the way we sing; for me there is more credibility in being described as being young or old souls.

In a similar way I also believe in karma as part of our lives because karma, like soul, is a part of us as humans that cannot be seen or touched. Karma is said to be our *'destiny as determined by our actions in a previous life'* and *'a force for good and bad'* – although I prefer to say not so good rather than bad. Our bodies are also said to have an aura – *'a subtly and pervasive quality or atmosphere seen as emanating from a person, place or thing'* and many people say they can see it around the body, which I presume gives rise to the statement often used that someone has a 'good feel' or a 'nice energy' around them. Whilst there have been times when I have 'seen' a white or glimmering glow around and close to the body's edge, I am, unfortunately, not one of those significant others who can claim to see auras as a vibrant and living energy with the naked eye. What I have seen is photographs of the body taken with a special 'Kirlian camera' that seems to show a rainbow of colours emanating from the human body; in fact I have such a photograph of my own. I see this multi-coloured pervasive quality or atmosphere as energy and that it offers the perfect opportunity to be the home for the energy of our soul, which is defined as *'the principle of life, feeling, thought and actions in humans, regarded as a distinct entity separate from the body, and commonly held to be separable in existence from the body; the spiritual part of humans as distinct from the physical part'*, a description that is in parts not unlike that of the aura.

My spiritual 'education' has often included discussions on centres of energy within our human body; indeed there are many therapists, and so-called 'alternative therapists', who work with them to heal the mind, body and spirit of us. I have been taught that there are seven major energy centres – called chakras – each of which is linked to a specific colour, and my Kirlian photograph seems to confirm that. They are:

Purple for the crown chakra on top of the head;

Indigo for the third eye or brow chakra;

Blue the throat;

Green the heart;

Yellow the solar plexus;

Orange the sacral;

Red for the root, or base, chakra at the base of the spine.

I believe these colours are representative of both our physical and emotional state as a snapshot of our well-being at the time they are photographed and will constantly change as our feelings change. The use of colours as a healing medium, by what I believe to be a transfer of energy between the client, the healer and the afterlife, can dramatically increase our well-being when we become out of balance and ill at ease – disease – through lifestyles that often take no account of the ethereal body as part of who we are.

Whether it is true that our soul exists as energy within and possibly around our body as part of our lives to communicate and link us with the afterlife remains, as yet, unprovable outside of my own belief. But if it does it asks questions about its purpose and how much influence it has on our human journeys. Does it influence the whole journey, just significant parts or none, either of which must presumably be decided upon before incarnating to Earth? And, depending on the answer, how does having a soul that can influence our decision-making process fit into the idea that we, as humans, have 'free will' – *'the power of acting without the constraint of necessity or fate; the ability to act at one's own discretion'*?

The answer is that we don't know, or at least I don't know, and because of that it leaves us once again to speculate and guess within the parameters that our own beliefs will allow. Of course, it is a fact that no matter how much sense our individual beliefs make they will remain as assumptions, speculations and best guesses based on a human way of thinking that may be as far away from the truth as it is possible to be. The only shred of evidence that even supports the practicalities of us having a soul is an experiment I have heard about when the body of a human in the latter stages of dying was weighed, and then weighed again immediately after death, when there was said to be a measurable loss.

My best guess, and thus my belief, is that we do indeed have a soul, which may or may not live as or within our aura, and may or may not have some level of influence over our human lives, having chosen us as a specific and suitable human to experience an incarnation on Earth as a great way to learn.

Should it be that my soul has chosen me because of the suitability of my circumstances around the time of my creation, i.e. parents, location and era, surely this only becomes possible through an understanding and acceptance that time, as we know it on Earth, does not apply in the afterlife. Simply because that is what will enable the soul in the afterlife to see some, or all, of the human life it is considering before making a decision to join or not to join; and if not to join then to choose another human that will better fulfil its expectations for an onward enlightenment and ascension from the experiences of the chosen human as its 'taxi'.

Whilst that still doesn't help us to understand how much influence, or none, the soul has once it has chosen to be incarnated and 'crossed over' the veil from the afterlife to join with its chosen human for the start the journey, by accepting that we have been chosen surely must give purpose to our lives, even if it is for the ultimate purpose of the soul's benefit of further enlightenment and ascension.

By accepting we, my soul and I, have a common purpose and a relationship I have to explore the extent and boundaries of it. In other words, what part do I play with my soul or what part does my soul play with me? Who am I? Am I the significant part or is that the role of my soul?

If I am a human without a soul, then my human life is my responsibility alone and at my death the only onward responsibility is what I have come to believe in at the time of my passing.

If I do have a soul, which has no responsibility other than choosing me and my life, then the soul will have a truly unique and pure experience of being human with no controls over the outcomes of its choices after incarnating. That, as we know, can leave its chosen human to its own devices in making either catastrophic or inspirational choices, or anything in-between – and will become a truly free-will experience; my human life will be my responsibility alone for the experience of the soul and at my death the only onward responsibility is for whatever I have come to believe in at the time of my passing.

A second option, with the soul and I having part responsibility, offers the same opportunities, but with a tailored free-will human experience achieved by assuming some level of control over me, its human taxi, by steering our journey together only over certain parts, that may not necessarily be considered crucial, but if they are will, I believe, become what I identify as crossroads.

Another option would be for the soul to have full responsibility and control, which would surely lead to the soul avoiding many of the very crucial and significant circumstances that were chosen to learn from in the first place and would thus not be a free-will experience in any form. For that reason I do not feel it is a viable option.

Whatever the role of our soul is, and from wherever it is achieved, I would still expect it to have a full awareness of the human experience, even if it cannot feel the emotions and live the dilemmas associated with it.

I was first introduced to the idea that we, as humans, have free will long after I began to knowingly take personal responsibility. There is no doubt that the notion of having free will further encouraged me to be responsible for my own decisions and their outcomes and I don't believe that will ever change. But with my growing belief that we have a soul that connects us to the afterlife, I began to wonder whether we can ever truly have free will as indicated by *'the power of acting without the constraint of necessity or fate...'* fate meaning *'the development of events outside a person's control'*, when we have a soul or some other mechanism that may have the ability to guide us at certain stages.

I imagine there are many of you who, while agreeing that we, as humans, have free will in our life, would argue that it must extend to the whole journey and not just specific parts and that's how it may be. If it is then that would mean that our soul is a silent and inactive partner and just along for the ride and the experience of being human is gained from awareness alone. The trouble with that is that it would also throw into doubt how karma, created in another life or incarnation, could be played out in this lifetime, because by definition it has to be something that can be experienced and neutralised in either this incarnation or another, or across many others, which surely means there has to be an element of our lives being pre-planned, especially so when, as many believe, it is played out with other souls from within or close to the same soul groups. It is of course also entirely possible that the circumstances of the human life chosen has been specifically chosen to encompass any karma that needs to be repaid, good or bad, and that the soul who has made those choices will have made them through an awareness, and/or an agreement, in conjunction with other souls who will be incarnating at or around the same time.

I believe in karma and having a soul and that our aura has the potential for being the home of our soul. I also believe that we, as humans, are utilised as a means to an end for the benefit of the soul's experience on Earth for its onward enlightenment at the time of our passing, and our role as the human in the relationship is irrelevant other than having the perfect circumstances of conception to suit the soul's purpose. What I call karmic relationships, where I have acted completely out of character from what I would have ordinarily considered to be my normal behaviour, strengthens my feeling that my soul, or some other life force, must have some sort of influence over my life over and above what I would have expected as a human living its life in accordance with my life script, written from the circumstances of my conception. In other words, our lives are meant to be how they are and not just down to chance.

Whilst I value everyone's personal opinion and concede my beliefs could be off track, I cannot convince myself that life's opportunity to learn could be so random as to be not chosen or indeed dependent on chance, unless of course it is specifically chosen to be so for the specific purpose of the incarnation.

If we are to save this beautiful world we live in from destruction, surely we have to have the ability to recognise our behaviours are contributing to it on some level. In order to change the world we have to change and raise our levels of consciousness through the awareness of a bigger picture, and I believe that is achieved in partnership with our soul's consciousness, which means our soul has to have some influence over our personal development as humans on a journey together.

I have considered the pros and cons long and hard and my thoughts always come back to the central question: Do we have a purpose here on Earth other than that of experiencing the random nature of our circumstances and their outcomes?

The life of Jesus, as a human being with a very advanced soul, and thus special, has never been emulated in its loving intent and influence, and adds perfect food for thought in the pros and cons of being on Earth as a human being with a purpose. If Jesus, as a human, had a very special purpose, which in my understanding was to raise the human consciousness – the Christ consciousness – then surely as fellow human beings we all have a purpose.

I believe that in the earliest days of my life in partnership with my soul, our circumstances would have been chosen to enable my human learnt behaviour to fashion our journey as planned with a relatively light touch to ensure it plays out as planned through my life script. Despite my poor start at school it has never held me back. I obtained a carpentry apprenticeship that has stood me in good stead all my life and similarly achieved a successful and fulfilling thirty-year Fire Brigade career. Many would say that was coincidental, but there are many other positive events that have quietly shaped and benefitted my life when I was unaware, lost and in need of assistance and guidance, all of which are very obvious in hindsight, but were most certainly not at the time. I see my life now, as it has played out, as perfect for me because it feels like it has been, as if I couldn't have planned it any better for myself had I done so, which of course I think I have.

All the unexpected events that have occurred over the course of my life do seem to have fitted together seamlessly so as not to be noticed or relied upon, and that is why I see them as part of the life force I call synchronicity and something to do with God, and his workers, who will subtly implement God's will into my life with a light touch, representative of being 'meant to be', whilst I was completely unaware and unable to achieve through a lack of knowing. That bias has slowly changed as we, my soul and I, have developed our instincts from our experiences, which were specifically chosen to teach us to become a knowing influence. Those instincts, our instincts, now somehow act as a bridge of communications between us, me and my soul, and ultimately with the afterlife and God. As our instincts grow, especially with the help of modalities such as meditation and mindfulness – being mindful – those communications will become stronger, helping the bias and influence to swing in the direction needed to achieve our purpose by the end of the journey, and to produce the picture planned for on completion of our lives as humans.

It is important to say that meditation, etc., is the circumstance I have chosen for my own unique journey and yours will be necessarily different and designed for your own life journey through your own experiences that will lead you to your own purpose by the opportunities given to learn from.

While I have often been tempted to see the direction I have taken to find a way through life to happiness and fulfilment by learning to love myself as a miracle, I can see now how it was all meant to be and hardly justifiable as such, although I do like to keep an open mind and my options open for the possibilities of a miracle, just in case synchronicity is a figment of my imagination.

Achieving enlightenment on our journey is not entirely dependent on our faith in something bigger in life, it can be achieved through our own determination to succeed, probably in partnership with our soul, but if we do have faith in a supernatural power it can help us whilst we are being tested. My faith has grown only since asking for help and has blossomed from an understanding that was initially supported by my curiosity and by guessing how life works, to be more like a knowing from deep within me that is almost impossible to convey unless you have experienced those of you own.

Many people who do not have a need to question their lives, with or without God, with or without a soul as a link to God, may see some of my questioning and occasional lack of faith as a possible hurdle to God or any other supernatural power, but I see it as being healthy because it has encouraged the free thinking I required to explore every possible angle and, as such, it indirectly became a way of asking for help in the earliest parts of my spiritual journey when my faith, for what it was, was at its weakest.

The existence of God, or other higher power, as a force that guides and teaches us from within via our soul through all journeys is made entirely more probable by God's acceptance that life as a human being will only ever be perfect when seen through his or her eyes as someone who sees and knows all. There are many ways to find God and the only faith required when we begin to look is in the hope and expectation that God will guide us in the process. A good place to start is linking angels etc., and other, yet to be identified, aliens and light beings, as ambassadors of a god who believes in us all as his children and trying to understand the possibilities for the existence and location of a soul within us as the ultimate home of God.

43

Mistakes and Blame

As humans we use the word 'mistake' a lot and it does reflect *an error in judgement caused by poor reasoning, carelessness or insufficient knowledge'*. But can we truly make a mistake in life when it has been chosen for the experience and made through an honest ignorance? What we see as mistakes are surely better thought of as opportunities to learn from during our search for wholeness. My earliest 'mistakes' were inevitable, but I gradually learnt from them, which finally led me to my ultimate breaking point, and an introduction to a spiritual awareness that aligned with my personal growth to inform an understanding that allowed me to take an informed, and thus better, control over my decisions.

The so-called 'mistakes' that I have made can seem trivial compared to the 'catastrophic' mistakes of others, especially those in a position to influence global events such as wars. That doesn't stop me from feeling guilty about my actions, especially the effect it has had on my children, something that I have found hard to eradicate from my life despite my children encouraging me to 'stop and get on with it', and believe me I have tried. But the guilt still lingers in me and it will probably stay that way as a necessary feeling for the expediencies of serving what I believe to be my soul's purpose.

How I have lived my life may seem to be less than perfect but because I have come to believe that it was for my perceived imperfections that I was chosen by my soul in the first place, I have also come to consider whether my mistakes as a human could be classified in some way as our mistakes. Certainly it would be very convenient for explaining many of the actions I am not particularly proud of, and the possibility of sharing the blame becomes a very attractive proposition. Although to begin with that thought was not a serious one, it was the beginning of trying to determine in my own mind my relationship with my soul, but whatever the truth of that relationship I have come to the conclusion that me, the human, must, first and foremost, take responsibility for how I think and act.

Why? Because, so far as I'm concerned, my soul is immortal and thus timeless, and I am not. My identity is real to me, but I can only guess at my soul's. I am the mortal being who has been chosen for the experiential journey from which my soul will disembark and return to the afterlife on my death; and then, if required, will reincarnate for further experiences by joining another human being from conception as it did with me. And that is why I, a human with a soul, must take personal responsibility while alive and the soul must assume an onward responsibility in the afterlife.

While here on Earth I will be judged and punished for my actions according to the law of the land upon which I live, and for those actions that are not deemed within the law, like values and morals, I will no doubt be judged by the standards of behaviour considered to be acceptable, or not, according to the beliefs and understandings of others, and that will be substantially different for everyone.

Whether my soul will feel any of the pain or anguish associated with my being judged and punished or not is a difficult call, but I am leaning towards a 'yes', so that it may also gain that experience, which is why it has chosen to join with me in the first place.

There are many humans who have the belief that at death they will either go to Heaven or Hell, but personally I do not believe there is a hell, despite the thought of it being a wonderful deterrent, because by doing so it perpetuates the very acts of violence and injustices on Earth that good-living people condemn in favour of striving to love each other. That is why I understand Hell as a 'Hell on Earth', rather than being a part of the experiential schools of learning that our soul will return to in the afterlife, to gain and assimilate the knowledge and understanding from all the experiences gained during its incarnation on Earth. In other words, they will somehow have to feel the pain, anguish and sorrow inflicted on others during the incarnation, as well as the joy and pleasure derived from helping others, as bad and good karma.

But what if we, as humans, are guilty of crimes against humanity and we pass away to death unpunished by the laws of the land and the soul is not accountable in any way? Doesn't that raise doubts about the point of being human in the first place through the issue of accountability? And what role would a god play? Would any god sanction the taking of a life? What if we have no soul or there is no god and no afterlife? What would be the point of being human when 'getting away with it' means just that? Surely there has to be accountability for our actions on Earth in some way; unless that accountability is served by us as a new human 'inheriting', through the choices of our soul, karma incurred in a previous incarnation and played out in the next. That seems to me to be entirely possible, but surely it would have to be arranged by some other superior life force in the hierarchy of the afterlife, possibly God! And if it is God, does that make God the ultimate arbitrator? Would God really allow the atrocities that man perpetrates against fellow man, or is God to the soul what the soul is to us as humans, an almost silent partner?

Whilst I do not doubt God, that we have a soul or that I am a human with responsibilities, it's just very hard to comprehend how the relationship works. Because by believing my soul has chosen me and other souls have chosen you means we are either very convenient as by-products of our parents' unison or created as meant to be, having been perpetuated by the choice of our souls since the beginning of time.

Of course there will always be debates and disagreements

about the fine line that exists between right or wrong, especially in war situations when following orders or 'fighting' to right a perceived injustice. It will also take an extraordinary amount of strength, compassion and understanding to forgive someone who has taken the life of a loved one in the name of God or any belief; such are the complexities of a life believed to be chosen for the experience when it involves pain and suffering.

The dilemma of all these thoughts and ideas are something I struggle with daily.

As such, it is important for our souls that as humans we become watchful that the experiences of mistakes, blame and guilt in particular do not lessen our willingness to fully take part in life and to avoid taking the personal responsibility so essential for our combined growth. In today's world of health and safety it would be the equivalent of becoming risk averse. My school reports sum up my early life so well in stating that I 'could have done better' and that had continued well into my fifties and I now feel that was absolutely meant to be for me and was the reason the soul, my soul, had chosen me in the first place as it suited our chosen life's purpose. That I have been a challenge to myself and my soul for all our years together, makes me feel proud to have been chosen and has given me a reason to try to do everything I do better in partnership with my soul and possibly with God. I have learnt that we can only achieve what our understanding will allow us to at any one time and not to ignore our deeper instincts that may be God, our soul, spirit guides, archangels, angels etc., one or more of whom may be trying to communicate with us.

My spiritually aware journey has shown me that by accepting we are not alone and that help can be available under the correct circumstances, we will gradually lessen the distance between the dualities of living as a human being, with a soul, to access our deeper instincts. As we do, if we do, the quiet voice of our soul from within will begin to emerge and become louder as it wills us forward with encouragement. To deny our soul's inner voice will create an imbalance within us where we can become ill at ease, and when we are ill at ease, or out of balance within ourselves, it can be a trigger for dis-ease as well as our continuing disappointments as our life dams up to stagnate our growth, as opposed to being in a flow, which makes it much easier to be encouraged and trusting of our instincts.

My inner voice grew in the form of Groundhog Days with every disappointment and frustration, created by the similarities of my decisions until I recognised they were trying to show me that I had to do something different. I could no longer deny that I was the common denominator and thus the only one who could change what I, and many others, had considered to be a chaotic and a damaging life.

I now understand only too well why those people who have seen my life as chaotic and who still see the need to apportion blame are the same people that are now thinking 'yes, but at what cost and damage', and they are right of course because that is how I would have felt. The cost and damage for me, and those who have had expectations that I was true, was in the heartbreak of the shattered dreams of believing we were 'in love' and together forever in a harmonious bliss, and the reality of trying to understand why those dreams did not materialise.

But the rewards of listening and learning from my actions have been phenomenal – albeit a long time coming – as I have learnt to love myself and thus another. Of course those rewards can all so easily be lost by us all in the reality of holding onto those chaotic moments when emotions were high and not so easily forgotten or forgiven outside of the truth of being real. Many hold on to the past and harbour the pain simply because it is easier than walking forward, or maybe it is because they know no different; but neither did I until I asked for help and was given it.

I have often found it easier to be a victim of life, and in truth I still do at times even now because it mimics my childhood and at the same time fulfils in some way my inner desire to be loved, but the sympathy I gained from being a victim also held me back, rather than helping me to understand and inspiring me to be different.

The emotional upheavals caused by my decisions have radiated out in ripples from the core of my being with a succession of broken hearts which was never my intention, but I do not see it as possible that we can live life without causing the ripples that spoil our dreams of perfection when they are made from a place of honest ignorance. Wouldn't that mean we feel there is nothing to strive for, when even striving to maintain an unhappy relationship, with ourselves or others, is an experience to learn from as humans. And if you can stretch your minds further to a continuation of life in some way that matters to you, the same ripples will surely widen the growth from those experiences to include the enlightenment of our soul and eventually to learn to love each other.

When we are young we could do some things better, but there is an allowance for age because we are expected to learn. As we get older we do some things better, but not everything, and there is less of an allowance. At some stage, as we reach adulthood, we are released into the world with the expectancy that we have learnt enough and there is little or no allowance.

When I was born within the ripples of my parents' lives I was innocent and trusting and when I finally 'flew the nest', having got married, I took on responsibility as an inexperienced adult who had not experienced the love or encouragement from my parents and innocently expected life to be the same as it was at home with my parents (and of course it was in many ways). My decision to leave my wife after seventeen turbulent and unhappy years of marriage, meant, by default, I was also leaving behind my innocent and trusting children to the legal word of agreed access once a week, which meant they were caught in the ripples that I had created, and by doing so I had perpetuated to them the cycle of my life as experienced with my parents.

Although it is too late for my children, breaking that cycle of passing on the ripples of my learnt behaviours and understanding life's choices better to avoid mistakes, blame and guilt has at least become part of my human purpose and my greatest challenge because the ripples we all exist within are multi-faceted and unique, and yet, I am also fully aware that within my own philosophical understanding of life, my children and their souls will also have chosen me as a parent. And in that regard, that they have chosen me as part of their circumstance, it makes me proud to be me despite me, because it means I was chosen as having something to offer them in their own life purpose, and of course that also means my parents had much to offer me. Maybe that is all about learning to take personal responsibility no matter how we achieve it on our soul's journey.

Consequently, I believe there is no one right way or wrong way to lead our lives, just the way our circumstances have led us. That those circumstances can lead us to be vulnerable to outside influence as we 'fight' to belong and to be part of something that makes us feel secure and acceptable is inevitable. But it is also inevitable that different circumstances will have different outcomes and we, as humans, will probably never know whether we have been successful in reaching our goal at the time of our passing, but our souls will. And when and if my soul incarnates again I am sure that it will choose a human who will listen better and trust more whilst developing its relationship for the purpose of enlightenment.

There will be many times when we try to change our lives, but we will find it hard if we remain within the influence of our family and other significant persons who very often, and for all the right reasons, will apply subtle pressures to stay as we are. Had I asked others for advice on whether I should have stayed in my marriage

I would have received a different answer from them all, but I didn't, although there were many that offered their opinions anyway! My father was one, but I would not change my decision.

If I had succeeded in the personal battle that had raged for years to stay for the sake of my children and not given into the temptations of a lust-driven love born from my lack of self-worth, would the ripples created have been any kinder or just different, and would they have increased the possibilities of making matters worse in the long run? That is something I will never know for sure in this lifetime because it didn't happen like that, so the only point of speculating is in the benefits of learning my own truth. It was to be many years hence until I began to understand that and is the reason why I had no choice but to get on with the job of living in the only way I knew how.

Learning to trust what life puts in front of us can be daunting and confusing, unless we can believe in a higher power that is trying to help us, and by us I mean humans collectively as well as me and my soul, and although being part of something bigger remains unproven outside the power of belief, I hope dear God that I am right with my feelings and beliefs because surely nobody can ever be perfect except in the eyes of a god or some other supernatural power.

Outside of that, we can only know what we have been taught and then discover for ourselves as we, the pupils, become the teachers and surely every action we take is about the multi-complexity of our interactive experiences, which, if we view in isolation, or as gains for one and a loss for another, we will be missing the point of a life designed for the experience of being human with a soul and a spiritual purpose.

That I have gained some understanding in that respect has become my own miracle by trusting in something I can only feel and I thank my god through the example Jesus has shown us all for guiding me to be without judgement while I discovered myself through the purpose of living.

44

Age and Change

The relationship with my wife before we were married was good. There was an incident involving the use and allocation of the wedding cars while planning the wedding that concerned me, but it went ahead despite the doubts that came with it. We had bought a house together before the wedding and moved in after, while we continued its refurbishment. Whilst it was completely different to living at home with my parents, the battles that were to come were still a shock; I guess it was to both of us, but they were largely masked and buffered by being busy and accepting the shared responsibility of young house owners with a mortgage to pay. My strong work ethic, learnt from my parents, continued as I worked hard 'doing up' the house, but gradually the cracks began to appear through our differences, something I didn't understand or know how to resolve, and consequently they never were. Seventeen years and two children later I left for another woman and the reality of that decision, had I the understanding to really think it through, would prove to be harder than I had ever imagined possible.

The memories of that unnecessary and extremely difficult time will remain etched in my mind forever, but there was one comment in particular from my wife that has remained uppermost in my mind when she said something to the effect of '...it's not fair, someone else is going to get the best of you now'. She was right of course, but at the time it puzzled me. Whilst it would take a long time for the best of me to be revealed, the important thing was not necessarily in the time it took, but being aware enough to recognise when it did. I see that statement, and not necessarily because it seemed out of character, as an early indicator of what I call now a knowing without knowing. It's the sort of statement that has two meanings; one born out of sadness and suitable for the immediate occasion and another that is deeper and beyond what I see as normal, probably from a soul level that is purely instinctive. Had that statement been made twenty years later, maybe I would have stopped, listened and searched for its deeper meaning. As it is, it has become another small piece of anecdotal evidence to add to the bigger picture in support of my belief in a force that is all knowing and here to help us.

I continued to 'fail' in relationships for all but the next twenty years, but I have come to realise that all my relationship experiences, and indeed those times of being on my own, have given me the opportunities to learn from, and as such can't be passed or failed with certificates of proof. My partners were my teachers in the classroom called Earth and I was also theirs. These were not exams to test academic ability or text book knowledge but experiences to grow from or stand still and stagnate. They were of, and for, the love of enlightenment and ascension to higher levels of understanding designed to reveal the best of me still to come that was hidden in a lack of self-worth.

It's an irony that my greatest learning came from being 'dumped' for the first time in my life by the woman who had finally had enough of my erratic behaviour and found her own worth. I will be forever grateful for the particular part she played in my teaching that had innocently encouraged me to extend my education to the University of Life.

When I trained as a carpenter and joiner I was taught that if you don't start a job right it won't finish right. You can cover up the problem or mask it with a high quality finish but the issue will always remain, no matter how well hidden and camouflaged. That is similar to how we, as humans, hide our learnt behaviours in our subconscious mind and inadvertently go to all sorts of lengths to cover them up, or maybe overcome them would be a better way to describe it. Although seeing life as a job of work may not be a great analogy for our lives as a human being, we could actually do a lot worse in trying to make sense of it from the point of view of choosing our circumstances to shape our experiences and learning.

As humans we will normally identify our lives by age through childhood, adolescence, adulthood, and possibly parenthood. At some stage our bodies will reach its physical optimum and by then we will have been expected to become independent adults, although that is clearly not always the case. It is even less likely, and certainly not a 'given', that we will have achieved the emotional intelligence and understanding required to support independent living as an adult, because that is something else we have to learn through the experience of living. With independent living comes a responsibility to make decisions about our futures and some of them will be more important than others. They will often be identified as 'crossroads', especially if life is seen as a journey. My first crossroad was undoubtedly choosing to get married and by default leaving what had been my home for twenty-two years. What I didn't leave behind were the behaviours learnt as a child from my parents and, crucially, the search for my mother's love that came with them.

Three years later, at twenty-five years of age, I had developed enough physically – just – to be accepted into the Fire Brigade, and the very nature of the training forced my emotional development by having to learn how to integrate myself to become a valued member of a team that depended on knowing each other to thrive and survive. That career changing decision would turn out to be the next important crossroad in my life and, although I began to 'grow up' quickly, it was not matched by my understanding, or an ability to live harmoniously with my wife as I never connected the two. Consequently, my marriage remained as much a mystery to me as before and was something that happened around me and not because of me. Despite that, my daughter was born a year after I became a fireman and my son three years later. We became a quaintly and ironically termed 'nuclear family' and, although as parents we had new responsibilities and less time to battle, we still managed it.

My third crossroad was my decision to leave the marriage and I spent most of the next twenty or so years acting like I was eighteen again and trying to neutralise and live with the inevitable outcomes of that decision. If I had to sum up how my emotional and personal awareness had grown in that time I would describe it at best as patchy, and at its worst naive and something else I could have done better; although it had improved proportionally the older I became; alcohol was by then playing an increasingly important part in my life.

My fourth crossroad at fifty years of age was not so much a decision, but my cry for help that had been fuelled by the alcohol and the growing realisation, disappointments and frustrations that, having left my wife, and many others, I seemed to be no better at being happy, content and fulfilled or at understanding relationships, or myself. Life was no better, different but not better. Although all my crossroads have shaped and perpetuated my life, this one at fifty would at least begin to supply the answers that I had asked a god I doubted for. I wouldn't call it a mid-life crisis, just an escalation to a point of despair and wanting to be different because all my Groundhog Days were showing me I had to be, although I didn't understand about Groundhog Days then either! My prayer – for surely that is what it was – was answered, as the poor quality finish that had been applied to my life to mask my needs began to be exposed as flaws, and bit by bit were being stripped away to make room for discovering the real me, and not some poor imitation, as I set about learning who I was and why.

Every crossroad in my life has provided me with an opportunity to think because that's what they do by demanding a decision, even if that decision is to carry on as normal, but by asking for help, this one in particular would usher in the most significant of changes by manoeuvring me into a spiritual church. That I was meant to travel in the new direction offered seems now to be an absolute certainty although at the time it was by no means certain that I would. What saved me from ignoring the new way of life was my complete ignorance of it because it soon became obvious, when sharing my new and very different 'spiritual' experiences with anyone who would listen, that there was some sort of taboo associated with it. That taboo still exists today and continues to divide opinions simply because so many somehow associate spirituality, as it was introduced to me, as communicating with the dead and thus evil and dangerous; maybe I was just lucky that dealing with the dead was a way of life for me in my work and as such held no such fears, but the days of seeing such things as lucky had long dissolved into those that are meant to be, and my work colleagues must have felt the same, unless they were keeping their opinions to themselves, because most of them, but not all, despite their surreptitious approach, didn't seem remotely interested in my new-found belief, other than the normal ribbing that goes on in team environment, and why should they unless it was meant to be for them?

That doesn't keep me from asking myself how something that has been so fundamental to my new way of looking at life, with a positive change for the better as a result, can be so alien to so many, especially to those who are also seeking answers? The answer of course is in what we have been taught to believe or in my case what I had not been, and that is why I find even writing this book so conflicting. Yes, it has been cathartic and yes, I get excited that my beliefs have changed my way of thinking and thus my life, but just because it was meant to be for me it doesn't mean it is meant to be for anyone else; that will depend entirely on your chosen journeys. My intention is not to dismiss or destabilise the beliefs of others but to share with as many people as I can a new way of thinking that challenges a taboo that keeps the door of opportunities so firmly locked by showing that nothing inside being spiritually aware is harmful.

Having said that, working with the dead before and after my

own introduction has shown me why it is such an emotive subject and why so many of us would not wish to challenge what we take comfort from in our individual beliefs. After all, there is very little other than our beliefs, and the occasional piece of anecdotal evidence, that in isolation is so easy to dismiss, that there is a continuation of life in some way after death. I can also see how exploring alternatives to your own beliefs and in particular your god could possibly be seen as insulting and thus a limiting factor, but it doesn't have to be seen as challenging anyone's belief, because surely it is in the very multitude of beliefs available as alternatives that should give us the clearest indicator that there are many pathways available on any search for fulfilment and happiness. That I have also come to see and understand why those who have 'found God' in their own particular way are so enthusiastic about sharing their own excitement of 'being born again', has been of use to me in understanding my own opinions and those of others.

My purpose in writing about my own experiences is not in trying to convince you to do the same, because that is an individual decision based on your own tolerances and the expectations you have for your life; it is purely to share the excitement of my new understandings and what I have learnt from them and to hopefully show how we can become blinded, and thus not open-minded enough, to be inclusive of all beliefs, no matter what they are, just because there is comfort in staying the same.

Reaching the age of fifty seems to be a common factor in the search for change and answers to a life previously accepted without thought, and there is some comfort for me in at least being 'normal' in that way. Mine was because I was lost and searching for answers to the mess I had caused to myself and others, but the most common reason for seeking change that I have come across is when looking for answers following the death or serious illness of a loved one, and surely there is no more challenging a situation than when the expectation of a long happy and fulfilling life together is taken or threatened; other factors include having your own life-threatening illness; reaching an age when as an adult without children you become disillusioned with life; or as a parent, the children leave home to live their own lives and instead of using the additional free time to focus on all the things that have yet to be achieved, either together or alone, the opportunity is allowed to slip away to become lost. The fear of change and the possibility of loneliness is such a powerful and limiting force which encourages us to metaphorically stay at home where it is safe by staying the same, but it can be both courageous and empowering to step outside of being normal!

On any journey the directions we take through crossroads are important and I could discuss all day what would have happened had I chosen differently at my first. But the truth of what I choose to believe about my life as a journey for the experience is that it has been shaped from the very beginning – sometime after conception and before birth – by the choice of my soul to choose me with my personal circumstances as ideal for our journey together. Even if you cannot believe or accept that you would have chosen your parents for how they would shape your onward life, the consequences of having randomly allocated parents are still exactly the same from conception onwards, but without the sense that choosing them purposely and carefully to fulfil your human purpose with meaning can have.

The decision to leave my wife without too much consideration of the consequences unsurprisingly proved to be controversial and life changing for my immediate family and to a lesser extent the extended family and close friends. But why it became controversial to anyone outside of the family I do not know because it was really nothing to do with them except, I believe, by doing so it sort of made them feel better about their own unhappy relationships and could be used as a justification to remain closed to new opportunities and 'make it work'.

With metaphors from that difficult time like 'be careful what you wish for' and 'the grass is not always greener on the other side of the road' ringing around my head, I have long since learnt that separation and/or divorce should have been a last resort and being able to speak my truth with honesty and being open about my feelings the first. Because I was not open and honest it made life much harder for everyone involved. How much easier it may have been had I made the decision in consultation with my wife or if I had stayed until the children were older and finished in full-time education I will never know. But I do believe that I would have had to face the same dilemmas of difficult choices, possibly with equally damaging emotional traumas, at some time in the future when the extended time living together could have made the break as hard, if not harder. Whether the passage of time would have changed the relationship is something else I will never know, but I doubt it and although I have never regretted the decision to part from my wife, I have regretted the way I went about it.

I had wavered knowingly at that particular crossroads of indecision for seventeen years while trying to be happy, and as soon as I had made the positive decision to stop thinking about leaving it was as if some force of life immediately decided to test that decision, when drunk with alcohol, with what seemed like an offer of true love that was too good to be true and was. I have spent years wondering whether the choice to leave in those circumstances was the 'wrong' decision, a 'mistake' or a 'failure', or whether it was meant to be as part of a sideways redirection at the crossroad to get me going forward later and thus somehow right, but I am yet to decide and think I never will, with the trauma and despair I brought upon my family a constant reminder.

As we cannot guess or know the outcomes of any of our decisions, be they crossroads or not, it seems to me that the only way to look at each individual part of our journey is as an essential part of reaching our destination.

In the early days, after finding myself in a spiritual environment, I tried to circumnavigate life's decision-making process by seeking the answers through the crystal ball of mediums and clairvoyants and I began to look for signs as confirmation of the way forward for every choice I had to make. It would take me many years to see the craziness of that approach to life and ditch it in favour of following my own instincts.

When I proposed to my future wife I was nineteen and I experienced feelings of joy and happiness for the first time in my life. I could have taken that as a sign for the right decision, and I did. Every other decision I had made up to that point in my life had been informed and guided by good-intentioned parenting, but I didn't understand that then either. I did try to make our marriage work, but because I wasn't real, making it work would be all it could ever be until I was. The longer and harder I tried, the deeper the hole I was digging for myself became. My favourite saying after our arguments had settled into the post-battle debrief was about getting off of the downward spiral our life had become and starting again from scratch. My father would have said 'you've made your bed now lie in it' and I did try for seventeen years until I slid full speed down the helter-skelter of life into the abyss of confusion.

45

God

I know there are many people who, like me, have questioned the role of God in our lives on Earth. My daughter, many years previously, whilst working on a school assignment, had asked me why God would allow so much unnecessary death and violence in the world. I struggled to answer it then and that's not changed a great deal even now and, as such, I have few expectations that I will find a definitive answer in this lifetime.

What has changed is our ability as humans to record scenes of death and violence on our personal recording devices, from every part of our planet, which depicts man's worst atrocities to his fellow man and to watch, if we can bear, from the relative comfort of our homes. This is no longer history written on stone or parchment, it is a visual reality that makes it extremely hard, if not impossible, to remain impassionate and to not become emotionally moved and angered by the gratuitous violence perpetrated in the name of individual beliefs, greed or pure thuggery. And maybe that's why the questioning of a god stops there for so many because it is so difficult to find an answer that does not question the existence of a god, or any other higher power that could surely put a stop to it. And yet I have come to believe that it is the very belief of a god or other higher power that will be the ultimate arbitrator of a system of justice that does not sanction violence in any shape or form.

Whatever our beliefs, be they that we are the children of God or not, or something entirely different, be they that we are part of the Universe or we stand alone as humans on Earth, our actions or inactions can never be irrelevant just because we think nobody or nothing is watching or caring. How can we ignore our own actions and reactions in the hope it will be someone else's problem or that it will either go away or stop? Because the reality is that it could be any of us next – although I hesitate to use the phrase 'there but for the grace of God' as a way of being lucky or unlucky. Surely we should expect ourselves to come together as humans in a community of common belief that violence, be it physical or emotional, with acts of aggression in the name of power and control, is not acceptable, whether we are led by leaders who feel they have to maintain loyalty to their own cause and peoples or not. Why do we allow ourselves to become divided by whatever particular religion, or none, that we choose to follow? Why do we allow ourselves to be divided by race or gender, or by status or wealth? We are all part of a community that is equal as humans with our own voice and that is the only belief that should matter. No religion or god should encourage loyalty through exclusivity and the fear of being disloyal and the implicit threat therein that we may not go to a place such as Heaven unless we conform to their doctrines and stringent ideologies. We can only excommunicate ourselves through our own fears because no loving god would expel us from worshipping whoever we choose to when it is done with a good and loving intention; let us be exulted by learning to love ourselves as individuals and being as good and loving of and towards each other as we can be by being a member of being a human. Surely it is enough to be loyal to the seeking of our own truths and becoming as real as we can be within our own realities, and not just in the way taught by others.

Why can we not come together for the higher purpose of mankind in a love for each other and celebrate our differences as the act of the ultimate worship? How can being dependent or conditional on a personal belief render us, as human beings living together and sharing Earth together, so powerless in our ability to demonstrate a togetherness of love and goodwill for a purpose greater than being human as guardians of the planet? Do we really think we will be abandoned at our death and denied passage to Nirvana ('*a place or state characterised by freedom from or oblivion to pain, worry, and the external world*') by celebrating the love that can be found in all religions and worshiping communities? Isolation in our individual beliefs has become limiting through the fear of not believing!

Let us all be free to celebrate being alive and having the ability to find comfort and solace in our own belief or none and that of others, no matter what it is or how it is celebrated, knowing we will be welcomed to the afterlife in whatever form we travel and no matter what decisions we have made in our lives for the experience of living our life to the full, without the threat that for some reason we will not be welcomed home from the experience. Is it not enough that we try to be as good and loving as we can be instead of becoming conditioned and increasingly apathetic through the fear of making a mistake? Would any god or any other supernatural power really only welcome those who have not lived life to the full to avoid the risk of punishment and shun those who have tried, sometimes against all the odds, to be good. Every one of us makes mistakes, it is inevitable, but every one of us has the opportunity offered to us in one way or another to make up for it by following what I understand as a predestined onward pathway as honestly as we can.

Although I was born into a Christian family I have never felt the need for a devotional and ritual adherence to religious practice as a necessity of faith. My belief is in there being no need to qualify for anything through a compliance with the religious rules of any faith and, accordingly, there is no right or wrong way to be, just an acceptance that there is more than one way. Whilst I have met a growing number of 'disillusioned' people from all manner of faiths who have describe themselves as being spiritual but not religious (SBNR), I see myself as being both, simply because I can be. In fact, believing in being spiritual has encouraged me to be more understanding and accepting of all religions.

My early religious beliefs were inherited from my parents and have rightly been reshaped by my recent experiences, and in particular that our individual journeys as humans are the foundations of our lives in this incarnation regardless of religion, or none. They provide what is a solid pathway for our soul's enlightenment through whatever direction we have chosen to travel and the understanding and experience gained by living and learning to be open-minded and accepting of diversity in all its forms. My spiritual connection through my instincts has informed me, as much as it can at the moment, that we are all able to utilise a different pathway to the same destination without judgement or precondition and we, the human collective, and we as individuals with a soul, will be reunited in astonishment as we hug and greet our so-called enemies on Earth as brothers and sisters in the continuing life I call the afterlife.

Although I believe in God, I still question every possibility around the truth, which could be thought of as agnostic, but I am not truly agnostic, I am the same as so many others who believe in parts of their own religions but not all; all I want is to be as real as I can be and challenge in a good and loving way what I do not know for sure; I want to love and be loved for being real and not have my life coloured in by a faith that guarantees a place in Heaven for being a good boy; I want to be able to be with my own opinions and be welcome by those with others as I welcome them without fighting or feeling threatened; I want to continue to be as good as I possibly can be on the journey that I see as being as real as it can be at the moment and an essential part of the destination yet to be confirmed, but hoped for as the home of my soul more than I could have ever imagined in order to confirm the purpose of being human that I have pinned my hopes upon.

Recently, I watched an interview with a young man of school age broadcast on television; he was about nine or ten and had fled his war-torn country of birth, leaving behind what was left of his family with plans to be with his brother in a country supposedly full of opportunities and where he had hopes for an education that would fulfil his ambition of one day becoming a doctor to help others. He was stuck on his own with thousands of others whose journeys of hope had been interrupted and was working in a factory, for what remuneration I do not know, but I suspect for food and shelter and just to stay alive. He did not complain, despite the obvious sadness and pain that could be seen in his eyes and confirmed by his forlorn appearance as he explained with an acceptance and bravery that his dreams had been shattered and that God must have changed his plans for him and made others. What an incredible belief in his god that showed! And in doing so he inspired me to believe in my own as well as his, should it be different.

How could I ever compare my life to that of this child as hard? I can't and won't, but I can believe and hope with all my heart that he is right, because otherwise I have got it wrong too. We are indeed living in a harsh world that continually throws my belief that lives are chosen for a purpose other than just surviving into doubt and it would be so easy to lose faith. This young child's message did so much to inform my own purpose and understanding and yet he was surely too young to understand, although not too young to suffer from those who fight each other in the name of God with blood on their hands.

PRINTED AND BOUND BY:

Copytech (UK) Limited trading as Printondemand-worldwide,
9 Culley Court, Bakewell Road, Orton Southgate.
Peterborough, PE2 6XD, United Kingdom.